BLACKING UP

BLACKING UP

The Minstrel Show

in Nineteenth-Century

America

Robert C. Toll

Oxford University Press

London   Oxford   New York

Copyright © 1974 by Oxford University Press, Inc.
Library of Congress Catalogue Card Number: 74-83992
First published by Oxford University Press, New York, 1974
First issued as an Oxford University Press paperback, 1977
Printed in the United States of America

OXFORD UNIVERSITY PRESS

London   Oxford   New York
Glasgow   Toronto   Melbourne   Wellington
Cape Town   Ibadan   Nairobi   Dar es Salaam   Lusaka   Addis Ababa
Delhi   Bombay   Calcutta   Madras   Karachi   Lahore   Dacca
Kuala Lumpur   Singapore   Hong Kong   Tokyo

Preface

"Our best poets and authors contribute to the progress of this our only original American Institution," a performer in 1863 proudly boasted about his profession. "Its songs are sung by Fifth Avenue belles and are hummed by modest serving-girls. Brass bands march through streets playing songs the newsboys will soon be whistling." To some mid-nineteenth-century Americans, it was "The only true American drama" or an "American National Opera." [1] But to most people it was simply "nigger minstrelsy." Performed by white men in blackface make-up, using what they claimed were Negro dialects, songs, dances, and jokes, minstrelsy literally swept the nation in the 1840's, from the White House to the California gold fields, from New Orleans to New England, from riverboats and saloons to 2500-seat theaters. For over half a century it remained the most popular entertainment form in the country.

With its images of Negroes shaped by white expectations

and desires and not by black realities, minstrelsy and its latter-day successors, like "Uncle Remus" and "Amos and Andy," deeply embedded caricatures of blacks into American popular culture. Besides its portrayals of Negroes, minstrelsy also "informed" its patrons about a wide range of important subjects, from plantations to cities, from fashions to morality, and from Indians to immigrants. Furthermore, as the first American popular entertainment form to become a national institution, it set many precedents and trends that strongly influenced its successors, especially burlesque and vaudeville. Thus, minstrelsy helped shape the way Americans conceived of and thought about each other and their country, as well as playing a formative role in the evolution of American show business.

But despite minstrelsy's great significance, critically important questions about it remain unanswered: Where did it come from? Why did white men blacken their faces to become entertainers? Why was blackface minstrelsy so popular that it dominated American show business for fifty years? What did the shows mean to and do for their audiences? How and why did minstrelsy change over the years? What explains its decline in popularity? What impact did the black people who first entered American show business as minstrels make on the public? What was life like for these early black entertainment pioneers? Did they attempt to alter minstrel stereotypes of black people? This book seeks to answer these and other questions about the minstrel show as a way to understand the thoughts, feelings, needs, and desires of the common Americans who shaped minstrelsy in their own image. Chapter I explains the social and entertainment contexts in which minstrelsy emerged, chapters II, V, and VII examine minstrelsy's evolution as an institution, and the other four chapters analyze its treatment of the topics that most concerned it.[2]

I want to thank the staffs of all the libraries I worked in for

Preface

their assistance, especially Jeanne T. Newlin of the Harvard Theatre Collection, Paul Myers and Dorothy O'Conner of the Theatre Collection of the New York Public Library at Lincoln Center, and Jane Van Arsdale and Kurtz Myers of the rare book and music departments of the Buffalo and Erie County Library. A small grant from the history department, University of California, Berkeley, helped finance my research, and a year spent as a research associate at the Institute for the Study of Community and Race Relations in Berkeley enabled me to complete work on the manuscript. I owe special debts to Alan Dundes for critically reading several versions of the text, to Lawrence Levine for his many suggestions, especially about Chapter VIII, to Richard Carlson for his general editing and his relentless battle against my wordiness and use of the passive voice, and to Leon Litwack for years of encouragement and for the countless hours he has spent patiently teaching me to write. Any errors or inadequacies that remain are, of course, my responsibility. My wife Judy worked beside me throughout much of the research and served as an indispensable sounding board for my interpretations. In the creation of this book, as in every other facet of my life, she is my partner.

R.C.T.

Oakland, California
July 1974

[1] *Charley Fox's Minstrel Companion* (Philadelphia, 1863), p. 5; *Democratic Review*, XVII (September 1845), 218–19; *Knickerbocker*, XXVI (October 1845), 333; quoted in Frank L. Mott, *A History of American Magazines*, 5 vols. (Cambridge, Mass., 1939), I, 429, 433–34.

[2] For a description of the materials, the analytical techniques, and the conceptual approach used for this study, see the Note On Method, page 281.

For Judy

Contents

BLACKING
UP

1 The Emergence of a "Common Man's Culture"

Professional popular culture, the business of amusing and entertaining large numbers of common people, emerged in the United States during the first half of the nineteenth century. After the War of 1812, many Americans expressed the need for native forms, symbols, and institutions that would assert the nation's cultural distinctiveness as clearly and emphatically as the war had reaffirmed its political independence. American elite groups, envisioning few social and institutional changes, looked forward to a cultural renaissance in which American artists and subjects would bring European forms and concepts to new heights of achievement. But, at the same time, new forces emerged demanding that "middling" Americans be able to shape the country in their own image. Besides political power and unhampered opportunities for economic and social mobility, they wanted a "common man's culture" that glorified American democracy and the average white man in contrast to

3

European aristocracy and effete "gentlemen." In response, traditional cultural media, like newspapers, literature, and stage entertainment, tried to satisfy the basically conflicting demands of both groups. Almost inevitably, entertainment in America fragmented into "highbrow" and "lowbrow," elitist and popular. Out of this turmoil came unequivocally popular forms that were both products of and responses to the way common Americans transformed old cultural institutions to meet their new needs and desires.[1] The minstrel show was the most important new form to grow out of this process.

These "new" audiences first emerged as a by-product of the nation's wildly accelerating urban growth. Between 1820 and 1860, Philadelphia quadrupled in population; New York City mushroomed from 410,000 in 1840 to 910,000 in 1860; by 1850, eight American cities had more than 100,000 residents. In this urban population explosion, the rural migrants faced an almost totally alien environment that forced them to make fundamental changes in their lives, thoughts, and culture. They had to endure dire living conditions, totally inadequate housing, and rampant disease. Furthermore, many of them saw their economic hopes dashed as the ranks of the poor and the wealth of the few rich citizens swelled as never before. This disparity gave urban common people's antielitist feelings a basis in reality as well as in ideology. New city dwellers also had to endure social and cultural anguish that in some ways was even more severe than their physical plight. Leaving the stable, socially secure world of the rural folk, they entered the chaotic, bewildering uncertainties of the city. They had to learn to live by clocks rather than by a natural calendar, to work to the rhythms of machines away from their homes and their families, and to live crammed together with strangers, some of whom might not even speak the same language.[2]

As part of this "culture shock," they had to learn to do

The Emergence of a "Common Man's Culture"

without the verbal arts—stories, songs, tales and jokes—that they had enjoyed with their previous neighbors. This meant the loss of much more than amusements, because in folk societies verbal arts taught values and norms, invoked sanctions against transgressors, and provided vehicles for fantasy and outlets for social criticism. They were central to group identity. They told people who they were and how to live with their neighbors.[3] These rural migrants, cut off from their folk groups, had to establish new definitions of themselves as Americans and to find new "rules" to govern and explain their situation. They desperately needed amusements that spoke to them in terms they could understand and enjoy, that affirmed their worth and gave them dignity. They needed a substitute for their folk culture—something that could establish a new sense of community and identity for them and their neighbors. These needs originated in cities but spread throughout the country as developments in transportation and communication greatly increased the flow of people, goods, information, ideas, and anxieties. By trial and error, popular arts emerged to fill these needs. Minstrelsy ultimately found the most successful entertainment formula.

Although statements about the "age of the common man" are sorely overworked and too simplistic, the transformation of America from a deferential to an egalitarian society proceeded at a rapidly accelerating rate in the decades after 1820. In the name of democracy and free opportunity for "middling" Americans, an egalitarian consciousness emerged that attacked aristocratic elements and special privilege groups.[4] It also produced the need for cultural forms that reflected the average man's nationalism and egalitarianism, glorified "plain people," were aggressively antiaristocratic and anti-European, and could replace rural folk culture with symbols that white "common men" could all unite around.

To satisfy these needs, entertainment became less formal in tone and turned to regional American folk culture for material to construct heroes for common Americans. Newspapers were the first to show the signs of popularization. After 1820, they became much more informal and entertaining, and their circulation grew. Led by the new weeklies aimed at a mass audience, newspapers made widespread use of native American folk humor, anecdotes, and tall tales. Bringing regional life into the cities, the two most popular weeklies, the New-York-City-based *Spirit of the Times* and the Boston-based *Yankee Blade*, filled their pages with the lore of the Southwest and New England respectively. With the down-home air of friends swapping yarns over the cracker barrel, American folk characters, speaking the dialects of the American backlands, delighted their principally urban audiences. As a spin-off from these successful weeklies, these characters appeared in "comic almanacks" and many other forms of inexpensive literature addressed to common people in their own language.[5]

Even though these characters were native American types, in American settings with American themes, produced by Americans, they did not satisfy the longings of the nation's "Better Families" and intellectuals for evidence that Americans had produced a society and culture as cultivated, civilized, and artistic as Europeans had. These elite groups were caught in a frustrating dilemma. They wanted a distinctively American culture, but their criteria and values were European. The American heritage that did exist—the taming of a rugged wilderness, the building of a society literally from the ground up, the great opportunities for social and material mobility, the humble origin of so many of the people, and the widespread material success—was the very antithesis of what Europeans thought a proper society should be. To cultivated people, the folk-based popular literature, which was roughhewn, dogmati-

cally unlettered, physically violent, and intensely antiaristocratic, was further evidence that Europeans were right when
they charged that Americans had no "respectable" culture. In
these decades, American formal artists and writers struggled to
tailor American realities to fit European forms and conceptions.
Their most noteworthy successes—the Hudson River school of
painters and James Fenimore Cooper—crafted aspects of the
American wilderness into models of European romanticism.[6]
Unlike popular artists, formal artists long had to wrestle with
this conflict between European standards and American realities.

The fundamental differences between antebellum popular
and formal culture that ultimately fragmented all American entertainment forms are clearly revealed by a comparison of the
backwoodsman in James Fenimore Cooper's Leatherstocking
novels and in the popular writing about Davy Crockett. Both
these characters were drawn from the American wilderness,
and both appeared in fiction. But the resemblance ends there.
Unlearned, natural, and instinctual, Cooper's Natty Bumppo
was uncorrupted, humble, and chivalrous—the romantic No-
bleman of Nature set in the American forest. In *The Last of the
Mohicans*, after he and his faithful Indian companions had rescued Cora and Alice, he rejected their offers of money with his
typical romantic language: "These Mohicans and I will do what
man's thoughts can invent, to keep such flowers, which though
so sweet, were never made for the wilderness, from harm, and
that without hope of any other recompense but such as God
always gives to upright dealings." [7] The fictionalized Crockett,
who appeared in a flood of popular literature between 1833 and
1856,[8] was the very antithesis of Natty. Crockett was a crude,
rowdy braggart: "I can walk like an ox, run like a fox, swim like
an eel, yell like an Indian, fight like a devil, spout like an
earthquake, make love like a mad bull, and swallow a nigger

whole without choking if you butter his head and pin his ears back." [9] Natty was an idealized son of the forest; Crockett, too, was fresh from the backwoods, but he claimed to be "half-horse, half-alligator, a little touched with snapping turtle." [10]

Although Natty was master of every situation, he lived in harmony with nature, killing game only for food and enemy Indians only for survival—and even then with a reverence for their nobility. Crockett, on the other hand, represented exploitative conquest—over nature, animals, men, and women. He laid waste to everything in his path, just for the sheer joy of it. In the frequent brawls that he provoked, he fought without regard for any rules, kicking, biting, and scratching to win. After his inevitable triumph, he arrogantly crowed over his victims. In even greater contrast to chivalrous Natty, Crockett boasted of his sexual prowess and his conquests of women. When accused of adultery during his congressional campaign in 1829, he reportedly replied, "I never ran away with any man's wife—that was not willing." [11]

Natty was the product of romanticism. To create him, Cooper took American material and fashioned it into a European pattern. Although Natty would have shunned it, he was perfectly suited for the best drawing room or parlor, for the most refined taste. In him, Cooper proclaimed to both Europeans and Americans that America could produce both literature and personal character that measured up to the highest European standards. The fictionalized Crockett, on the other hand, was the substance of America forged into a defiant repudiation of European criteria. He was the common, unwashed American raised to the level of superman. With both feet planted in the frontier, he towered over it, thumbed his nose at convention, challenged all comers—and won.

Other regional types, like Mike Fink, the swaggering, two-fisted riverboatsman, and Brother Jonathan, the debunking, rapier-witted Yankee, joined Crockett in popular literature. Drawn from American folklore, all of them had humble origins, taunted the pretentious, and mocked "aristocratic" refinements.[12] Although both popular and formal literature addressed themselves to defining America and Americans, they spoke to different groups with different concerns, values, and needs. Thus, literature, a form produced and consumed by individuals, quickly splintered into popular and elite forms.

Unlike literature, however, stage entertainment was a socially based form that took much longer to fragment. Requiring a theater, costumes, production staffs, and actors as well as writers, stage shows had huge operating costs that required large attendance at each production. Thus, in the early nineteenth century when drama was struggling to survive in America, it was concentrated in population centers, continually striving to broaden its audience base. Until urbanization and transportation developments greatly expanded the number of potential patrons, economic necessity forced all theatergoers into the same audience even as they became much more diverse. The common people clustered in American cities quickly took to stage entertainment because it so closely resembled the verbal arts of their rural folk communities, in which artists narrated, acted, sang, and danced before live audiences who participated in the performance.[13] Furthermore, since stage entertainers were necessarily responsive to their audiences, the large numbers of vocal "middling" Americans who flocked into theaters had a greater influence on the content of the shows than the more reserved "Better People" in the audience. Although men like playwright-producer-director William Dunlap had labored tirelessly in the first two decades of the nineteenth century to legitimize American theater by producing American actors and plays that could rival Europe's best, stage entertainment in America after 1830 was increasingly dominated by popular tastes, not by artistic criteria, by the rapidly growing urban middling and lower classes, not by traditional elites. "The rapid increase in population in newly formed cities," a visiting actor, William Davidge, complained about American theater, "produces a style of patrons whose habits and associations afford no opportunity for the cultivation of the arts." [14]

Although there is little precise information about the composition of nineteenth-century theater audiences, abundant superficial descriptions indicate that the various sections of the theater attracted different social and economic groups. The expensive box seats offered privacy, prestige, the greatest measure of decorum, and a place for proper ladies to sit. In general, the "Better People" went there to be seen and to see each other, as well as to see a play. Below the boxes, in front of the stage, was the pit, where the "middling" classes sat. Depending on the circumstances and the disposition of the commentator, the people in the pit were both attacked as crude ruffians and praised as good people interested in the productions. But there was no question about the nature of the gallery, which was located in the upper reaches of the theater and occupied by what were thought to be the lowest reaches of society. If Negroes were allowed into the theater at all, the management confined them to part of the gallery. With the blacks sat those who could only afford the cheapest seats in the house, those who preferred the company of "rowdies," and those who preferred its excellent throwing angle. It was from the gallery that missiles of all sorts rained down on unpopular performers or in response to unpopular material. Social whispering might sweep the boxes, but loud bellows rang from the gallery patrons who actively and vociferously participated in the performances.[15]

Audiences could house such diverse groups largely because going to the theater in these years was primarily a social occasion, and each section of the theater was a society of its own.

The Emergence of a "Common Man's Culture"

In the boxes, socialites and would-be socialites paraded their newest fashions and hair styles. Some even complained that there was too much light on the stage and too little in the boxes so that it was difficult to "recognize a friend across the house." In the gallery and the pit, women nursed babies, men spit tobacco juice on the floor, told jokes, cracked peanuts, ate lunches, and drank liquor. They stamped their feet in time to the music and sang along, sporadically hollering back and forth to each other. Davy Crockett would have been perfectly at home there. People got in fights, others competed with the performers, and still others somehow snored through it all.[16]

For all their own activity, audience members, especially the gallery and pit, did not ignore the performers. Whenever they enjoyed a speech, song, or bit of acting, they cheered and demanded encores. Since many actors relied on the proceeds from "benefit nights," performances given at the end of a run from which the actor got the proceeds, they learned to play to the audience. Broad humor and comedy, ad libs with local allusions, and exaggerated sentimentalism, all had great appeal to those who were "indifferent to subtler dramatic beauties." When they were displeased, people in the gallery and the pit hissed at the performers and shouted out their preferences. Frequently, they demanded that orchestras play patriotic songs and other popular music instead of scheduled "sonatas and other airs." Positioned in front of the pit in a direct firing line from the gallery, the orchestras, who knew they might find themselves deluged with "apples, stones, and other missiles," usually complied. At the Bowery Theater in New York City in 1833, for example, patrons displeased with the overture, demanded "Yankee Doodle" instead. When they prevailed, they "evinced their satisfaction by a gentle roar." [17]

Minstrels seem to have drawn the sorts of rowdy, expressive people who usually occupied the pit and the gallery for theatrical entertainment. Early minstrel programs frequently listed "Rules of Hall" which pleaded with the audience not to whistle during the performances and not to beat time with their feet. Similar problems still existed in 1875 when Duprez and Benedict's Minstrels published a satirical "Rules for Visiting a Place of Amusement" that revealed a great deal about the "normal" actions of a minstrel audience. "As soon as you have been seated," the "rules" began, "eat peanuts, whistle and stamp your feet so everybody will know you're an old theatre-goer." After the show began, the guide urged audience members to keep time with the music, to whistle or hum along with any songs they knew, and to shout out the answers to conundrums before the endmen could. "If you recognize anyone in the gallery holler to them," it continued. When things get dull around you, do something to amuse the audience. Finally, the guide reminded, be sure and bring lots of tobacco to smoke and chew. "Spit all over the floor; if there are any spittoons they're meant for ornamentation;" and try to "spit so a lake will form at your feet. If there be many ladies and children in the audience, take out your pipe or segar, smoke, enjoy yourself; you paid to come in, didn't you?" [18]

The antebellum minstrel show, which enjoyed its greatest popularity in Northeastern cities, drew audiences that were, if anything, more demonstrative than other theater audiences of the period. When they were pleased, they roared for encores and, at times, even threw money. When they were mildly displeased they disrupted performances with hisses and shouts. But when they felt cheated, they could become violent. They mobbed inferior troupes that had passed themselves off as famous companies and then presented third-rate shows. They also drove poor or unpopular performers from the stage with barrages of anything they could find to throw including rocks and nails. Although poor companies could survive by playing

The Emergence of a "Common Man's Culture"

one-nighters and not revisiting the scenes of their past failures, in the long run the boisterous audiences had their way. Minstrel troupes either shaped their shows to suit the tastes, needs, and desires of their audiences or were replaced by companies that did.

Far from being apologetic about their assertive behavior, theater-goers took pride in the power they exerted. "We (the sovereigns) determine to have the worth of our money when we go to the theatre," a Boston correspondent boasted in 1846. "We made Blangy dance her best dances twice; we made Mrs. Sequin repeat 'Marble Halls' . . . and tonight we are going to encore Mrs. Kean's 'I Don't Believe It' in *The Gamester*. . . . Perhaps we'll flatter Mr. Kean by making him take poison twice; the latter depends upon the furor of the moment." [19] Audiences not only got encores when they wanted them, they also got new plays that spoke directly to their nationalism and egalitarianism and new stage characters that made heroes of "common" white Americans.

Before audiences defined blacks, in minstrelsy, they forged positive stage images of themselves. Between 1826 and 1836, actor James Hackett established the Yankee as the most significant American stage character. This "simple" rustic, Brother Jonathan—proud, independent, morally strong, brave, and nationalistic—delighted audiences throughout the country with his triumphs over "high-falutin'," pretentious characters and scheming, immoral city slickers. Coming out of the American countryside, dressed like a bumpkin, and speaking a rural dialect, he pierced through the hypocrisy and corruption of "civilized" society with his biting wit and stinging commentary. He took all the jibes directed at common Americans for being uncivilized and unrefined and turned them into a debunking counterattack against those very standards of civilization and refinement. A model of what common Americans liked to think they were, the Yankee possessed the good traits of Europeans stripped of their decadence, pretension, and corruption. He represented the American Everyman, arisen and triumphant. A blend of fact, fiction, and fantasy, he provided a symbol ordinary Americans could identify with and believe in.[20]

The backwoodsman, the boasting frontiersman who roared of his superhuman powers and deeds in so much of the popular literature of the period, rarely appeared on stage, probably because of the difficulties in staging his incredible feats without making them appear laughable. The option of having characters on stage swap the greater than life yarns of the frontier lacked sufficient dramatic action to make this a regular occurrence. But, occasionally, as in *Gamecock of the Wilderness*, the Yankee and the Frontiersman appeared together on stage as part of a trend to combine or unite the two native white folk types. Although they retained their basic differences, the low-keyed understatement of the Yankee and the arrogant ballyhooing of the Frontiersman, both used dialects rich in homely metaphors, both boasted of having what were supposed to be faults, and both defeated pretentious aristocrats. Similarly, in the widely popular melodramas, rural heroes who were pure of heart and motive inevitably won out over corrupt, immoral city slickers. These rural characters with the strength to triumph over every adversity fed the identity-hungry egos of the growing numbers of Americans who were experiencing the jolting shocks of urbanization.[21]

But these rural characters were not alone in this process. By the late 1840's, a legendary urban "common man" had joined the Yankee and the Frontiersman in the pantheon of white American folk heroes. Beginning with "The Fireman's Frolic" and "Life in New York, or Firemen on Duty" in 1831 and 1832, urban firemen, "B'howery B'hoys," as these frequently rowdy citizens were called, began to be featured in plays.[22] These culminated in the tremendously popular character of Mose the B'howery B'hoy, the New York City volunteer fireman who first appeared in 1848. Volunteer firemen were familar indeed to urban audiences because they were the only firefighting forces in most antebellum cities. Although they were often charged with corruption and extortion for fire "protection," [23] volunteer firemen proved very popular stage characters, perhaps because the firemen most likely extorted money only from the wealthy, or perhaps simply because they were recognizable urban common men who, on stage, had many desirable traits.

Mose the B'howery B'hoy, an unlikely combination of East Side swell, gutter bum, volunteer fireman, brawler, and heroic protector of the weak, was a physical man who loved to fight both men and fires, especially men. "I'm bilein' over for a sousin' good fight with someone somewhere," he bellowed like Davy Crockett. "If I don't have a a muss soon, I'll spile." Faced with fires and especially with people trapped inside burning buildings, Mose became a daredevil with a strong streak of sentiment and chivalry worthy of a melodramatic hero. After he had saved a baby from death in a fire, he recalled, wiping a tear from his eye, that its mother "fell down on her knees and blessed me. Ever since dat time I've had a great partiality for little babies. The fire-boys may be a little rough outside, but they're all right there. (Touches breast.)" Besides his heroics and sentimental rescues, which were dramatically played out on the stage with elaborate sets and props, Mose also defended the plain people of the Bowery against urban corruption. He saved Linda the cigar girl from molesters, helped a rural migrant recover the goods he had been cheated of by city slickers, protected old men from muggers, and thwarted "silver-tongued seducers." [24] In every theatrical city in the nation, Mose strutted across the stage with puffed-out chest and puffed-up ego. In this somewhat coarse, belligerently egalitarian man of action, who was tough on the outside but sentimental and chivalrous, in his rowdy way, within, theater audiences again chose a decidedly antiaristocratic hero who glorified the American common man in contrast to immoral city slickers and effete, corrupt "gentlemen."

In 1849, the inherent, but previously subdued, conflict between European-oriented elite groups and antiaristocratic common people in antebellum theater audiences burst into open combat during the Astor Place Riot in New York City. Theatrical riots, directed at "arrogant" English actors, whom the nationalistic b'hoys felt had insulted America or Americans, had occurred since 1825, when "mobocratic rowdies" in Boston used "a fusilade of missiles both hard and soft" to force Edmund Kean, the prominent British actor, off the stage because he reportedly complained that Americans did not take plays seriously. Even British actress Fanny Kemble's preference for the English style of horseback riding provoked an attempted riot.[25] Thus, it was nothing new when a New York City audience, invoking the name of nationalism, assaulted British tragedian Charles Macready who was engaged in a running battle for audiences, acclaim, and status with the leading American actor Edwin Forrest. After being bombarded with rotten eggs, vegetables, and chairs, Macready resolved to return to England immediately.

But a group of prominent New Yorkers, including Washington Irving and Herman Melville, greatly expanded the scope of the incident when they persuaded Macready to continue so that such rowdy behavior would not be allowed to destroy public order.[26] With police and soldiers standing by, great crowds gathered at the theater on the night of the next performance. After police arrested some of the demonstration leaders, a full-fledged battle erupted in the theater and on the streets outside. It escalated until the troops opened fire on the mob. When the bloody fighting finally ended, thirty-one rioters and spectators had been killed and 150 people had been injured— civilians, policemen, and soldiers.[27]

There were many major riots in antebellum American cities, but most of them were directed against various minority scapegoats—Catholics, abolitionists, and blacks.[28] Thus, the Astor Place Riot, with its class conflict, seemed to many writers a much more disturbing phenomenon. "There is now in our country, in New York City," the *Philadelphia Ledger* lamented, "what every good patriot has hitherto considered it his duty to deny—a high class and a low class." "The B'hoys of New York and the 'Upper Ten' are as divided as the white and red roses of York and Lancaster," The *Home Journal* ominously observed. "Let but the more passive aristocratic party select a favorite and let there be but a symptom of a handle for the B'hoys to express dissent, and the undercurrent breaks forth like an uncapped hydrant." [29]

Against the background of aggressively antiaristocratic popular culture heroes, of frequent urban riots, and of basic conflicts over the course of America's cultural development, the violent reaction to Macready was almost predictable. Just as their favorite stage character might have done, the b'hoys in the audience and their supporters in the street took action to humiliate Macready, "the pet of princes," and his upper-class American allies. To do this they even confronted armed soldiers and baited them. "Take the life out of a freeborn American for a bloody British actor! Do it," dared a "burly ruffian" baring his chest through his red flannel much as Mose might have done, saying "ay you daren't." [30] The attitudes expressed in the theater riot and in the popular stage characters were parts of a fundamental struggle between aristocrats and "middling" Americans. It was not a battle for goods; it was a battle over defining the nation and its values, and it was fought in the arena of popular culture.

After mid-century, sparked by the shocking revelations of the Astor Place Riot which made the unbridgeable cultural gap between American "common people" and "elite groups" unavoidably obvious, stage entertainment began to divide into specialized forms, offering distinctive attractions and appealing to different groups. In the 1830's, when all theatergoers still attended the same theater, a typical evening's entertainment consisted of a full-length play, whose acts were interspersed with variety specialities—dances, popular songs, black-faced acts, jugglers, acrobats, trained animals, and novelties like a "Monkey Man," whose act a critic lauded by exclaiming, "an ape itself could not do it better." [31] Regardless of the tone of the major feature, the company concluded the hodgepodge amusement package with a rollicking farce. But beginning in the 1850's, people in large cities and other major market areas could choose between different types of productions including legitimate theater, opera, symphony music, melodrama, variety, the circus, and minstrelsy. Even where the range of choices was not that wide, the distinction between popular and formal stage performances, between high and low brow culture, had become well established, which allowed both of them to develop more fully. Minstrelsy was the first new entertainment institution to emerge out of this turmoil.

More than any other individual, P. T. Barnum pioneered the techniques that made popular entertainment successful and paved the way for minstrelsy. Viewing public amusement strictly as a business in which entertainment was "merchandise" subject to the laws of trade like any other goods, he realized that he could make a fortune if he could persuade large numbers of people to each pay a small amount of money to be entertained. He solved the problem of how to find attractions with broad general appeal by resolving to offer the public "such a variety, quantity, and quality of amusement, blended with instruction all for twenty-five cents, children half price, that my attractions would be irresistible, and my fortune certain." Starting with the American Museum in New York City, a typical collection of natural and unnatural curiosities, he added features, including a theater, until he had a dazzling array of over 600,000 displays, wonders, and freaks, all packaged as a perfectly respectable educational institution. For one price of admission, the public could study working models of Niagara Falls and of new machines; it could see giants and midgets, elephants and trained fleas, a "Feejee mermaid" and a bearded lady, statues of scriptural characters, waxwork displays of the horrors of intemperance, American Indians doing war dances, an English Punch and Judy show, fancy glassblowers, and a knitting machine run by a dog. When people tired of all this, they could go into the "lecture room" and see a popular play or variety bill at no extra cost.[32] Like the verbal arts, Barnum's Museum was more than just amusement. Many of the features actually did teach his customers about the wider world they were just beginning to discover, while it also gave them shared experiences to talk about.

Although Barnum's Museum was the largest and grandest in America, it was not a new idea. Small urban museums, actually freak shows, and traveling menageries, featuring acrobats, clowns, and exotic wild animals, had existed for decades. Barnum's real genius stemmed from his understanding that, whatever the merits of his attractions, promotion was the key to success in popular entertainment. "At the outset of my career, I saw that everything depended upon getting people to think, and talk and become curious and excited over and about the 'rare spectacle.' " Long before twentieth-century advertising men trained in psychology learned to stage public relations stunts and "media events," Barnum had perfected the process. He admitted hiring acts that had no entertainment value because they would provoke free "plugs" in the newspapers. When he went into the burgeoning circus business in 1851, he imported Ceylonese elephants, and dramatically paraded them up Broadway in New York City to the delight of the public and press. After he temporarily withdrew from the circus business in 1855, he stationed one of his elephants on his farm and had it plow the same field over and over every time a train passed in order to attract attention for his museum and other ventures.[33] With these and the many other sensational stunts he used to stimulate public interest, Barnum demonstrated many of the promotional techniques that minstrelsy used as it grew and matured.

In the thirty years after the War of 1812, then, the forces demanding a "common man's culture" had transformed American entertainment. Virtually all of the old cultural forms, which had tried to accommodate highly vocal middling Americans into their audiences by making extensive use of American folk culture, had fragmented. Besides serious literature and arty journals, there were now inexpensive popular books and folksy weeklies, dominated by greater-than-life American folk heroes. Similarly, in addition to complex drama and comedies of manners, theaters now offered uncomplicated plays in which "simple" Americans won out over corrupt, money-grubbing schemers and pretentious aristocrats. Also reflecting average people's great demand for entertainment that they could understand and enjoy, menageries, acrobatic troupes, and equestrian shows grew in scale and began merging into traveling circuses that honeycombed the nation. Led by P. T. Barnum, entertainment entrepeneurs, sensing the great financial potential of the rapidly expanding markets produced by the revolutions in transportation and the explosions in urban population, began consciously catering to mass audiences and working to create public interest and attendance. With all the conditions present for an entertainment explosion, when a new, uniquely American popular culture form, the minstrel show, emerged on the scene, it became an instant rage and a national institution virtually overnight.

NOTES

¹ For the growth of American popular culture, see: Carl Bode, *The Anatomy of American Popular Culture, 1840–1861* (Berkeley, Cal., 1959); Foster Rhea Dulles, *A History of Recreation*, 2nd ed. (New York, 1965), pp. 84–168; David Grimsted, *Melodrama Unveiled: American Theater and Culture, 1800–1850* (Chicago, 1968); Francis Hodge, *Yankee Theater: The Image of America on the Stage, 1825–1850* (Austin, Tex., 1964).

² Stuart Blumin, "Mobility and Change in Antebellum Philadelphia," in Stephen Thernstrom (ed.), *Nineteenth Century Cities*, (New Haven, 1969, paperback ed.), pp. 199, 204–6; Norman Ware, *The Industrial Worker: 1840–1860*, (New York, 1964, paperback ed.), pp. 10–17. Carl N. Degler, *Out of Our Past*, (New York, 1962, paperback ed.), pp. 314–20; Ralph Turner, "The Industrial City: Center of Cultural Change," in Carolyn Ware, ed., *The Cultural Approach to History* (New York, 1940), pp. 228–42. Roger Lane explains Boston violence in this period as a response to "culture shock"; see: Roger Lane, "Urbanization and Criminal Violence in the 19th Century: Massachusetts as a Test Case," in Hugh Davis Graham and Ted Robert Gurr, eds., *Violence in America*, (New York, 1969, Signet ed.), pp. 453–55.

³ William Bascom, "Four Functions of Folklore," *Journal of American Folklore*, LXVII (1954), 333–49, "Folklore and Anthropology," *Journal of American Folklore*, LXVI (1953), 283–90; see also the articles on "The Functions of Folklore" in Alan Dundes, ed., *The Study of Folklore* (Englewood Cliffs, N.J., 1965), pp. 277–337.

⁴ The political manifestations of this development have been extensively studied and debated. For example, see: Lee Benson, *The*

Concept of Jacksonian Democracy (Princeton, 1961); Marvin Myers, *The Jacksonian Persuasion* (Stanford, Cal., 1957); Arthur Schlesinger, Jr., *The Age of Jackson* (Boston, 1945).

[5] The best survey of folk culture in these years is Richard M. Dorson, *American Folklore*, (Chicago, 1959, paperback ed.), chapters 2 and 6; Dorson's bibliographies are the best entry to the wide range of primary and secondary literature on this subject; also see two pioneering works: Walter Blair, *Native American Humor* (New York, 1937) and Constance Rourke, *American Humor* (New York, 1931).

[6] Daniel Boorstin, *The Americans: The National Experience*, (New York, 1965, Vintage ed.), parts six and seven; Benjamin T. Spencer, *The Quest for Nationality: An American Literary Campaign* (Syracuse, 1957).

[7] James Fenimore Cooper, *Last of the Mohicans*, (New York, 1960, Washington Square Press ed.), p. 44.

[8] Dorson, *American Folklore*, pp. 202–8.

[9] *Davy Crockett's Almanac*, Vol. I, No. 3 (1837), p. 40, in B. A. Botkin, ed., *Treasury of American Folklore* (New York, 1944), p. 28.

[10] *Sketches and Eccentricities of Col. David Crockett of West Tennessee* (New York, 1833), p. 164, in Botkin, *Treasury . . .* , p. 56.

[11] *Old Times in West Tennessee* (Memphis, 1873), pp. 175–76, in Botkin, *Treasury . . .* , p. 27.

[12] For various interpretations of these characters, see: Blair, Dorson, Rourke, and Jesse Bier, *The Rise and Fall of American Humor* (New York, 1968), pp. 52–77.

[13] There are, of course, important differences between homogeneous folk groups, in which performers are members of the group and all expression is in-group, and popular culture, where the performer-creator is not usually a member of the same group as the audience. But there are important similarities. As several important folklorists have pointed out, the social functions of verbal art are best understood when seen as theater (Melville Jacobs, *The Content and Style of an Oral Literature* [Chicago, 1959], p. 211; Daniel Crowley, *I Talk Old Story Good* [Berkeley, 1959]). Similarly, popular theater in the mid-nineteenth century, when audiences were extremely vocal, served as a vehicle for establishing a common identity for "middling" Americans, in a sense, a national American "folk," who shared symbols, norms, values, definitions, and perceptions.

23

The Emergence of a "Common Man's Culture"

¹⁴ William Davidge, *Footlight Flashes* (New York, 1867), p. 202, quoted in Dulles, *A History of Recreation*, pp. 100–101. Dunlap's efforts are described in chapter one of David Grimsted, *Melodrama Unveiled*.

¹⁵ The section on theater audiences is drawn primarily from: Grimsted, *Melodrama Unveiled*, pp. 46–78.

¹⁶ Hodge, *Yankee Theater*, pp. 25–26; Grimsted, *Melodrama Unveiled*, pp. 58–59.

¹⁷ Grimsted, *Melodrama Unveiled*, p. 65; New York *Mirror*, X (Mar. 9, 1833), p. 287, quoted in Hodge, *Yankee Theater*, p. 18.

¹⁸ Duprez and Benedict's Minstrels, *Minstrel Daily Herald* (advertisement in newspaper form), Feb. 25, 1875, Harvard Theatre Collection, hereafter referred to as HTC.

¹⁹ *Spirit of the Times*, October 24, 1846, quoted in Grimsted, *Melodrama Unveiled*, p. 64.

²⁰ Hodge, *Yankee Theater*, see also: Richard M. Dorson, "The Yankee on the Stage," *New England Quarterly*, XIII (1940), 467–93; Richard Moody, *America Takes the Stage: Romanticism in American Drama* (Bloomington, 1955); Rourke, *American Humor*; and Blair, *Native American Humor*.

²¹ Rourke, *American Humor*, pp. 65, 67.

²² Arthur H. Quinn, *A History of the American Drama from the Beginning to the Civil War*, 2nd ed. (New York, 1943), p. 304.

²³ Elizabeth Geffen, "Violence in Philadelphia in the 1840's and 1850's," *Pennsylvania History*, XXXVI (October 1969), 405–6; Lane, "Urbanization and Criminal Violence in the 19th Century: Massachusetts as a Test Case," p. 451.

²⁴ All preceding quotations by Mose are drawn from Richard M. Dorson, "Mose the Far-Famed and World-Renowned," *American Literature*, XV (1943), 288–300.

²⁵ Richard Moody, *The Astor Place Riot* (Bloomington, 1958), pp. 24–26; Grimsted, *Melodrama Unveiled*, pp. 66–67.

²⁶ Moody, *Riot*, pp. 130–31.

²⁷ *Ibid.*, pp. 116, 131–72.

²⁸ Between 1830 and 1860 there were at least 35 major riots in Baltimore, Philadelphia, Boston, and New York alone: Richard M. Brown, "Historical Patterns of Violence in America," *Violence in America*, pp. 50–51; Lane, "Urbanization . . . ," p. 455; Geffen, "Vi-

olence . . . ," pp. 386–98; Leonard Richard, *Gentlemen of Property and Standing: Anti-Abolition Mobs in Jacksonian America* (New York, 1970) analyzes the nature and motives of some of the riots and rioters.

[29] *Philadelphia Ledger*, May 14, 1849; *Home Journal*, May 12, 1849, quoted in Moody, *Riot*, pp. 228–29.

[30] Grimsted, *Melodrama Unveiled*, p. 74; Moody, *Riot*, p. 154.

[31] Grimsted, *Melodrama Unveiled*, pp. 99–105.

[32] P⍳ T. Barnum, *Struggles and Triumphs, or Forty Years' Recollections of P. T. Barnum Written by Himself* (Buffalo, 1873), pp. 72, 135.

[33] *Ibid.*, pp. 135, 146, 151, 357–62.

2 The Evolution of the Minstrel Show

As the first new popular entertainment form to grow out of the turbulent 1830's and 1840's, the minstrel show escaped most of the problems that plagued other stage entertainment. It was unabashedly popular in appeal, housed in its own show places, performed by middling Americans, focused on humble characters, and dominated by earthy, vital, song, dance, and humor. Every part of the minstrel show—its features, form, and content—was hammered out in the interaction between performers and the vocal audiences they sought only to please. "I've got only one method," J. H. Haverly, the greatest minstrel promoter, explained, "and that is to find out what the people want and then give them that thing. . . . There's no use trying to force the public into a theater." [1]

Besides this responsiveness, minstrels combined the folk-based themes and lore of other forms with Barnum's flair for promotion and added a compelling new figure—the black man.

By addressing themselves to race in the decades when white Americans first had to come to grips with what the position of blacks would be in America, while at the same time producing captivating, unique entertainment, blackfaced performers quickly established the minstrel show as a national institution, one that more than any other of its time was truly shaped by and for the masses of average Americans. Even though it was always extremely flexible, minstrelsy gradually evolved standard patterns and features that crystallized as audiences came to expect and demand their favorites and as performers found it increasingly necessary to plan their shows, which rapidly grew in size and complexity as well as popularity. The minstrel form and conventions that emerged in its formative first decade not only restructured American popular stage entertainment, they also revealed its huge audiences' central concerns, needs, and desires.

White men in blackface had portrayed Negro characters since well before the American Revolution. But until the War of 1812, Negro characters in popular songs were either comic buffoons or romanticized Noble Savages. Both types used dialects that owed more to Englishmen than to Afro-Americans. After the War of 1812, when the quest for a distinctly American culture dominated the arts, however, blackfaced characters became increasingly Afro-American. Ironically, an Englishman, Charles Matthews, first built Negro stage characterizations on detailed observations of black Americans. While visiting America in 1822, he studied Negro dialect, transcribed songs, lore, speeches, and sermons, and eagerly collected "scraps and malaprops." While attending a performance of the African Theater Company, a resident Negro theatrical troupe in New York City, Matthews heard the audience demand that the black actor playing Hamlet stop his soliloquy and sing "Possum up a Gum Tree." Matthews' use of this song in his act, "A Trip to America," was the first certain example of a white man borrowing Negro material for a blackfaced act.[2]

By the late 1820's, blackfaced white American performers like George Nichols, Bob Farrell, George Washington Dixon, J. W. Sweeney, John N. Smith, and Thomas D. Rice toured the nation, performing alleged Negro songs and dances in circuses and between the acts of plays. Like much of the rest of American culture, the melodies for many of these songs were of British origin. "Zip Coon" was related to an Irish song; "Sich a Getting Up Stairs" to an English Morris dance tune; "My Long Tail Blue" followed a Scottish folk song; "Jim Crow" resembled an Irish folk tune and an English stage song; and "Gumbo Chaff" was practically identical to the English song "Bow Wow Wow." But the lyrics drew heavily on American frontier lore and at least resembled Afro-American dialects while portraying comical images of blacks. "Coal Black Rose" described the struggle between two black men for Rose:

I ketch hold of Cuffee, I take him by de wool,
I ketch hold of Cuffee, he try away to pull
But I up wid a foot, and kick him on de shin,
Which put him breafless on de floor and make de nigger grin.

"My Long Tail Blue" told of a Negro dandy frivolously boasting about his clothing; "Clare de Kitchen," a series of unrelated verses, mixed animal fables with common humorous themes; similarly, "Zip Coon" interspersed comic love with topical verses:

I tell you what will happin den, now bery soon
De Nited States Bank will be blone to de moon
Dare General Jackson, will him lampoon,
An de bery nex President will be Zip Coon.[3]

Throughout the late 1820's traveling blackfaced performers grew in popularity and continually added to their repertoires. One of these "Ethiopian Delineators," Thomas D. Rice, while on tour in 1828, saw an old Negro, his right shoulder deformed and drawn up high, his left leg gnarled with rheumatism, stiff and crooked at the knee, doing an odd-looking dance while singing: "Weel about and turn about and do jus so;/Ebery time I weel about, I jump Jim Crow." Aware that any "peculiar" song or dance had great public appeal, Rice recognized this as excellent material for a stage act. He learned the song and dance, added new verses, "quickened and slightly changed the air," made himself up to look like the original—even to wearing his clothes—and took to the stage. His new act created a public sensation and took him on a triumphant tour of major entertainment centers, including dancing "Jim Crow" in New York City in 1832 and in London in 1836. Throughout the 1830's blackfaced entertainment gained in status and popularity; in the early 1840's two and even three minstrels banded together as song-and-dance-acts, but blackface remained only a part, though a prominent one, of other entertainment forms.[4]

Until the great impact of Harriet Beecher Stowe's novel *Uncle Tom's Cabin* after 1851, blacks were only minor characters in drama and literature.[5] In American drama, Negroes assumed the comic relief role that the ignorant Irish servant played in England, supplemented by some images of happy slaves.[6] Beginning in the 1830's "Ethiopian Delineators" strongly influenced these other stage portrayals of Negroes. In 1834, for example, just a few years after T. D. Rice first "jumped Jim Crow," Sambo, a loyal, trusting black servant in the play *The Patriot*, made his entrance singing: "Weel about—turn about—do just so, and eb'ry time weel about, Jump Sambo." [7] These minstrel-influenced comic parts culminated in Zeke, the malaprop-spewing servant in Anna Cora Mowatt's 1845 hit comedy

The Evolution of the Minstrel Show

The Fashion, which contrasted the European affectations of American elite groups to the noble simplicity of Adam True-man, a model stage Yankee. Just as the white "aristocrats" ridiculously aped Europeans, Zeke ludicrously tried to be something he was not—a white man. His opening speech indicated the tone of the play and of his character:

> Dere's a coat to take de eyes of all Broadway! Ah, Missy, it am de fixin's dat make de natural *born* gemman. A libery for ever! Dere's a pair ob insuppressibles to 'stonish de colored population.[8]

Although Negroes were featured no more prominently in pre-*Uncle Tom's Cabin* literature than in drama, the portrayals of them were more diverse and less influenced by minstrelsy. Beginning with Washington Irving's *Salamagundi* in 1817, the flat-nosed, big-lipped, "dancing darky" with the ear-to-ear grin became a nineteenth-century literary fixture. But Irving also described Negro storytellers and fishermen. James Fenimore Cooper added free Negroes who were proficient frontiersmen and superior sailors, and he made his Negro servants crafty and anxious to poke fun at their masters as well as loyal and deferential. In Cora, in *Last of the Mohicans*, he also created one of first "tragic Octoroons"—light-skinned "mixed blood" characters with the feelings and sensitivities of whites who were condemned to live as blacks. Even William Gilmore Simms, a Southern defender of slavery, created diverse black characters ranging from obsequious servants to brave freemen. But his typical Negro character, as it was in literature generally, was the happy slave who loved his master and refused to leave him even when offered freedom. Although antislavery writers saw the plantation as a brutal, cruel place for slaves, they portrayed blacks as passive victims, even when they idealized them as Christ-like martyrs. In fact, opponents of slavery made nearly all their rebellious slaves mulattoes, who had presumably gotten their love of freedom from their white ancestors.[9] Thus, although the conflicting sides in the debate over slavery had completely opposite views of the institution, they had rather similar views of black slaves' character. Even though these pre-*Uncle Tom's Cabin* portrayals of Negroes were only scattered minor characters in at best moderately widespread entertainment vehicles, they did reveal general American cultural tendencies to cast Negroes as inferior to whites and to use them for comic relief. But before *Uncle Tom's Cabin* it was minstrelsy that had the greatest impact on the Northern public's images of blacks.

In February 1843, four blackfaced white men, wearing ill-fitting, ragtag clothing, took the stage in New York City to perform for the first time an entire evening of the "oddities, peculiarities, eccentricities, and comicalities of that Sable Genus of Humanity."[10] The four men, Billy Whitlock, Frank Pelham, Dan Emmett, and Frank Brower, who billed themselves as the Virginia Minstrels, each had had experience as blackfaced entertainers with circuses, but they had no idea how popular blackface minstrelsy would be as a separate entertainment form. Having found themselves out of work in New York City during the disastrous 1842–43 entertainment season, they merely hoped that by increasing their numbers they would improve their box office. Their choice of name fits the same opportunistic pattern. Besides taking the name of a famous Southern state to enhance their claims of authenticity, they called themselves "minstrels" instead of the more common "delineators" because of the great success of the Tyrolese Minstrel Family which had recently toured America.[11] Even though by accident, the Virginia Minstrels appeared at the right time. They were instant sensations. In late 1843 the company left for a successful English tour, during which it dissolved for basically personal reasons, but also because the performers still thought of themselves as singles, not as a troupe. What they left behind, however, was a minstrel-mad public and a bevy of imitators that reshaped American popular entertainment.

Minstrelsy swept the nation in the mid-1840's. Indicating its rapid acceptance, in 1844, only a year after the first minstrel show, the Ethiopian Serenaders, a blackface minstrel troupe, played at the White House for the "Especial Amusement of the President of the United States, His Family and Friends." In subsequent years, minstrels entertained Presidents Tyler, Polk, Fillmore, and Pierce,[12] as well as countless common Americans throughout the nation. In response to the seemingly insatiable public demand, innumerable minstrel troupes appeared. It is impossible to determine how many there were, even in the first decade of minstrelsy, partially because of inadequate records but also because amateur and amateurish troupes appeared almost everywhere, usually only for short runs. When large numbers of people trekked across the continent in search of California gold, for example, minstrelsy quickly established itself there. First presented in 1849 by local amateur groups scattered throughout the gold fields, minstrelsy by 1855 claimed five professional troupes in San Francisco alone.[13] Similar developments occurred wherever people were concentrated and transportation was available, especially along the Mississippi River, the rapidly expanding rail lines into the Northwest, and in the burgeoning cities of the Northeast.[14]

Antebellum minstrelsy enjoyed great popularity throughout the nation, but few famous troupes, in fact, traveled widely before the Civil War. The Buckley Serenaders visited California in 1852 and toured what later became the Southern minstrel route—Baltimore, Louisville, Savannah, Charleston, Mobile, Memphis, and New Orleans, and then up the Mississippi—but this tour was very unusual for a major troupe. Generally, the traveling companies before the war were local performers touring their own region, many exploiting the names of famous troupes. For example, at least fifteen minstrel companies, many with famous names, performed in Memphis between 1845 and 1860. But most of them were either the same basic personnel using different minstrel names or different performers masquerading as the same famous troupe.[15]

Although blackface entertainment was born in the Mid-West and South, the minstrel show itself began and matured in the cities of the Northeast. Philadelphia, Boston, and New York either gave birth to most of the famous companies or served as their permanent homes. The reason major troupes did not travel was the success they enjoyed in these cities, where it was not uncommon for minstrel companies to have consecutive runs of a decade! Ordway's Aeolians in Boston, Hooley's Minstrels in Brooklyn, and E. P. Christy's Minstrels in New York each ran ten years straight; in Philadelphia, Sanford's Minstrels ran seven years and Carncross and Dixey's ran nine; Wood's Minstrels bested all others by running for fifteen years in New York City.[16]

New York City, the birthplace of the minstrel show, was by far its greatest stronghold until after the Civil War. Virtually all the major developments in minstrelsy began there, primarily because the intense competition eliminated poor performers and forced innovations. From mid-1840 to mid-1850, five or six major companies regularly played there; during the 1850's, ten major minstrel houses thrived and three famous troupes played in the same block on Broadway. Minstrels performed in large theaters like the Chatham, Bowery, and Old Park, in Barnum's Museum, in converted churches and synagogues, in a showboat that toured the New York vicinity, and in their own newly built theaters, which they sometimes christened "Ethiopian Opera Houses." With these massive audiences, it is not surprising that the *Literary World* observed in

33

The Evolution of the Minstrel Show

1849 that minstrelsy convulsed "the b'hoys and their seamstress sweethearts," probably many of the same b'hoys who fought in the Astor Place Riots and cheered the antics of Mose.[17]

Everywhere it played, minstrelsy seemed to have a magnetic, almost hypnotic, impact on its audiences. "A minstrel show came to town, and I thought of nothing else for weeks," Ben Cotton recalled of the first time he saw minstrels in the 1840's in Pawtucket, Rhode Island. George Thatcher, later a minstrel star, had comparable feelings when as a boy in Baltimore he saw his first show. "I found myself dreaming of minstrels; I would awake with an imaginary tambourine in my hand, and rub my face with my hands to see if I was blacked up. . . . The dream of my life was to see or speak to a performer." After Dave Wambold, later a minstrel tenor, attended his first minstrel show in Newark, New Jersey, his parents could not keep him in school because "he was wont to play truant and get up minstrel performances among his companions." Similarly, Joel Chandler Harris, Stephen Foster, M. B. Leavitt, and Al G. Field—all later important in American popular culture—were stagestruck boys who played minstrelsy in their youth. Minstrels had truly captured the imagination of the nation.[18]

But why was minstrelsy a national senation? What gave it such great appeal for Northern white common people of all ages? As it evolved into an entertainment institution over the years, it became a major vehicle through which Northern whites conceptualized and coped with many of their problems. Analysis of these "deeper" meanings, which is the major subject of this book, provides the fullest understanding of the reasons for minstrelsy's popularity and longevity.

But, first of all, minstrelsy had to establish itself as an amusement that masses of people would pay to see. Although blackface makeup and portrayal of Negro characters were synonymous with minstrelsy from its inception, the form had enough other attractions to have made it at least a temporary success. It offered antebellum Americans an irresistible entertainment package. Like Davy Crockett's tall tales and Mose's braggadocio stunts, minstrelsy brought the vitality and vigor of the folk into popular culture. Furthermore, minstrelsy was not only responsive to its audiences, it was very much like them. It was immediate, unpretentious, and direct. It had no characterization to develop, no plot to evolve, no musical score, no set speeches, no subsidiary dialogue—indeed no fixed script at all. Each act—song, dance, joke, or skit—was a self-contained performance that strived to be a highlight of the show. This meant that minstrels could adapt to their specific audience while the show was in process.

To these general entertainment appeals, minstrelsy added the promise of satisfying white Northerners' growing curiosity about blacks and especially slaves at a time when slavery was becoming a major national controversy. Unlike earlier blackface entertainers who focused on vaguely western Jim Crow or urban Zip Coon, the Virginia Minstrels and their successors claimed that their infectious music, captivating dance, and rollicking humor represented the "sports and pastimes of the Virginia Colored Race, through medium of Songs, Refrains, and Ditties as sung by Southern slaves." [19] Although most Northerners did not know what slaves were like, they believed or wanted to believe that black slaves differed greatly from free, white Americans. Thus, minstrels emphasized Negro "peculiarities," described themselves exotically as "Ethiopian Delineators" and/or "Congo Melodists," and called some of their acts "Virginia Jungle Dance," "Nubian Jungle Dance," "African Fling," and "African Sailor's Hornpipe." [20] Probably more convincing than anything else, minstrel performances looked different enough to be authentic.

1. This sheet music cover represents common early minstrel images of Northern and Southern Negroes. Note the contorted bodies and physical caricatures used to stress slaves' "peculiarities."

Boston Minstrels, "Ethiopian Melodies," Boston, 1843, Harvard Theatre Collection.

The Virginia Minstrels combined the raucous qualities of the frontier with what audiences believed were Negro song, dance, dialect, and humor and presented them with a vitality, exuberance, and rapid-fire pace previously unknown on the American stage. They were something new, unusual, and compelling. They burst on stage in makeup which gave the impression of huge eyes and gaping mouths. They dressed in ill-fitting, patchwork clothes, and spoke in heavy "nigger" dialects. Once on stage, they could not stay still for an instant. Even while sitting, they contorted their bodies, cocked their heads, rolled their eyes, and twisted their outstretched legs. When the music began, they exploded in a frenzy of grotesque and eccentric movements. Whether singing, dancing, or joking, whether in a featured role, accompanying a comrade, or just listening, their wild hollering and their bobbing, seemingly compulsive movements charged their entire performance with excitement. They sang and danced rousing numbers and cracked earthy jokes.[21] From beginning to end, their shows provided an emotional outlet. Most of all, the performers seemed to have fun and succeeded in involving the foot-stomping, whistling, shouting audiences in the festivities.

Some early minstrel troupes based their appeals more on sentimental, emotional material than on the robust humor and music of the Virginia Minstrels. The songs of Stephen Foster epitomize this approach. Foster himself had starred as a blackface singer with an amateur theater group when he was only nine years old. While in his teens, he had seen "Jim Crow" Rice perform and tried unsuccessfully to sell him some songs. In the late 1840's Foster's songs, especially "Old Uncle Ned" and "Camptown Races," enjoyed great success with many minstrel troupes. After 1850, Foster sold E. P. Christy, leader of the popular Christy Minstrels, many of his most famous songs, among them "Old Folks at Home" (first published under E. P.

The Evolution of the Minstrel Show

Christy's name) and "Massa's in the Cold Ground." [22] His songs enjoyed greater popularity than those of any other minstrel songwriter.

Everything Foster wrote was romantic, sentimental, and emotionally moving. On the plantation, he found warm, happy images of family and home, free from all problems. His fictional slaves, though he shunned that word, were happy and carefree, contented old men or exiles longing to return. His drippingly romantic love songs were about aged mothers with grey hair and gentle eyes or fragile, delicate women in the grave or close to it. He intensified the emotional impact of many of his love songs by directing them toward dying or dead lovers, which also ensured that the love was free of sexuality. The pure love for a departed mother, the lifelong devotion to the dying lover, the serene death of a contented old slave—all these flowed from Foster's pen and from minstrel stages. Foster's songs offered the unsettled Northern public welcome symbols of escape from their frustrating, new lives: distance in time (childhood, old age, the "good old days"), distance in space (the South), distance from reality (dreams), and distance from life (death). [23] Besides giving whites ludicrous caricatures of blacks, minstrelsy, through songs like Foster's, also created an idealized world that had all the virtues that Northern society seemed to lack.

By 1845, minstrelsy in New York City drifted toward the "refined" melodic approach to minstrelsy and away from the earthy vitality of its folk roots. The Ethiopian Serenaders, basking in the glory of their White House triumph, evidently sought the respectability of "high" culture by cleaning up their show and concentrating on blackfaced "concerts." In 1846, they left for a successful English tour. In their absence, the Christy Minstrels opened in New York. Within a year, that troupe surpassed all other minstrel companies in popularity and, along with Barnum's Museum, became a mandatory entertainment stop for the city's rural visitors.[24] Using Foster's songs, they kept the sentimental, "refined" music and restored the robust comedy, song, and dance of the Virginia Minstrels. They had found the ideal minstrel blend. In 1847, when the Ethiopian Serenaders returned from England, the *Spirit of the Times* warned them that they were too elegant and sedate in their formal wear and their musical manner to compete with the humor of the Christys who "accomplish what is the legitimate object of their costume and colored faces, namely the personation of the witty Negro. At Palmo's [where the Serenaders were playing] we listen and are pleased but leave with little desire to return." After seeing the Christys, however, "we listen and laugh and desire to go again and again." [25] Minstrel audiences obviously wanted to laugh at Negro characters and to enjoy their "peculiar" music and dance as well as being serenaded with lyrical popular music that appealed to their "tender" emotions.

Because early minstrels created plausible black characters, some Northerners, probably a substantial number of the gullible public that had seen few Negroes and were still unfamiliar with minstrel conventions, mistook minstrels for real Negroes. When Al G. Field, himself later a minstrel, first saw minstrels, he thought they were black men. And in the 1860's, a country visitor to Boston believed blackfaced performers were actually Negroes.[26] Furthermore, after the Civil War, when black people first became minstrels, whites were astonished at the diversity of Negroes' skin color. Realizing that some audience members believed that they were Negroes, early minstrels tried to make it quite clear that only their makeup and some of their material was black. During their English tour in 1846, for example, when the Ethiopian Serenaders were charged with not being real Negroes, they issued no denials. The minstrels, an Englishman observed, resented any implication that they had

2. This sheet music cover contrasts minstrels in blackface and makeup with portraits of them as respectable white men.

"Songs of the Virginia Serenaders," Boston, 1844, Harvard Theatre Collection.

even the "least drop of black blood in their veins; so they lost no time in publishing portraits of themselves with the white faces bestowed upon them by nature." [27] The minstrel sheet music that flooded America in the early years when minstrelsy was still a new form also emphasized that minstrelsy was a white man's charade by featuring portraits of the groups in formal wear without their makeup, sometimes accompanied by contrasting illustrations of them in costume and blackface. Minstrels also put material into their shows to stress the point. "Why am I like a young widow?" a comedian asked. After the line was slowly repeated, he fired back: "Because I do not stay long in black." [28] With such devices, minstrels established their identities as professional entertainers—and as white men.

Although primarily Northern and white, the Virginia Minstrels and their many successors claimed to be authentic delineators of black life.[29] But were they? In one important sense, the question is easily answerable. Blackface minstrels were not authentic, even in intention. They were not ethnographers, but professional entertainers whose major concern was to create stage acts that would please their audiences. The issue, then, is where the minstrels obtained the material they transformed into blackfaced stage acts. Did they draw on Afro-Americans for more than color?

Like other antebellum entertainers, minstrels drew on Anglo-American folklore, especially on the volatile frontiersman who was better suited to minstrels' flamboyant style than the understated Yankee. Reflecting nationalistic boosterism, minstrels advocated expansion to Texas, Oregon, and Cuba; offered to fight in Maine's border dispute with Canada; and taunted Europeans, especially the British, for their weaknesses and vices. In the best tradition of Mike Fink, blackfaced riverboatmen sang, danced, and fought their ways up and down rivers as far apart as the Susquehanna and the Mississippi.[30]

The Evolution of the Minstrel Show

Although some of these songs bore little resemblance to river lore, others had an authentic ring. In work-song style, the refrain "Pull away merrily, Row boys row" punctuated the verses of "The Darky's Boat Song." Other songs had similar patterns: "De Singing Darkey of de Ohio," "Dance Boatmen Dance," and "Banks of de Ohio." [31] And as blackface roarers, rivaling the likes of Davy Crockett, minstrel characters trumpeted their own boasts:

> My mammy was a wolf, my daddy was a tiger
> I'm what you call de ole Virginia nigger;
> Half fire, half smoke, a little touch of thunder
> I'm what dey call de eighth wonder.

A number of other blackface roarers bragged about their powers. "I wip de lion of de west," one claimed. "I wip my weight in wildcats," another boasted; "I eat an alligator." [32]

Like the literature of the frontier, minstrelsy also made extensive use of tall tales. In 1848, one character bragged in song that he had scratched out a panther's eyes with his toenails, bent a tree till it had a hump like a camel, and pulled a steamboat out of the water with a fishing pole. Another character successfully defended himself against various animals after a punitive master tied him up as a scarecrow. He killed a buzzard by blowing in its face, blinded a panther by scratching out its eyes with his toenails, and escaped when a weasel gnawing on his leg ate through his bonds. [33] Others sang of sailing down the Mississippi on the backs of alligators with teeth like broad swords or on logs that turned into sea serpents. These characters steered the sea creatures by their tails and could, without breathing, ride them for miles underwater. When one of these blackfaced characters found his entrance to a river blocked by a giant catfish he simply sailed his boat right at its mouth and turned it inside out. [34] In portraying such incredible exploits, which were typical of the Western lore that played such an important part in the emergence of American popular culture, minstrels used familiar material guaranteed to please their audiences.

But what was so striking about early minstrelsy was that it seemed unique. Although minstrels' strange and exaggerated gestures and makeup account for part of this appearance of distinctiveness, strong evidence exists that as part of their effort to capture the native vitality of America and to establish themselves as authentic delineators of Negroes, white minstrels selectively adapted elements of black as well as white folk culture. Even though early blackface entertainers were almost all Northern white men, they had ample opportunity to learn about black music, dance, and lore while traveling widely in the South and West before minstrelsy became a sedentary, urban form. They were constantly on the lookout for material to construct unique stage acts with a strong folk appeal. And since they could shape the lore they adapted into nonthreatening images of Negroes as harmless curiosities, there was no reason for them not to follow the examples of Charles Matthews and T. D. Rice and "borrow" material from Negroes.

Since cultural interaction between blacks and whites was common in Southern frontier areas, minstrels probably unwittingly included elements of black culture in some of what they thought was white frontier lore. Both South Carolina Negroes and white boatmen knew "Possum Up the Gum Tree"; Negro firemen on the Mississippi sang "Clare de Kitchen"; and a Negro banjoist at a white frontier frolic in Tennessee in the early 1830's played "De Ole Jaw Bone." Furthermore, black and white backwoodsmen both danced many of the same jigs and reels.[35] The blend of Afro- and Euro-American musical and dance styles, which later became common in American popular culture, began on the frontier and was first given wide exposure by minstrels.

The Evolution of the Minstrel Show

The importance for minstrelsy of the reciprocal relationship between white and black cultures was strikingly evident in the career of William Henry Lane, "Master Juba," one of the few Negroes in early minstrelsy and the most famous dancer of his day. Although he specialized in the "jig," an Irish folk dance, at a time when everyone was familiar with it, he was widely acclaimed as a unique dancer. Whether playing a New York City dive or starring with a white minstrel troupe, his act began with imitations of the other famous dancers of his day and climaxed when he "show[ed] his own jig." Praised by Charles Dickens and many other critics for his unusual style, he consistently defeated John Diamond, the greatest white minstrel dancer, in a series of challenge dances after 1845, with "the manner in which he beats time with his feet." His rhythm set him off from all the others. He had learned a European dance, blended it with African tradition, and produced a new form, an Afro-American dance that had a great impact on minstrelsy.[36]

Such blendings of black and white dances pervaded early minstrelsy and help account for its appearance of uniqueness. The normal direction of the adaption, however, was from blacks to blackface, and the "borrowers" were white men who consciously learned from blacks. Thomas D. Rice's "Jump Jim Crow," the first blackface act to win widespread fame, was also the first clear instance of a minstrel using an Afro-American dance. Since the melody to "Jim Crow" was a familiar English tune and the words were neither unusual or especially clever, it must have been the dance that made Rice's performance such a public rage. Descriptions of the "hop," the rhythms, and the peculiar shoulder and arm movements involved in the dance strongly suggest that it was a variation of a characteristically Negro shuffle in which the feet remain close to the ground and upper-body movements predominate. "Jump Jim Crow" was, thus, probably the first of many Afro-American dances to become a worldwide success.[37] The "Essence of Old Virginia," one of the most famous minstrel dances with which the early plantation finales often closed, was also characterized by the sliding steps of Afro-American shuffles in contrast to the high stepping tapping of Irish "jigs." "If a guy could really do it," ragtime composer Arthur Marshall said of "The Essence," "he sometimes looked as if he was being towed around on ice skates . . . the performer moves forward without appearing to move his feet at all." [38] Ultimately, minstrels refined this Afro-American dance into the extremely popular and influential "Soft Shoe." Through the years, minstrels continued to get many of their new dances from blacks. In the 1850's, Dave Reed, a white minstrel, emerged with a dance he said he learned from Negroes when he was working on Mississippi riverboats. Again, its peculiar arm and hand movements strongly resembled Afro-American dances, the "Buzzard Lope" and the "Ring Shout," which lends credence to Reed's claim. In the 1880's James McIntyre, of the famous minstrel team McIntyre and Heath, claimed to be the first to introduce the syncopated "Buck and Wing," a combination time-step and hop that became a popular twentieth-century tap dance. Although his claim is doubtful, the dance's Afro-American origin is not.[39] "The Walkaround," another speciality in minstrels' plantation finales, featured competition between individuals within a circle formed by the rest of the company. Like the others, this dance almost certainly journeyed from Africa through Afro-Americans on plantations to minstrels on theatrical stages.[40]

Although no other area of early minstrelsy was as strongly indebted to blacks as the dance, it is clear that minstrels borrowed other material as well. George Nichols, a blackface circus clown who was one of the pioneers of minstrelsy, learned some of his "original" songs, like "Clare de Kitchen," from anonymous blacks on the Mississippi and from two New Orleans Negro singers, Picayune Butler and "Old Corn Meal." Little is known about Butler, from whom Nichols got "Picayune Butler Is Going Away." But "Corn Meal" was a street vendor who appeared on stage with his horse and cart in New Orleans in 1837 and again in 1840, performing minstrel songs and his own material, which included his vending song "Fresh Corn Meal." T. D. Rice probably borrowed from "Corn Meal" when Rice visited New Orleans in 1835, 1836, and 1838. During his second visit there, he prepared a skit entitled "Corn Meal" certainly derived from the black performer.[41] In 1856, some twenty years later, when Buckley's New Orleans Serenaders were playing in Savannah, G. Swaine Buckley, the troupe's singing star, saw a Negro vendor with a small donkey cart selling melons by calling his wares in a chanted song.[42] Buckley was so taken with this "grotesque outfit" that he later amused J. W. McAndrews and other troupe members with an account of it. Realizing a good thing, McAndrews found the vendor the next day, learned his song and routine, and bought his whole outfit—clothes, cart, and donkey. Turning the Negro's sales pitch into a blackface act, McAndrews became "The Watermelon Man," a part he continued to play until his career ended in 1895, almost forty years later.[43]

Although blackface performers rarely credited specific material to blacks because they wanted to be known as creative artists as well as entertainers, many early minstrels claimed that they did "field work" among Southern Negroes while they were traveling. The individual claims are rarely as confirmable as Dave Reed's, but since these performers had both the opportunities and the motives to do it, and since Afro-American culture did influence minstrelsy, these claims probably represent what at least some minstrels did to find new material. Billy Whitlock, one of the original Virginia Minstrels, spent a great deal of time in the 1830's touring the South with circuses, learning to play the banjo, and shaping his act. He claimed that when he was not performing, he would "steal off to some negro hut to hear the darkies sing and see them dance, taking a jug of whisky to make things merrier." Ben Cotton, a minstrel specializing in portrayals of Southern Negroes, also claimed he closely studied blacks when he worked on Mississippi riverboats. "I used to sit with them in front of their cabins," he recalled, "and we would start the banjo twanging, and their voices would ring out in the quiet night air in their weird melodies. They did not quite understand me. I was the first white man they had seen who sang as they did; but we were brothers for the time being and were perfectly happy." From somewhere, perhaps from sessions such as these, banjo tunes with complex rhythms, that had no European antecedents and showed strong evidence of African polyrhythms, emerged in minstrelsy in the 1840's. These few dozen syncopated banjo tunes may have been the first evidence of the evolution of American jazz from the interaction of European melodies with African rhythms.[44]

Early in his life, E. P. Christy, leader of the influential Christy Minstrels, had considerable experience with Southern Negroes. In 1827, in New Orleans, he supervised a ropewalk worked by slaves, whose singing fascinated him. While in New Orleans, he reportedly was a regular visitor at what he called "the Congo Green", the area usually known as Congo Square where blacks gathered to sing, dance, and celebrate whenever they could. There Christy studied Negroes' "queer words and simple but expressive melodies." After leaving the South, Christy gained fame as a traveling blackface musician and comic singer. In the late 1830's he settled in Buffalo, New York, worked as a blackface entertainer, and allegedly continued to draw material from Negroes, especially One-legged Harrison, a singer in a Negro church, with whom he claimed to visit and "trade down home talk." [45] In 1842 or 1843, he formed a minstrel troupe in Buffalo. A few years later, when the Christy Minstrels stunned audiences and moved to the forefront of minstrelsy, they doubtless brought parts of Afro-American culture with them.

Lending further credence to the argument that they did draw material from blacks, early minstrels incorporated elements of Afro-American folklore and beliefs into their shows. As ex-slaves later did, minstrels portrayed "jumping the broom" as a way slaves "wed widout any bodder" and described the "Patting Juba" dance that was common among antebellum slaves.[46] They also included superstitions that closely resembled Afro-American folk beliefs. They advertised, for example, that the song "We Are Coming Sister Mary" was "founded on a superstition that exists among the slaves that when one of their number is about to die they are forewarned by singing spirits" or "in a dream song." Such beliefs were common in black folk tradition.[47] Several minstrel songs incorporated other superstitions and beliefs also found in black folklore. Some warned, for example, that heads should be shaved before burial, while others attested to the importance of the devil in black tradition.

> White folks say de debils dead
> An buried in a tan vat
> De nigger say he raised again
> And turned into a ram cat.[48]

This traditional association between cats and evil was also expressed in songs which told of young girls mysteriously killed by a black cat pressing "his clay cold lips" to her beating breast or by a "snowy white" old tomcat "drinking" a girl's breath "like cream." [49] Such material, which was only a minor part of minstrelsy, is significant because it is additional evidence that minstrels did observe and learn from the black folk and because superstition became a major feature of whites' stereotypes of blacks.

Minstrels made extensive use of nonsense humor, fantasy, and animal fables that they almost certainly derived from Afro-American folk song and narrative, which relied heavily on animal symbolism, used indirection and guile to voice protests or attack adversaries, and featured victories for the weak over the strong. Anglo-American tradition, on the other hand, was direct and "realistic," employed overt protest, and presented direct conflicts, in which the strong always won out.[50] Minstrel songs reveal traits of both traditions, which again reinforces the point that minstrels eclectically selected their material with their eyes on its entertainment value, not on its origins. Since minstrels' early songs were often little more than series of unconnected fragments held together only by a common chorus, it was quite easy for them to add any items, themes, or verses that they liked to their repertoires.

Reflecting this versatility, early minstrel songs often included verses about raccoons, possums, jaybirds, alligators, frogs, chickens, hounds, and other animals, whose exploits were both "nonsensical" (in that they lacked social meanings) and quite pointed. A typical example of a nonsense or non-pointed verse was:

> Dare was a frog jumped out de spring,
> It was so cold he couldn't sing,
> He tied his tail to a hickory stump,
> He rared an pitched but he couldn't make a jump.[51]

Like the black folk, minstrels also used animal verses that described ordinary hunting scenes, narrated the actions of animals who talked and behaved like people, and reflected the symbolic expression black verbal tradition used to portray conflict:

> Jaybird pon a swinging limb
> Winked at me I winked at him
> Cotched up a stone hit him on de shin
> And dats de way we sucked him in.[52]

Still other minstrel verses described the weak outsmarting the strong, another dominant theme in Afro-American lore:

> A Bull frog dress'd in sogers close
> Went in de field to shoot some crows;
> De crows smell powder and fly away
> De Bull frog mighty mad dat day.[53]

Two versions of "Jim Crack Corn" indicate that minstrels used the techniques of both Anglo- and Afro-American lore in their animal songs. Both were directed against the master. The common version, which might have come from any source, used realistic symbols: the blue tail fly bit the master's horse, causing it to throw him to his death, after which the singers often gloated over their master's accidental demise.[54] Another version, however, used characteristic Afro-American aggressive fantasy to express antimaster violence, which the narrator, almost in complicity, made no attempt to interrupt: a fly "big as an elephant" was in the master's shoe and proceeded to devour him as he put it on.

> Poor mass did scream, de fly didn't care
> He eat till de shoe alone war dere
> An all ob de ole Massa dat we could spy
> Stuck out ob de troat ob de Blue Tail Fly.[55]

Many minstrel nonanimal fantasy songs also reflected similar feelings and methods. One female slave, for example, had such a huge "mouf" and nostrils that her master used to hang his clothes on them. In retaliation, she swallowed his hat and coat, and when he took her with him to a tailor shop, she "swallowed tailor and all." [56] As a result of living in a discriminatory caste system, the black folk learned to use features of whites' negative stereotypes of Negroes as at least psychic weapons against whites, as this minstrel song did. The presence of these distinctively Afro-American themes and techniques in minstrelsy further supports the view that minstrels borrowed from black culture. Moreover, minstrelsy also portrayed crafty black slave tricksters, whose constant verbal battles to outwit and ridicule their masters closely resemble the John and Old Master stories of Afro-American folk tradition. [57]

The link between minstrelsy and black folk song has long been recognized, but it has been assumed that this indicated "the white man in the woodpile"; that is, that the black folk simply absorbed minstrel songs into their repertoires. [58] Although some blacks no doubt did this, it is also clear that early minstrels used Afro-American dances and dance-steps, reproduced individual Negro's songs and "routines" intact, absorbed Afro-American syncopated rhythms into their music, and employed characteristically Afro-American folk elements and forms. Black and white Americans influenced each other. In their formative years, many blackfaced performers traveled all over the country consciously drawing vital and distinctive material from the native folk. There was no reason for entertainers portraying black characters to ignore Afro-American material, and every reason for them to use it. When a new generation of untraveled, urban minstrels emerged, minstrelsy seemed to its audiences to be losing its authentic flavor and tone. In fact, this lack of what audiences perceived to be credible Negro portrayals was the most common reason contemporaries gave for the decline of minstrelsy. [59] After Negroes had become minstrels and essentially pre-empted "Negro Subjects," white performers like J. W. McAndrews and McIntyre and Heath, who claimed they had studied blacks and probably had, were the only white minstrels to retain their reputations for Ethiopian delineation.[60]

Besides confirming the folk origins of American popular entertainment, minstrelsy's borrowing of Afro-American culture is of great significance because it was the first indication of the powerful influence Afro-American culture would have on the performing arts in America. It does not mean that early minstrels accurately portrayed Negro life or even the cultural elements that they used. They did neither. In the process of creating their stage images of Negroes, Northern white professional entertainers selectively adapted elements of Afro-American folk culture into caricatures and stereotypes of Negroes.[61] These negative images of blacks did have some elements of black culture in them, however twisted and distorted the overall effect was. Thus, when white Americans later came in contact with Afro-Americans, whites who were disposed to confirm the caricatures could do it by focusing on the familiar elements, like superstition, love of music and dance, and the "childish" belief in "silly" animal fables and by ignoring everything else about blacks. Minstrelsy was the first example of the way American popular culture would exploit and manipulate Afro-Americans and their culture to please and benefit white Americans.

Although minstrelsy became an American entertainment fixture virtually overnight, it took almost a decade for minstrels and their audiences to evolve a standard pattern for the minstrel show. Until the debut of the Virginia Minstrels, blackface entertainment had consisted of individual songs and dances and a smattering of short comedy skits. Thus, the Virginia Minstrels inadvertently began to shape the conventions of the minstrel show when they structured their performances. To improve the coordination of the show, they arranged their chairs in a semi-circle, with the tambourine and bones (simple rhythm "clackers") players on the ends; to give the performance the aura of a real party and to provide continuity, they interspersed comic repartee between their otherwise unconnected songs and dances; to add laughter, they closed the first part of their two-part show with a stump speech (a humorous "address" on a topical subject delivered in heavy malaprop-laden dialect); and to stress their authenticity as "Ethiopian delineators," they concentrated on songs and dances about Southern Negroes, usually concluding with a rousing plantation number. All of these features became standard parts of the show in later years. Besides that, the instruments they used—the fiddle, banjo, bones, and tambourine—became the core of the minstrel band. But, minstrelsy still had only minimal structure.[62] From its inception, it had such versatility and flexibility that it could immediately respond to its audiences' preferences in both form and content.

By the mid-1850's, minstrel companies had grown larger, performers had become more specialized, featured roles had emerged, and minstrelsy had arrived at the basic three-part structure that it thereafter retained. The basic minstrel format, which resulted from audience-performer interaction and extensive experimentation, reveals a great deal about the entertainment appeal of minstrelsy. In the first part, the entire company appeared in a semicircle and followed a standard pattern that included jokes and comic songs interspersed between "serious" songs and dances performed by individuals with the full cast often singing the choruses. Besides the humor and songs done in dialect, there were nondialect songs and material that commented on current events and social problems. The first part regularly closed with a lively group song and dance number.

The most important features of the first part were its specialty roles. Although rarely given public acclaim, the interlocutor, who was seated in the center of the company and acted as the master of ceremony, was essential to the success of the first part. With a precise if somewhat pompous command of the language, an extensive vocabulary, and a resonant voice, the interlocutor personified dignity, which made the raucous comedy of the endmen even funnier. When the endmen mocked his pomposity, audiences could indulge their anti-intellectualism and antielitism by laughing at him. But when he patiently corrected the ignorant comedians with their malaprop-laden dialects, audiences could feel superior to stupid "niggers" and laugh with him. "He is the minstrel mentor to a brace of African Telemachuses," T. Alston Brown, a theatrical manager, critic, and historian observed, "always the same genial, gentlemanly, unruffled creature surveying the endmen . . . with the smiling forbearance which comes of innate superiority." [63] His stage directing role, however, was at least as critical to the show. As onstage director, the interlocutor orchestrated the loosely structured, heavily improvisational first part to meet the particular audience's tastes. Although unnoticed by the audience, his talent for knowing when to draw out or cut off comedians, when to change to a different type of humor, and whether to vary the prearranged musical selections largely determined the difference between a good and bad first part. Thus, good interlocutors, who seemed to do nothing, were among the most sought after and highest paid minstrels.

The musical star of the first part was the romantic balladeer, usually a tenor, who sang sentimental love songs that provided an outlet for tender emotions and a chance for the ladies in the audience to sigh, to weep, or to do both. "The untimely death of his unusually attractive sweetheart is the customary burden of the genteel minstrel's song," Olive Logan, a noted actress and a minstrel fan, observed. "Willows or cypress incessantly wave their melancholy boughs over the lone, dank grave by the rippling river's side, of Cynthie Sue or Lily Dale." [64] Many of these strikingly handsome, melancholy singers became matinée idols. Women, longing for men who were not afraid to express love or sorrow, wanted to comfort them for their losses and to hear their dulcet tones serenading their new-found loves.

On the ends of the semicircle sat the greatest stars of most companies, the comedians, Brudder Tambo and Brudder Bones—named for their instruments. Made up to give the appearance of large eyes and gaping mouths with huge lips, set apart by brighter, more flamboyant dress, and using heavier, more ludicrous dialects, the endmen contorted their bodies in exaggerated gestures and twisted their words in endless puns in order to keep the audience laughing. An endman caught in a shipwreck in the Erie Canal pulled out a bar of soap and washed himself ashore. The chicken crossed the road to get to the other side. Firemen wore red suspenders to hold up their pants. And the audience howled. "The pun and the conundrum were mighty popular with our grandfathers," Lew Dockstader, himself a great minstrel comedian, recalled. "They screamed over both." [65] At the same time that they laughed down at the stupid blackface characters, audience members also learned the intricacies of the language and the staccato pace of urban life. Endmen also delighted audiences with their physically funny performances of comedy songs. "He stands upon his chair in excitement frantically rattling the bones," Olive Logan wrote of a typical Brudder Bones performance. "He dances to the tune, he throws open the lapel of his coat, and in a final spasm of delight . . . he stands upon his head on the chair seat and for a thrilling and evanescent instant extends his nether extremities in the air." [66]

With their seemingly endless store of riddles, puns, and "one-liners," endmen made great impressions on audiences everywhere, but nowhere greater than in small towns. Wherever they went, several leading minstrels pointed out, the endmen's jokes were in the mouths of the "town humorists" for weeks after the shows.[67] Indeed, endmen with their "new" rapid-fire humor seemed primarily responsible for the minstrels being the most desired entertainment form in these towns. When the advance agent for Theodore Thomas and his orchestra arrived in a small Michigan town in the early 1880's, for example, he went to the editor of the local paper to ask for a plug and to inquire about the financial prospects for a first-rate musical aggregation. "If you have two durned good end men you'll do well," he replied. "But if you ain't got good end men our people won't patronize the show." [68]

The second part of the show, the variety section, or olio, offered a wide range of entertainment to the audience and allowed time to put up the closing act's set behind the curtain. Song and dance men, acrobats, men playing combs, porcupine quills, or glasses, and any number of other novelties might appear in this miscellaneous section. Other than diversity, its distinctive feature was the stump speech. Usually given by one of the endmen, it was a discourse as much on the infinite possibilities for malaprops as on the chosen subject.

> Feller-fellers and oder fellers, when Joan of Ark and his broder Noah's Ark crossed de Rubicund in search of Deca-moran's horn, and meeting dat solitary horseman by de way, dey anapulated in de clarion tones of de clamurous rooster, de insignification of de—de—de—de hop-toad am a very big bird—du da—du da day—does it not prove dat where gold is up to a discount of two cups of coffee on de dollar, dat bolivers must fall back into de radience of de—de—anything else, derefore at once and exclusively proving de fact dat de afore-mentioned accounts for de milk in de cocoa-nut!

The typical stump speech was considered a "marvel of grotesque humor" that was "just such an oration as a pompous darkey, better stocked with words that Judgement" might give.[69]

Over the years, the stump speaker became one of the major minstrel comedy specialists. Each of these stars had his own special style and topics. While some limited themselves to "nonsense," others used their ludicrous verbosity to express "serious" social criticism. Ad Ryman, for example, regularly "lectured" on education, temperance, and women's rights. But whatever their content, stump speakers regularly got laughs by combining the physical comedy of endmen with their verbal pomposity. While discoursing on education with "mock dignity and absurd seriousness," Ryman, on one occasion, concluded by "diving under the table and standing rigidly upon his head with heels in the air, sending the audience into screams of laughter." If the stump speaker did not fall off the podium onto the floor to punctuate his oration, one fan reminisced, the audience felt cheated.[70] They were rarely disappointed.

After the olio, the curtain rose for a one-act skit closing the show. Before the mid-1850's these finales almost invariably were set on Southern plantations. With the entire troupe on stage in "darky" costumes, usually neat, bright-colored theatrical "farm wear," the skits featured individual songs and dances and concluded with a rousing group song and dance number.[71] In the early 1850's, beginning with parodies like the "new serio-comico-tragico-melodramatical negro version of Macbeth" staged by Henry Wood's Minstrels on April 26, 1852, minstrels began to close their shows with comedy sketches lampooning current events or entertainment hits. When George Christy, the comedy star of the Christy Minstrels, joined Wood's Minstrels, the company created such a rage with their farces that many others followed their example.[72] All of these nonplantation skits were basically slapstick comedies, featuring Negro

The Evolution of the Minstrel Show

low-comedy types with their malaprop-laden dialect, and nearly always ending in a flurry of inflated bladders, bombardments of cream pies, or fireworks explosions that literally closed the show with a bang. Although Bryant's Minstrels, led by Dan Bryant's caricatures of plantation Negroes and Dan Emmett's pro-Southern songs, including "Dixie," sparked a revival of plantation finales in the late 1850's,[73] the farce or parody was becoming a standard closing act of the now formalized show.

By 1860 minstrelsy had been transformed. It had gone from unorganized individual acts to a structured entertainment form, from primarily musical to heavily comical, from a concentration on plantation material to a more diversified show. But its basic appeal remained the same. The reason minstrels drew so much better then *Othello*, although both were dark, the editor of the *Clipper* explained in November 1860, was that "people favor mirth more than melancholy" and are "more ready to laugh over the oddities of a darkie on a Virginia plantation than to weep over the solemnity of a noble Moor." Minstrelsy provided common Americans with folk-based earthy songs, vital dances, and robust humor as well as with beautiful ballads and fine singing that they could enjoy at reasonable prices. It also provided a nonthreatening way for white Americans to cope with questions about the nature and proper place of black people in America. In this regard, as in almost every other, the editor of the *Clipper* properly concluded that minstrelsy had "truly democratic associations." [74]

NOTES

[1] Haverly Mastodon Minstrels, n.p., May 31, 1880, program, HTC.
[2] For the quest for an American culture, see: Benjamin T. Spen-

cer, *The Quest for Nationality* (Syracuse, 1957) and Francis Hodge, *Yankee Theater* (Austin, Tex., 1964); for the African Theater, see Herbert Marshall and Mildred Stock, *Ira Aldridge: The Negro Tragedian*, (Carbondale, Ill., 1968, paperback ed.), pp. 28–48; for a detailed account of British characterizations of the Negro, their transplanting in America, and their Americanization, see Hans Nathan, *Dan Emmett and the Rise of Early Negro Minstrelsy* (Norman, Okla., 1962), chapters 1–3.

³ Nathan, *Dan Emmett . . .* , pp. 159–82; Charles Haywood, "Negro Minstrelsy and Shakesperean Burlesque," *Folklore and Society: Essays in Honor of B. A. Botkin*, ed. Bruce Jackson (Hatboro, Pa., 1966), p. 78, argues that many early minstrel songs were based on Scotch-Irish sources; song quotations are from: Foster S. Damon, *Series of Old American Songs* (Providence, 1936), n. p.

⁴ See Carl Wittke, *Tambo and Bones* (Durham, N. C., 1930), p. 24, for references to the many conflicting claims about the geographical origin of the "Jim Crow" routine and for details of Rice's career; Nathan. *Dan Emmett . . .* , pp. 62–66.

⁵ Richard Moody, *America Takes the Stage: Romanticism in American Drama* (Bloomington, Ind., 1955) p. 60; William R. Taylor, *Cavalier and Yankee*, (New York, 1963, paperback ed.), p. 287.

⁶ Sterling Brown, *Negro Poetry and Drama* (Washington, D.C., 1937), pp. 103–4; Moody, *America Takes the Stage*, p. 62.

⁷ Quoted in: Moody, *America Takes the Stage*, pp. 68–69.

⁸ Anna Cora Mowatt, *The Fashion*, in: Myron Matlaw, ed., *The Black Crook and Other Nineteenth-Century American Plays* (New York, 1967), p. 32.

⁹ Sterling Brown, *The Negro in American Fiction* (Washington, D.C., 1937), pp. 6–10, 17–47.

¹⁰ Virginia Minstrels, Dublin, Ireland, 1844, program, HTC. Although from Ireland, this program is typical of their early appeal.

¹¹ Nathan, *Dan Emmett . . .* , pp. 143–58; Nathan's detailed account of the origin and fate of the Virginia Minstrels is definitive.

¹² *Ethiopian Serenaders Booklet*, London, England, September 12, 1844, HTC; Sam Sanford played at Tyler's wedding celebrations and later carried a letter of introduction from President Polk to England; "Interview with Sam Sanford, Boston *Globe*, Oct. 28, 1882, clipping in Boston Public Library. The Boston Harmoneons played for Polk on June 18, 1846; see obituary of L. V. H. Crosby (n.p., n.d.), and

program reprinted in a clipping (n.p., n.d.), both in HTC. George Kunkel's troupe entertained both Fillmore and Pierce; see Stewart McCauley, *Songs of Kunkel's Nightingale Opera Troupe* (Baltimore, 1854), p. v.

[13] Edmond M. Gagey, *The San Francisco Stage: A History* (New York, 1950), pp. 31, 64–65; George R. MacMinn, *The Theater of the Golden Era in California* (Caldwell, Idaho, 1941), pp. 431–34, 436.

[14] Harry R. Edwall, "The Golden Era of Minstrelsy in Memphis: A Reconstruction," *West Tennessee Historical Society Papers*, IX (1955), 35; Phillip Graham, *Showboats: The History of an American Institution* (Austin, 1961), p. 24; Wittke, *Tambo and Bones*, pp. 72–76, 79–80; Marion S. Revett, *A Minstrel Town* (New York, 1955), pp. xv–xvi.

[15] Wittke, *Tambo and Bones*, pp. 72–80; *Buckley's Ethiopian Melodies, No. 4* (Philadelphia, 1857), p. vi; Revett, *A Minstrel Town*, pp. xv–xvi; Graham, *Showboats*, p. 24; Edwall, "The Golden Era of Minstrelsy," pp. 35, 39.

[16] Wittke, *Tambo and Bones*, pp. 66–72.

[17] *Ibid.*, pp. 66–67; Graham, *Showboats*, p. 24; *Literary World*, V (July 7, 1849), 1, quoted in Mott, *History of American Magazines* (Cambridge, Mass., 1939), Vol. I, pp. 433–34.

[18] "Interview with Ben Cotton," New York *Mirror*, July 3, 1897, Walsh Collection, clipping, Theatre Collection, New York Public Library at Lincoln Center, hereafter referred to as NYLC; "The Only Thatcher's Autobiography," in Thatcher Minstrel program, n.p., n.d. [1882?], NYLC; obituary, New York *Herald*, November 11, 1889, clipping, HTC; Bernard Wolfe, "Uncle Remus and the Malevolent Rabbit," *Commentary* 8 (July 1949), 40; John T. Howard, *Stephen Foster* (New York, 1953, paperback ed.), pp. 119–20; M. B. Leavitt, *Fifty Years of Theatrical Management* (New York, 1912), p. 19; Al G. Field, *Watch Yourself Go By* (Columbus, 1912), pp. 113–14.

[19] Virginia Minstrels, Dublin, Ireland, 1844, program, HTC.

[20] Harmoneons, Philadelphia, January 30, 1844, program, HTC.

[21] Nathan, *Dan Emmett . . .* , pp. 123–26.

[22] Howard, *Stephen Foster*, pp. 83, 124–25, 194.

[23] Carl Bode, *The Anatomy of American Popular Culture* (Berkeley, 1959), pp. 26–29, makes this perceptive observation about Foster's escapism. For a fuller discussion of early minstrelsy's emotional appeals, see chapter 3.

²⁴ George C. Odell, *Annals of the New York Stage*, 15 vols. (New York, 1927–49), Vol. V, pp. 131, 223, 307.

²⁵ *Spirit of the Times*, Oct. 16, 1847, quoted in Odell, *Annals* . . . , Vol. V, pp. 377–78.

²⁶ Field, *Watch Yourself Go By*, p. 113; Anon., "Reminiscences" (n.p., July 26, 1902), clipping, HTC.

²⁷ "Nigger Minstrelsy," *Living Age* (Feb. 12, 1862), p. 398.

²⁸ Lew Dockstader, "The Search for the Oldest Minstrel Joke," n.p., Dec. 25, 1916, clipping, NYLC.

²⁹ Of seventy-five leading minstrels born before 1840, three were from the South, two of these from border cities. (More came from Europe.) One-third were from New York and the majority were from the Northeast. Compiled from T. A. Brown, *A History of the American Stage* (New York, 1870), and Edward Leroy Rice, *Monarchs of Minstrelsy* (New York, 1911).

³⁰ "New Jim Brown Bout de Sputed Territory," *Jim Along Josey Roarer* (New York, n.d. [mid-1830's?]); "Maine Boundary Question," *Negro Forget Me Not Songster* (Philadelphia, 1848), pp. 77–78; "Brother Jonathan and John Bull" and "Taxation of America," *Uncle True Songster* (Philadelphia, 185–), pp. 140–44; Bob Farrel, "Sich a Gitting Up Stairs" (n.p., n.d. [late 1830's], sheet music; Nathan, *Dan Emmett* . . . , pp. 56, 321–23.

³¹ Murphy, West, and Peel Minstrels, "The Darky's Boat Song," n.p., 1853, sheet music, HTC. All others are in *Woods Minstrel Songs* (New York, 1855), but were done earlier by many other troupes.

³² "Juba," *De Susannah and Thick Lip Melodist* (New York, 1850), pp. 49–50; Charles White, "Hard Times", *New Illustrated Melodeon* (New York, 1848), p. 51; E. P. Christy, "Away Down in Old Virginia," *Christy's Plantation Melodies #1* (New York, 1851), p. 47; "Jim Crow" (New York, n.d. [late 1820's]), sheet music, and "Jim Crow" (New York, n.d.), quoted in Nathan, *Dan Emmett* . . . , pp. 55–56.

³³ Charles White, "I Must Go to Richmond," *Illustrated*, p. 55; "Walk Jawbone," *Deacon Snowball's Negro Melodies* (New York, 1843), Elias Howe, *Ethiopian Glee Book #4 Containing Songs Sung by the New Orleans Serenaders* (Boston, 1850), pp. 216–17, *Negro Melodies No. 3, Rose of Alabama* (Philadelphia, 1864), pp. 17–19.

³⁴ "Pompey Smash," *De Susannah*, pp. 75–78; Howe, *Ethiopian Glee Book #3, Christy Minstrels* (Boston, 1849), p. 135, and another ver-

sion cited in Cecil Patterson, "A Different Drum: The Image of the Negro in Nineteenth Century Popular Song Books," doctoral dissertation, University of Pennsylvania, 1961, p. 89. For a sample of frontier lore, see B. A. Botkin, *A Treasury of American Folklore* (New York, 1944), pp. 2–50.

[35] Nathan, *Dan Emmett* . . . , pp. 186–88, 153; Constance Rourke, *American Humor*, (New York, 1931, Anchor ed.), p. 79.

[36] Marian Winter, "Juba and American Minstrelsy," *Dance Index*, VI (1947), 23–47; Nathan, *Dan Emmett* . . . , pp. 73–74, 81–83; Marshall and Jean Stearns, *Jazz Dance* (New York, 1968), pp. 44–47; for a detailed analysis of minstrels' heavy debt to Afro-American dance, see Stearns, pp. 35–63.

[37] For a detailed examination of this dance, see Stearns, *Jazz Dance*, pp. 40–42.

[38] From unpublished notes by Rudi Blesh and Harriet Janis, quoted in Stearns, *Jazz Dance*, pp. 50–55.

[39] Winter, "Juba and American Minstrelsy," p. 38; Stearns, *Jazz Dance*, p. 47; "Interview with James McIntyre," New York *Herald-Tribune*, Nov. 10, 1935, quoted in Stearns, *Jazz Dance*, p. 50.

[40] Winter, "Juba and American Minstrelsy," p. 40; Rourke, *American Humor*, p. 78; Nathan, *Dan Emmett* . . . , pp. 236–37; Stearns, *Jazz Dance*, pp. 50–51.

[41] T. A. Brown, "Early History of Negro Minstrelsy," New York *Clipper*, May-August 1913; T. A. Brown, "The Origin of Negro Minstrelsy," in Charles H. Day, *Fun in Black* (New York, 1874), p. 6; J. J. Jennings, *Theatrical and Circus Life* (St. Louis, 1882), p. 368; Henry A. Kmen, *Music in New Orleans: The Formative Years, 1791–1841* (Baton Rouge, 1966), pp. 244–45; Nathan, *Dan Emmett* . . . , p. 183.

[42] For a discussion of Negro street vendors' songs, see Willis L. James, "The Romance of the Negro Folk Cry in America," *Phylon*, XVI (1955), 15–30.

[43] Leavitt, *Fifty Years of Theatrical Management*, p. 31.

[44] New York *Clipper*, Apr. 13, 1878, quoted in Nathan, *Dan Emmett* . . . , p. 71; "Interview with Ben Cotton," New York *Mirror*, 1897, clipping, NYLC. For a musicological analysis of these syncopated tunes that concludes that they must have been derived from Afro-Americans and may have been the origin of jazz, see Nathan, *Dan Emmett* . . . , chapter 13.

[45] "Authentic Memoir of E. P. Christy," *New York Age*, 1848,

clipping, HTC; Buffalo *Express*, Feb. 17, 1895, clipping, Buffalo Public Library.

⁴⁶ *Pop Goes the Weasel Songster* (Philadelphia, 1853), pp. 192–93; *Buckley's Songbook for the Parlor* (New York, 1855), pp. 25–26; Botkin, *Lay My Burden Down* (Chicago, 1945, Phoenix ed.), pp. 65, 86, 91, 124; "Old Wurginny," *Negro Melodies No. 3*, pp. 8–10; for examples of the "juba" dance among slaves, see Dena Epstein, "Slave Music in the United States," Music Library Association, *Notes*, XX (1963), 378–79.

⁴⁷ Christy Minstrels, 1854, and Wood and Christy Minstrels, 1855, programs, HTC. Newbell N. Puckett, *Folk Beliefs of the Southern Negro* (Chapel Hill, N.C., 1926) cites numerous Negro death omens and dream warnings.

⁴⁸ Charles White, *White's Serenaders' Song Book* (New York, 1851), p. 79. Puckett records the importance of the devil and the familiar linking of cats and evil in Afro-American tradition. Roger Abrahams points out that "Ram Cat" is still used by blacks in the West Indies and means "approximately the same as 'Tom Cat'—lover," Letter, Nov. 26, 1970.

⁴⁹ S. S. Purdy, "Sally Green," *Paul Pry Songster and Black Joker* (New York, 1865), pp. 45–46; "Africa's Daughter," *World of Negro Songs* (Philadelphia, 1856), pp. 49–51.

⁵⁰ Rourke, *American Humor*, pp. 75–76, 81–83, points out that nonsense and fantasy are absent from Anglo-American humor; animal songs and tales abound in black tradition; for an introduction to Afro-American folklore and how and why it differs from Euro-American lore, see Richard M. Dorson, *American Folklore* (Chicago, 1959) and *American Negro Folktales* (New York, 1967), and Roger Abrahams, *Positively Black* (Englewood Cliffs, N.J., 1970).

⁵¹ J. W. Sweeney, "Jenny Get Your Hoe Cake Done" (New York, 1840), sheet music, HTC.

⁵² J. W. Sweeney, "Jawbone" (n.p., 1840), sheet music, HTC, and many other minstrels; black folk versions of this verse are in Langston Hughes and Arna Bontemps, eds. *Book of Negro Folklore* (New York, 1958). pp, 220–21, Thomas Talley, *Negro Folk Rhymes* (New York, 1922), pp. 14–15; Dorothy Scarborough, *On the Trail of Negro Folksongs* (Hatboro, Pa., 1963, reprint ed.), p. 191; *Frank C. Brown Collection of North Carolina Folklore* (Durham, N.C., 1952), Vol. III, pp. 201–2.

[53] "Clare de Kitchen," Boston, 1832, sheet music in Damon, n.p., *Ethiopian #3*, and many other minstrel songsters; black folk versions are in Talley, *Negro Folk Rhymes*, p. 20; *Brown Collection . . .* , Vol. III, p. 496; see also discussion of black minstrel versions in chapter 8.

[54] Virginia Minstrels, "Jim Crack Corn," New York, 1846, sheet music, HTC, and many other minstrel companies; folk versions are in Scarborough, *On the Trail of Negro Folksongs*, pp. 202–3, and *Brown Collection*, Vol., pp. 496–97.

[55] Ethiopian Serenaders, "Jim Crack Corn," n.p., n.d. [1846?], sheet music, HTC.

[56] "Gal from the South," *Woods Minstrel Songs*, p. 26, George Christy, *George Christy and White's Melodies* (Philadelphia, 1854), p. 85; for folk versions, see Scarborough, *On the Trail of Negro Folksongs*, p. 68; Newman I. White, *American Negro Folksongs* (Hatboro, Pa., 1965, reprint ed.), pp. 153, 155; and Howard Odum and Guy B. Johnson, *The Negro and His Songs* (Hatboro, Pa., 1964, reprint ed.), p. 236.

[57] For a discussion of Negroes' aggressive use of whites' stereotypes of blacks, see Abrahams, *Positively Black;* for a discussion of these tricksters and the many other antislavery sentiments expressed in minstrelsy, see chapter 3; for an introduction to and a sample of John and Old Master stories, see Dorson, *Negro Folktales*, pp. 124–71.

[58] Newman White offered this explanation for the 104 minstrel correlations he found for the 680 songs in his collection of Afro-American folk songs. Besides his book, already cited, see his "Whiteman in the Woodpile," *American Speech*, Vol. IV (1929), 28–47.

[59] For examples of this widely held viewpoint, see Sam Johnsing, "The Decadence of a Black Art," *New York Dramatic News*, Dec. 27, 1902; "Negro Minstrelsy—Ancient and Modern," in *Maga Social Papers* (New York, 1867), p. 286; "The Last Minstrel," n.p., June 23, 1879, clipping, Boston Public Library.

[60] For a discussion of the decline of minstrelsy and the impact of black minstrels, see chapters 5 and 7.

[61] For analysis of minstrelsy's portrayals of Negroes, see chapter 3.

[62] Nathan, *Dan Emmett . . .* , pp. 143–58.

[63] Brown, "Early History"; contrary to widespread belief interlocutors did not usually appear in whiteface: "Why Lew Dockstader Tops the Minstrel Heap," *Morning Telegraph*, May 3, 1903, re-

fers to the interlocutor in the old-time minstrel show contrasting his ebony makeup to his lack of "darky dialect." Ed Marble, *The Minstrel Show* (New York, 1893), makes no mention of anyone appearing in whiteface. Pictures of troupes confirm the use of whiteface in the 1890's, perhaps a part of the general use of whiteface in the minstrel show; see discussion of this in chapter 5.

[64] Olive Logan, "The Ancestry of Brudder Bones," *Harper's*, Vol. LVIII (1879), 692.

[65] Lew Dockstader, "The Search for the Oldest Minstrel Joke," n.p., Dec. 25, 1916, clipping, NYLC.

[66] Logan, "The Ancestry of Brudder Bones," p. 689.

[67] Frank Dumont, "The Golden Days of Minstrelsy," New York *Clipper*, 1914, clipping, NYLC; "Why Lew Dockstader Tops the Minstrel Heap," *Morning Telegraph*, May 3, 1903.

[68] Clipping (n.p., n.d. [early 1880's?]), HTC.

[69] James Sutherland, *From Stage to Pulpit by Bob Hart* (New York, 1883), p. 9; *Frank Brower's Black Diamond Songster* (New York, 1863), p. 12.

[70] New York *Clipper*, Apr. 20, 1872; clipping (n.p., n.d.), HTC; in the mid-twentieth century, "Professor" Irwin Corey continues this comedy tradition, although not in blackface.

[71] For minstrelsy's treatment of the plantation, see chapter 3.

[72] George Odell, *Annals of the New York Stage*, 15 vols. (New York, 1927–49), Vol. VI, p. 172; see also the program and playbill collections in HTC and NYLC.

[73] Nathan, *Dan Emmett* . . . , chapter 15.

[74] New York *Clipper*, Nov. 10, 1860, Dec. 15, 1860.

3 Images of Negroes in Antebellum Minstrelsy

It was no accident that the incredible popularity of minstrelsy coincided with public concern about slavery and the proper position of Negroes in America. Precisely because people could always just laugh off the performance, because viewers did not have to take the show seriously, minstrelsy served as a "safe" vehicle through which its primarily Northern, urban audiences could work out their feelings about even the most sensitive and volatile issues. During the sectional crisis, minstrels shaped white Americans' vague notions and amorphous beliefs about Negroes into vivid, eye-catching caricatures as they literally acted out images of blacks and plantation life that satisfied their huge audiences. Like every other aspect of the show, minstrelsy's racial content grew out of the intimate interaction between the performers and their vocal patrons. When public opinion shifted, the content of minstrelsy shifted. Thus, minstrelsy's portrayals of slavery and blacks reveal the evolution and functioning of American racial stereotypes better than any other source.

Before the Civil War, when the structure of the minstrel show gradually evolved from eclectic diversity to a standard pattern, minstrel racial content underwent equally profound and even more significant developments. Before the mid-1850's, minstrel portrayals of blacks contained much more than the ludicrous images of incompetent Northern Negroes and of happy slaves for which minstrelsy is infamous. They also included diverse black common people: hunters and fishermen thrilling to the joys of the catch; young lovers flirting and courting; black frontiersmen and riverboatsmen embodying American strength and independence; husbands and wives living happily together; heartbroken lovers pining for their sweethearts; and various characters voicing social commentary. Most important of all, many minstrel troupes, before the mid-1850's, expressed fundamental ambivalence about slavery by portraying both positive images of happy plantation blacks and negative condemnations of the cruelty and inhumanity of slavery in the same shows.[1]

Although they completely rejected any notion of the equality of the races and had no commitment to the welfare of Negroes, minstrels for a decade were sensitive to charges that slavery was brutal, oppressive, and undemocratic at the same time that they were attracted to romanticized proslavery arguments. In the early 1850's, however, slavery became the center of a struggle that threatened to destroy the Union and to allow millions of blacks to challenge whites for land, jobs, and status. After that, minstrels' objections to slavery and their diverse black character types virtually disappeared, leaving only contrasting caricatures of contented slaves and unhappy free Negroes. This change helped the Northern public to overlook the brutal aspects of slavery and to rationalize racial caste rather than face the prospect of fundamental social and political change.

From the outset, minstrelsy unequivocally branded Negroes as inferiors. Although it offered its audiences no heroic white characters, it provided even more certain assurances of white common people's identity by emphasizing Negroes' "peculiarities" and inferiority. Even sympathetic black characters were cast as inferiors. Minstrels used heavy dialect to portray Negroes as foolish, stupid, and compulsively musical. Minstrel blacks did not have hair, they had "wool"; they were "bleating black sheep," and their children were "darky cubs." They had bulging eyeballs, flat, wide noses, gaping mouths with long, dangling lower lips, and gigantic feet with elongated, even flapping heels. At times, minstrels even claimed that Negroes had to have their hair filed, not cut; that when blacks got sick and pale, they drank ink to restore their color; and that people could grow "niggas" by planting their toes in the ground. Besides picturing blacks as physically different and inferior, minstrels set them off culturally. Minstrel blacks would rather eat possum and coon than anything else; after working all day, they could sing and dance all night without rest; and they had different standards of beauty. Male minstrel characters described ideal women with feet so big they "covered up de whole sidewalk" or lips "as large as all out doors," or so large a lover could not kiss them all at once.[2] In every way, minstrels emphasized, blacks fell far short of white standards.

Minstrels also emphasized the subordinate status of Negroes by building it into the structure of their early shows. In the 1840's when the form of the shows still varied widely, the minstrel troupes that featured "refined" music often opened with a "concert" performed in formal wear and without blackface makeup. While they labeled the parts of the show containing Negro material "As Northern Dandies," "As Dandy Darkies," "As Southern Darkies," or "As Plantation Darkies," they titled the concerts "As Citizens." [3] The distinction was as clear as black and white. Only whites were citizens; only whites played refined music; blacks were peculiar and grotesque musically (culturally) as well as physically, whether Northern or Southern.

Minstrels had no doubts about how to portray Northern Negroes. Like the vast majority of white Northerners, minstrels "knew" blacks did not belong in the North. When they could not get rid of blacks, Northern whites forced them to live like inferiors and then used their behavior as "proof" that Negroes were inherently incompetent people who had the same opportunities as everyone else but could do nothing with them. [4] Minstrels shared in this self-fulfilling prophecy by consistently caricaturing free Negroes as silly black buffoons. They also used these laughable characters to express their dissatisfaction with the unhealthy direction that Northern society seemed to be taking. In the most obvious way, ludicrous minstrel blacks represented negative social trends carried to their most absurd extremes. But they also voiced biting social criticism from a position much like that of the classical Fool. To make this social criticism palatable and to further ridicule free Negroes, minstrels channeled most of the endmen's jokes and comic songs into these portrayals. To minstrels, Northern blacks, above all else, had to be people to laugh at.

Wearing skintight "trousaloons," a long-tailed coat with padded shoulders, a high ruffled collar, white gloves, an eyepiece, and a long watch chain, Count Julius Caesar Mars Napolean Sinclair Brown and other "aristocratic niggers" and "Dandy Broadway Swells" preened and pranced across the minstrel stage on their way to "De Colored Fancy Ball" and their other continual parties. While illustrating just how ridiculous Negroes could be when they tried to live like white "gemmen," these characters also lampooned frivolous whites who wasted their lives in unproductive dilletantism. The tendency for common people to aspire to be members of the upper class as soon as they had enough money to affect the appearance deeply troubled democratic minstrels. Minstrelsy's completely self-centered dandies, who thought only of courting, flashy clothes, new dances, and their looks, epitomized these pretentious upstarts at their worst.[5]

Further emphasizing how foolish they were, these egocentric "dandy darkies" claimed to be handsome, even though they had the exaggerated physical deformities common to all minstrel blacks. "Dandy Jim," for example, boasted that every time he looked in the mirror, he knew he was "de best lookin' nigger in de country." After proudly bragging about the size of his "beef-steak lips," he described going to a ball "wid lips combed out an' wool quite tall." Besides stressing just how superficial and ludicrous these self-styled aristocrats really were, these songs, which linked pretentious white dandies with the baseless vanity of these ugly blacks, must have delighted the white common people in the audience. Although directed at whites as well as blacks, these parodies, which were performed in blackface and dialect, so neatly reinforced what whites wanted to believe about Northern Negroes that they permanently became popular stereotypes of urban blacks.

To complement their pretentious dandies, minstrels created ignorant, malaprop-speaking low-comedy types. Using the incompetence and stupidity of these laughable imbeciles, who had to learn everything the hard way, as models of how *not* to do things, minstrels explained new inventions, current events, scientific principles, and city life. Minstrel blacks got tricked out of their money by con-men, run down by trolleys, shocked by electric batteries, and jailed for violating laws which they did not understand. While foolishly discoursing on things they knew almost nothing about, they actually imparted some information while also assuring Northern whites that, no matter how bewildered or inept they felt, blacks were much worse off than they were. Pontificating on natural laws, a typical Brudder Bones observed that the world *obviously* did not rotate. If it did, he confidently pointed out, everything would fall off once a day. Another figured that he could get to China in four hours by ascending in a balloon, letting the world turn under him, and then landing in China.[6] With such material, minstrels educated their audiences just as certainly as Barnum's Museum, but they did it with laughter, not with exhibits.

Reflecting their antielitist views, minstrels also used their black characters to lambast professional men who considered themselves better than common people. To minstrels, lawyers were agents of the devil who belonged in hell. Doctors usually operated on patients to remove their money-belts and freely used what minstrels claimed was their "license to kill." When Brudder Bones went to get a doctor for his sick employer, for example, he brought back a doctor, a lawyer, an undertaker, and a gravedigger to save himself some trips. Because it gave them a chance to combine anti-intellectual jibes at "gentlemen" with portrayals of pretentious blacks spouting tongue-twisting, mind-scrambling language, education was minstrelsy's most popular professional target. With great pomposity and empty heads, "edjumkated" blacks felt they could explain anything, even the abstract subtleties of transcendentalism:

> Transcendentalism is dat spiritual cognoscence ob psychological irrefragibility, connected wid conscientient ademption ob incolumbient spirituality and etherialized connection— which is deribed from a profound contemplation ob de irregability ob dose incessimable divisions ob de more minute portions ob subdivided particles ob inwisible atoms dat be-

> come ana-tom-catically tattalable in de circumambulatin
> commotion ob ambiloquous voluminiousness.

But anti-intellectual minstrels were not against *all* knowledge,
as a black character made clear in explaining his experience on a
ferry ride:

> When I got out a little piece from the shore, de man axed
> me if I knowed anyting about frenologism. I told him no.
> Ah, says he, den one quarter of your life is gone. Finally he
> says, does you know anyting about grammar. I told him no.
> Ah, says he, den one half ob you life am gone . . . He axed
> if I knowed anyting about dickshionary. I told him no and
> he say tree quarters of your life is gone. We hit a rock and
> den I axed him if he knowed how to swim. He said no. Den
> says I, de whole four quarters of your life am gone—shure.[7]

Although minstrels created a wide range of urban black
characters, some of whom closely resembled whites, and used
some jokes and puns that did not depend on race and dialect,
the vast majority of their Northern Negro material focused on
caricatures of strutting dandies and worthless ignoramuses. In
the 1850's, when slapstick farces began to replace plantation
skits in the featured closing slot on the program, mindless black
simpletons, with heavy "nigger" dialects and a natural propen-
sity to run around the stage bopping each other on the head
with inflated bladders, added further emphasis to minstrels' portrayals of Northern Negroes as lazy, pretentious, frivolous, im-
provident, irresponsible, and immature—the very antithesis of
what white men liked to believe about themselves. As such,
they served not only as ego-boasting scapegoats for whites but
also as confirmation that Negroes could not play a constructive
role in a free society and did not "belong" in the North.

Minstrels consistently and unequivocally rejected Northern Negroes, but slavery proved much more difficult and troubling for them. Until the 1850's, slavery seemed primarily a distant, abstract subject that served more as a test for white Northerners' ideology and a projection for their emotional needs than as a tangible, immediate reality. As egalitarians, who believed in every individual's right to unhampered personal opportunity and liberty, and as nationalists, who saw America as a model democracy, they abhorred the presence of human slavery in their country. But as insecure people, who were uncertain about their own status and identity because of the fundamental social flux in the antebellum North, they welcomed the stability and certainty provided by an inferior caste and the fixed hierarchy of slavery. Deeply concerned about the survival of the family and other basic social institutions that seemed imperiled by urbanization and modernization, they found the idealized model of loving, secure families described by defenders of slavery very attractive and comforting. But they also felt anguish at the inhumane cruelty and the destruction of black families detailed by abolitionists and ex-slaves. Torn between their beliefs and their needs, their desires and their fears, they used deeply moving, highly emotional language to express strong negative feelings about the brutality of slavery even as they warmly endorsed the positive images of the happy plantation.

From its beginnings, minstrelsy presented the plantation as a predominately happy place. Since early minstrels initially based their appeal on the authenticity of their portrayals of "the Sports and Pastimes of the Virginia Colored Race," [8] they made the slave party the central feature of their early shows. This not only created a festive, lighthearted mood but also suggested that when minstrels sang, danced, and told jokes, they were authentically representing Southern blacks. Besides establishing minstrels as entertainers, this emphasis on the plantation party also inculcated the idea that Southern Negroes were just frolicking, playful children: "Niggas' hearts am bery gay/ Dey tink ob nothin but to play." For these minstrel "dancing darkies," daytime was nothing more than the necessary interval between their nightly romps. "The way for to do right," one minstrel character observed, was "just leave the white folks use the day, and niggers use the night." [9] In addition to singing, dancing, playing music, and feasting, many of these characters looked forward to seeing their benevolent masters at their boisterous festivities.

> He often comes to see our sports—a fine segar
>   he quaffs.
> 'Case de merriment of niggers often makes him
>   laugh. [10]

With minstrel troupes throughout the country performing such material in virtually every show during minstrelsy's near century of existence, this caricature of the happy-go-lucky, child-like Southern Negro who loved to entertain whites became a fixture in American popular culture.

But before the mid-1850's, as part of the undercurrent of opposition to slavery that they regularly expressed, minstrels also portrayed plantation Negroes mischievously playing jokes on and jibing with their masters. Since these incidents closely resemble the legendary battle of wits in Afro-American folklore between a generic slave character, John, and his "Old Master," they may be among the authentic folk materials that minstrels borrowed. [11] Whatever the source of the material, at the same time that minstrels portrayed plantation Negroes as empty-headed, grinning darkies devoted to their masters, they also gave their audiences a chance to laugh *with* sly black characters who used deception and guile to outsmart gentlemen. These antiaristocratic black tricksters must have seemed especially amusing to color- and class-conscious white common men, just as linking grotesque black dandies with white swells did.

Many crafty minstrel blacks found ways to mock their masters and still avoid punishment. "We try to fool him [the master] bad when we can," one such character explained. Although most minstrel plantation parties were thrown by the master in the quarters, some minstrel slaves, like the heroes of black folktales, threw their own parties in the Big House with "borrowed" supplies whenever their masters were away. Other slaves laughed openly at their masters. At one party, while "Ole Cuff" was playing his banjo, his master appeared, told him to leave, began to dance with his partner, and finally took his banjo. But "de way he make it play, he set Ole Cuff a laffin. Den massa run away." Other characters mocked their incompetent masters for being unable to saddle horses or for running into posts while chasing chickens; one even called his master a "stout old fool." Somewhat more indirectly, but in the same derisive vein, Caesar told his "massa" he was saving his money to buy a place in heaven. When his master laughed at him and said if that was possible he would have bought one years ago, Caesar, playing dumb, replied that he would buy one in hell then, "Case massa, I'be lived wid you a good many years, and I am bery anxious to stay wid you forever." [12] Other minstrel tricksters bragged that they stole from their masters. One took a bottle of brandy and, when caught with it empty, said in characteristic trickster fashion, "de nigger smoove him down" by joking that he guessed the bottle had broken. Another boasted that "Massa bought a bran new coat and hung it on de wall. Dis nigga's gwine to take dat coat, and wear it to de ball." [13] From the slaveowners' point of view, such "typically Negro" behavior, which fit white expectations, was acceptable though not desirable. For minstrels it was a way to acknowledge slave discontent and to get a laugh at the master's expense without being too serious.

75

Negroes in Antebellum Minstrelsy

Like the black folk, minstrel slaves also used white stereotypes of blacks as weapons against their owners. Playing on his
master's assumption of his stupidity, a minstrel slave named
John subverted the plantation by feeding green tobacco to
sheep, eating oats meant for the horses, making his master's
tea out of bitter leaves, and even beating the master's coat while
he still had it on. "Jasper Jack," a common early minstrel character, found many ways to torment his owners and other
whites: he served his master and mistress monkey leg for dinner instead of pork; at a party, when he saw a German baron
steal a sausage, he shouted: "German sassige bery rich—
German baron bery poor!"; he caused a jackass to buck his mistress to the ground; when she complained that a quart of ale
he had poured was sour and lacked a frothy head, he told her:
"Put your own white head, marm, in de jug." Finally, in
the ultimate trickster turnabout, he married his Boston-born
mistress.

> But death lay Jack massa by de heels
> And Jack soon love widdy missy he feels
> She take come-passion, him wounds she heals
> Dey dance same night de bridal reels! [14]

Although the minstrels' fundamental ambivalence about
slavery pervaded all their plantation material before the mid-
1850's, it was most glaring when they portrayed the highly
emotional family images on which the cases both for and
against slavery rested. Like the proplantation literature, minstrelsy's favorable treatment of slavery stressed the plantation as
one big happy family, with the master and mistress as parents
and the slaves as their children. Focusing on the deep and en-
during bonds within this idealized, interracial family, minstrels
presented the theme of racial subordination in its most favorable light by equating it with the child's properly loyal defer-
ence to his loving parent. "He loved us as few masters do," a

Christy Minstrel character boasted for himself and many others. Again and again, minstrel blacks recounted how their kind masters took care of them, gave them all they wanted to eat, indulgently let them play and frolic, and proudly helped them set up their own households within the broader plantation home, like a model extended family. According to minstrels, some masters even gave their newlywed slaves their freedom as a wedding present, a present the happy couple often refused so they could stay in their beloved plantation home.[15]

As part of these romanticized family-centered images, minstrels often portrayed happy scenes of courtship. In sharp contrast to the way they lampooned prancing Northern dandies, minstrels used serious sentimental language to describe these idealized plantation romances. To give their love songs greater emotional appeal for white audiences, minstrels also created the alluring "yaller gal," who had the light skin and facial features of white women combined with the exoticism and "availability" of Negroes. Almost always described as extremely beautiful and highly desirable, she, like the desirable white woman, was hard to win and harder to hold, but never coarse or mannerless. Only black women had these undesirable traits—never the sweet, graceful yellow girls. These were not comedy parts. Black women furnished the laughs. Yaller gals, generally called "octoroons" outside minstrelsy, provided coquettish flirtations, happy romances, and sad, untimely deaths. Considering whites' preference for light-skinned Negroes and the large number of mulattoes in America, minstrels' creation of the yellow girl for their emotional love songs is not surprising. Nor is it surprising that they located them on plantations, which they envisioned as ideal domestic settings. What is surprising is that there were no yellow men in minstrelsy![16]

In the late 1830's and early 1840's some blackfaced performers had portrayed Northern Negro dandies who bragged

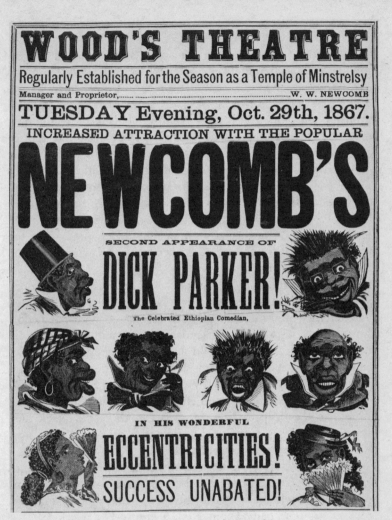

3.   This playbill is typical of the caricatures of Negroes that minstrels plastered all over the nation. Note the great contrast between the attractive "yaller gals" in the bottom row and the grotesque caricature of the black woman in the second row left.

Newcomb's Minstrels, New York, Oct. 29, 1867, Harvard Theatre Collection.

about courting white women. But even as a joke, this suggestion of interracial romance, especially between white women and black men, was unacceptable for minstrelsy, which consistently described Northern Negroes as inept, ridiculous, and repulsive inferiors. Although Negrophobes used frightening images of sexually aggressive black men to justify white repression and control of Negroes, minstrels did not use these scare tactics. To justify caste for their egalitarian audiences, minstrels portrayed Negroes more as emotional children to be protected and guided for their own good than as serious threats to whites. The only attractive minstrel-made Negro male was the practically asexual "Old Darky." Appealing black men were too much of a threat to whites and especially to the white men who fashioned minstrelsy.

To create the Old Darky, one of their most moving symbols of the idealized plantation family, minstrels blended together the intense sentimentalism associated with old people about to die, with lifelong friendships, and with loving family ties. These white-haired, "Old Uncles" possessed what nineteenth-century Americans considered the sentimental qualities of the "heart" without the balancing qualities of the "mind." They represented feelings and emotions in their pure form. To emphasize the deep, loving ties between these old black men and their masters, minstrels frequently described the slow death of one and the anguish and grief of the other. Stephen Foster, the master of maudlin sentimentalism, especially emotional death scenes, produced the most popular songs of this type. "Old Uncle Ned," performed by virtually every minstrel troupe, was nominally about Ned, a kindly Old Darky, but it actually focused on his master's devotion to him. Throughout Ned's long illness, his master lovingly nursed him, and when Ned finally died, "Master's tears down his cheeks ran like rain." [17] Paralleling the master-as-mourner theme, the sentimental Old Uncle frequently shed torrents of tears at the loss of a beloved master, without whom there seemed to be no reason for living. Like orphaned children with no one left to turn to, bereaved Old Darkies often wanted only to join their deceased masters in their graves.[18] These songs, which like other minstrel sentimentalism probably appealed mainly to women in the audiences, presented male characters who were not afraid to express the tender emotions that Northerners usually considered "feminine sensitivities." Complementing the gentle, emotional master who was featured in proplantation literature, the Old Uncle provided a model of a tender, expressive common man—one who loved, laughed, and cried.

With the beloved Old Uncle went the other half of the familiar matching set—the plantation "Mammy" or "Old Auntie." The most famous of these characters, "Aunt Dinah Roe," was a matriarch as tough as necessary and as tender as needed. Everyone loved her, "boff de black and de white," and with good reason:

> She'd joke wid de old folks and play wid de child
> She'd cry wid de sorrowing, laugh wid de gay;
> Tend on de sick bed, and join in de play
> De fust at de funeral, wedding, or birth
> De killer ob trouble and maker ob mirth
> She spoke her mind freely, was plain as de day
> But never hurt any by what she might say
> If she once made a promise, it neber was broke.[19]

As the song summed her up, she was "more dan a mudder," much more. She was an American counterpart to the European peasant, the Earth-mother. The Darky Uncle and Aunt offered white America openness, warmth, devotion, and love. The romanticized plantation served as a sanctuary where they and the natural family ties they epitomized had a chance to develop and mature, immune from the forces of "progress." Moreover, in this mythic world, Negroes wanted only a chance to play and to love and serve their beloved white superiors. White Americans wanted desperately to believe it was all true.

But even as it fully elaborated its idealized images of the plantation, minstrelsy could not ignore the moving antislavery case made by abolitionists and ex-slaves.

> Some massas love dar darkies well,
> And gib em what dey want,
> Except it is dar freedom
> And *dat* I know dey won't.[20]

Focused on oppressed common people and especially on broken families, minstrelsy's criticism of slavery had the perfect blend of sentimentalism and egalitarianism to appeal to mid-nineteenth-century American audiences. One of the most popular early minstrel songs, for example, strikingly contrasted the happy courtship, love, and marriage of "Lucy Neal" and her black suitor to the heartless cruelty of whites.

> Oh, dars de wite man comin, To tear you from
> my side;
> Stan back you wite slave dealer, She is my be-
> trothed bride.
> De poor nigger's fate is hard; De wite man's
> heart is stone.
> Dey part poor nigga from his wife, An brake
> dare happy home.

Although minstrel troupes varied the details, the song always focused on happy black lovers being cruelly torn apart. The Congo Melodists' Lucy died of heartbreak after her husband was sold for committing a petty theft. In another version, the master's motivation was that he "only lub de money bag"; again, Lucy died of grief.[21]

Building on this powerful emotional image, minstrels charged that heartless masters often prevented slave lovers from marrying so they could have the beautiful yaller gals for themselves. When a rich white man fell in love with "Dinah Clare," for example, he courted her against her will and vowed to have her for his own. But she dramatically chose to die rather than live with a white man. Similarly, "Rosa Moon," a "colored virgin" (a very unusual description of a Negro woman in minstrelsy), rejected her master's courting in favor of a slave, prompting her master to sell her rather than to let her marry a black man.[22] Although minstrels did not titillate their audiences with the lurid detail which some abolitionists used, they clearly charged that white masters, like the worst kind of immoral aristocrats, coverted and exploited Negro women against their will. Women who refused these powerful white men were sold or committed suicide.

Minstrels also complained that money-hungry masters, seeking to maximize their profits, broke up happy slave families whenever it suited them. Using the emotionally powerful image of the Old Uncle against slavery, minstrelsy charged that greedy slave owners even threw loving Old Darkies out into the cold when they grew too old and feeble to work. One of these old Negro characters warmly reminisced about the great pleasure he and his wife had gotten from their eight children:

> We've watched our little nigger boys
> A playing on de Green;
> A happier day of sweeter joys
> Dis nigger neber seen.

But then he abruptly shattered this idyllic family scene by describing how sad he felt when he had to tell his wife that their master had decided to sell him because "I'se gitten old." [23] By creating the very antithesis of Old Uncle Ned's devoted, loving master, minstrels revealed how fully they realized that their cherished image of the loving bonds between kindly masters and their loyal "servants" was not always true.

Although destruction of slave families was the most biting charge minstrels leveled against slavery, it was certainly not the only one. Slave characters bitterly criticized immoral masters who drank too much and loved to "hug the girls but missus doesn't know it." One minstrel slave's mistress was so stingy and cruel that she wanted to feed her slaves "on atmosphere and dress them in nature's blouses." She even caused a consumptive slave to cough himself to death by feeding him only tobacco leaves.[24] Others protested that masters made blacks work long hours with no wages and brutally beat them for returning a little late from a holiday or for crying for departed lovers. They also claimed that in the middle of the night black bodies were secretly buried in river mud.[25]

For oppressed minstrel slaves, even inconsequential acts could result in sadistic torture. In South Carolina, for example, a driver caught a slave bringing an ear of roasted corn to his home and made him chew the cob until his gums bled and then dance barefooted on sharp rocks while the driver laughed at him. After locking him under the barn and giving him only corn leaves to eat until he caught "Choler-o-phoby," the driver tied the slave up as a scarecrow and left him for the elements and animals. After he had successfully warded off a panther with only his toenails and had driven off a buzzard by staring it down, he thought he was doomed when a hungry eagle confronted him. The eagle, however, winked at him and screamed: "I'se de bird ob de free/And won't eat de meat ob slavery." If the American Eagle—the bird of the free—saving a poor, oppressed black man from slavery did not bring cheers from the b'hoys in the audience, nothing would have.[26]

Despite the suffering that some of their slave characters had to endure, minstrels rarely suggested any slave retaliation except for the tricksters' "pranks." But before 1850, minstrelsy occasionally included black slaves who openly resisted oppression: "White man come to take my wife/I up and stick em with a big Jack knife." [27] In the 1830's, a minstrel song commented on the Amistad Mutiny, in which black slaves seized a Spanish ship and ordered the navigator to sail to Africa. Undercutting the real thrust of the event, the song emphasized that Americans caught the blacks (the navigator actually tricked them to the United States) and beat them up. It failed to mention that the black rebels actually had killed a number of Spaniards and had won their freedom in an American court. Furthermore, the song had a frivolous "Hey Get Along Jim Along Josey" chorus and abruptly shifted from verses about the mutiny to ones about happy Louisiana slaves, strutting Northern dandies, and President Martin Van Buren. [28]

Minstrelsy gave similar, though somewhat more extensive treatment to Nat Turner's Rebellion. In the late 1840's several companies performed "Uncle Gabriel the Negro General." Although the Christy Minstrels in 1847 billed it as "A Description of the Northampton Insurrection," other companies correctly placed the revolt in Southhampton. By focusing on the betrayal and capture of Uncle Gabriel, a "nigger genral" who was "de chief ob de unsurgents," minstrels avoided mentioning the whites killed in the rebellion. The fullest version reported that a black boy named Daniel accidently betrayed Gabriel, that whites "fought him and dey caught him," after which they convicted him and then "hung him and swung him." [29] Even though treatments of both revolts centered on whites punishing the rebels, such events and themes did not appear at all in minstrelsy after 1850. These few early references indicate that minstrels, during their first decade when they felt ambivalent about slavery, had considerable freedom in portraying whatever seemed of topical interest. At the same time that they glorified the plantation and argued that whites should control blacks, minstrels also could strongly express their revulsion at the brutal aspects of slavery, to the point of acknowledging that some slaves violently revolted. Only a few years later, such themes would have been unthinkable on the minstrel stage. For all the public controversy it provoked, John Brown's Raid evidently went unmentioned in minstrelsy.

Minstrelsy's treatment of runaway slaves clearly reveals its fundamental ambivalence about slavery. To explain the fugitive's motivation, minstrels pointed to the injustices of bondage. Some black characters ran away seeking the vague promises of freedom: "Our masters de may go to Guinea/In the Free States we will dwell." Others fled from the brutality and suffering. But most ran away in order to reunite their families, to get married, or to live happily as husband and wife—domestic reasons that Northern whites could wholeheartedly endorse. While women, in the best sentimental fashion, grieved themselves to death when their husbands were sold, men often ran away in search of their lovers. On occasion, black family ties actually prevented husband and wife from leaving together. After a long argument, Dinah refused to go with Pompey to "de states dat am free" where "how happy, happy we will be" because she was determined to stay where their baby was buried.[30] In this case, minstrels portrayed motherhood as exerting an even stronger pull on a black woman than the promises of matrimonial joy in freedom. Worthy of the best romantic heroines in contemporary women's fiction, who often had to choose between duty and happiness, Dinah's sacrifice had broad emotional appeal to sentimentally inclined audience members.[31]

Although minstrels sympathized with oppressed slaves and could understand why they would want to run away, they almost never portrayed a happy or successful fugitive. Unlike abolitionists, minstrels offered no Frederick Douglass, no William

Wells Brown, no Soujourner Truth to testify to the rich potential of ex-slaves. Minstrels could not portray positive images of runaways, even as proper subordinates to whites, because fugitive slaves ran to the North, and Northerners wanted no part of Negroes. Minstrel ex-slaves either became pretentious dandies, incompetent fools, or joined the growing chorus of minstrel blacks who longed to return to their Southern homes where they "belonged." For each unhappy slave they described, minstrels portrayed a number of happy ones. For every one that had to flee from a brutal master, minstrels described others who were given their freedom by benevolent masters. Some emancipated slaves refused to leave their idyllic plantation homes. Others left but before long felt compelled to return: "Shaw! what's de use ob going 'mong strangers in de West?/We'd best stay here, whar we are near, wid old massa an' de rest." [32]

The homesick ex-plantation character gave minstrels an ideal device for asserting that Negroes had no place in the North and that those who had experienced both the plantation and freedom realized it. Those that left soon regretted it. Minstrel ex-slaves complained that in the North they could find no jobs and no friends; they had nowhere to go and no one to turn to. "Dis being free," one such character concluded, "is worser den being a slave." [33] Minstrelsy did not dwell on the difficulties that ex-slaves had in the North, however, because that would seem to support the reformers who claimed that Northern Negroes were unfairly denied opportunities. Instead, they focused on ex-slaves' glowing recollections of the joys of plantation life. They wove an appealing web of nostalgia that included loving masters, happy black families, abundant food, beautiful yaller gals, rewarding hunts, and nightly parties. These repentant runaways were invariably men; women presumably would never have been foolish enough to have left such happy homes.

These sentimental songs sharply contrasted the stable, loving families of an idyllic rural life to the harsh realities and social chaos of cities. Again, minstrelsy's black characters served as projections for the fears, needs, and desires of Northern white audiences. By focusing on caricatures of frolicking Negroes in the idealized plantation family, minstrelsy created a state of perpetual childhood that audiences could vicariously participate in and feel superior to at the same time. It had to be a happy, carefree life; any cruelty or mistreatment had to be condemned and eliminated. Had slaveowners reformed their institution to remove its most glaring inhumanities, minstrels and their audiences probably could have accepted it from the beginning. As it was, minstrelsy had to attack the injustices of slavery that were so widely publicized in the North. But these "exceptions," which also provided important emotional outlets for the audiences, did not keep minstrels from believing in the romanticized plantation myth. This adult fairy tale was too precious, too badly needed, to be discarded or destroyed because of blacks.

During minstrelsy's first decade, roughly from 1843 to 1853, then, its Northern urban audiences could at the same time cry over the destruction of black families and over the beauty of the loving, interracial plantation family; bemoan the cruelty to slaves and also the forlorn fate of runaways; respect the bondsman's intense feelings and desire for freedom and the contented slave's love for his master; and laugh *with* black tricksters making fools of white aristocrats and also *at* foolish black characters. Because the minstrel show's structure did not require continuity or consistency and because minstrelsy's antislavery sentiments contained no call to action, audiences could do all of this on the same night without feeling that Negroes were their equals or that they had to reconcile their contradictory feelings about slavery. For a decade, Northern audiences could view slavery as little more than part of the minstrel show.

Most white Americans act out their need for racial subordination only when they feel that their own interests and values are challenged. The 1850's were just such a time. The accelerating agitation of black and white abolitionists for full exercise of Northern Negroes' rights, the intensified pitch of the propaganda battle over slavery, the enforcement of the fugitive slave law in the North, the increased use of race as a political issue, the controversy over *Uncle Tom's Cabin,* and finally the outbreak of a virtual civil war in Kansas—all combined to make slavery and race seem real and immediate threats to white Northerners.[34] By the mid-1850's, everything Northerners were committed to—national destiny, social order, their own status, the plantation myth, and the Union itself—seemed at stake.

Confronted with issues that brought them face to face with their ambivalence on race and struck at the heart of their principles and self-interest, white Northerners had to make excruciatingly difficult choices. Some stood with the advocates of abolition and Negro rights; some joined the growing Republican party pledged to stopping the spread of slavery and to reserving the territories for free white labor; others sided with the racial demagoguery of the Democrats; many equivocated; and most probably hoped for another compromise.[35] But as the struggle intensified, the options seemed to narrow. To accept slavery where it existed in its present form appeared to be the only alternative to destruction of the Union. Seeing only these choices, great numbers of Northern whites seemed content to overlook their ideological and emotional misgivings and to compromise with slaveowners in order to preserve the Union and to maintain social order.[36]

But the people who made this choice still had to rationalize it with the American Creed. As always, minstrelsy both reflected and helped shape popular thought. After the mid-1850's the tone of minstrelsy sharply changed as its folk and antislavery content virtually disappeared.[37] Romantic and sentimentalized images of happy, contented slaves and nostalgic old Negroes looking back to the good old days on the plantation completely dominated minstrel portrayals of slaves. In drawing these images, white Americans rejected the humanizing content of folklore and the complexity of human diversity for the comforting façade of romanticized, folksy caricatures. They thrust aside wily black tricksters and antislavery protesters for loyal, grinning darkies who loved their white folks and were contented and indeed fulfilled by working all day and singing and dancing all night.

Minstrels repeatedly contrasted these simplified images of Southern Negroes to their caricatures of Northern blacks who were either pretentious dandies, ridiculous failures even in the useless world of fashion, or foolish and inept low-comedy types that minstrels prominently featured in their increasingly popular slapstick farces. Minstrels also expanded the role of ex-plantation Negroes who were unhappy in the North and longed for the comfort and security of their "place" on the plantation. With all indications that slaves were unhappy or mistreated purged from the shows, minstrels in the late 1850's incessantly hammered out their simplified rationalization: on the plantation Negroes were happy, contented, and fulfilled; off it, they were ludicrous and/or helpless incompetents. Blacks *needed* the plantation. Racial subordination did not conflict with the American Creed. It was the nation's gift to Negroes.

In their mocking response to the greatest contemporary sensation concerning slavery—the smashing success of *Uncle Tom's Cabin*—minstrels unequivocally expressed their new position on slavery. Published in 1852, *Uncle Tom's Cabin* was the first popular novel with blacks as its central characters. In it,

Harriet Beecher Stowe used every sentimental and romantic device of the period to portray slaves as human beings who suffered inhumane indignities and felt the same pain and anguish that whites would have felt. The novel opened in an idyllic Kentucky plantation that was a model of inter-racial happiness. But then a slavetrader forced the benevolent but impoverished master to sell some slaves to pay off his debts. When Eliza Harris learned that her young son was to be sold, her maternal love forced her to take him and run away to the North. Ultimately, after dramatically outracing her pursuers across the frozen Ohio River to freedom in Cincinnati and after emotional speeches about mother-love and the sanctity of the family, she was reunited in Canada with her husband George, who had earlier run away rather than submit to being property and not a free man.

When loyal, devoutly Christian Uncle Tom learned that he, too, was to be sold, he refused to flee with Eliza. He felt it was his Christian duty to accept the Lord's will. On the way to be sold in the deep South, Tom met Evangeline St. Clare, Little Eva, a saintly young white girl who possessed the innate purity and wisdom that nineteenth-century romantics believed children and other innocents had. Eva persuaded her father to buy Tom. At the St. Clare plantation, Eva radiated her Christian love for all God's children, including the frolicking Topsy, an ignorant, unloved, free-spirited young slave. Slavery weighed heavily on Eva's heart, however, and she finally died a slow, sentimental death. The angel of goodness had been destroyed by the sins of slavery. Eva's father's death again forced Tom's sale. At a vile slave auction, he was bought by Simon Legree, a brutal, immoral slavedriver who had turned his plantation into an agrarian factory, the antithesis of a loving home. After refusing to whip other slaves, Tom died a Christlike martyr's death at Legree's hands.

Harriet Beecher Stowe had hoped to appeal to white

Southerners by attacking slavery as an institution that was un-healthy for whites as well as blacks. Her principal human villain, Simon Legree, was a Northerner. She also portrayed idealized images of plantations and white Southerners when uncorrupted by commercialism. And she created caricatures of laughable slaves. But her portrayals of the cruelty, suffering, and destruc-tion caused by slavery were so powerful and moving that the overall effect of the novel was to exacerbate the sectional conflict. Instead of reaching a large Southern audience and persuading it that its "peculiar institution" was bad for the South, *Uncle Tom's Cabin* became a runaway bestseller in the North and was banned in most slave states as subversive literature. Defenders of slavery also produced a number of literary rebuttals to it, as Mrs. Stowe's novel itself became an issue in the increasingly shrill and menacing propaganda war over slavery.[38]

The vivid characters, moving images, and melodramatic scenes in *Uncle Tom's Cabin* provided such great material for dramatic productions that theatrical promoters quickly capital-ized on them. In 1853, after success in Troy, New York, a stage version of the novel written by George L. Aiken opened in New York City. Even though it focused on Little Eva, who re-turned at the end of the play to rise triumphantly into the clouds in a morally assuring climax, the Aiken version retained the antislavery content of the novel, including the sale of the slaves and the death of Uncle Tom. William Lloyd Garrison, who had attacked the novel in the *Liberator* for urging slaves to accept their lot and for advocating colonization, enthusiastically praised the Aiken stage play: "If the shrewdest abolitionist amongst us had prepared the drama with a view to make the strongest anti-slavery impression, he could scarcely have done the work better." The Aiken version proved so popular that it ran an unprecedented 325 consecutive performances.[39]

The play's striking success compelled other theater man-

agers to enter rival productions, which, from the very beginning, presented plantation bondage "unmarred" by Mrs. Stowe's
antislavery images. The most famous and widely performed
pro-Southern version of *Uncle Tom's Cabin*, written by Henry J.
Conway, opened in New York in P. T. Barnum's American
Museum in November 1853 during the Aiken version's long
run. Advertising his show as the only "just and sensible dramatic version of Mrs. Stowe's book," Barnum claimed it showed
the cruelties of slavery but did not "foolishly and unjustly ele-
vate the negro above the white man in intellect or morals." It
was a "true picture of negro life in the South," Barnum in-
sisted, "and instead of turning away the audience in tears the
author has wisely consulted dramatic taste by having Virtue triumphant at last." Scenes like the slave auction were treated
lightly and the production ended happily with Uncle Tom
being melodramatically rescued from Simon Legree just in the
nick of time.[40]

The competition between the Aiken and Conway versions
of the play quickly took on more serious overtones than a simple battle for theater patrons waged in newspaper advertisements and the other extensive promotions. Outraged by the
Conway version, Garrison charged that "Barnum has offered
the slave-driver the incense of an expurgated form of 'Uncle
Tom's Cabin' . . . which omits all the strikes at the slave system, and has so shaped his drama as to make it quite an agree-
able thing to be a slave." As the competing versions came to be
identified with the factions warring over slavery, fist fights
broke out on the streets and in neighborhood saloons between
the emotionally charged partisans.[41]

The National Theater continued to offer the antislavery
Aiken version of the play until May 1854, when it no longer
drew well enough to justify continuing it. By this time, the potential audience had been diminished because the play had been

presented in many nearby cities which previously had provided the National with a large part of its audience. The other New York productions had also taken their toll. But most importantly, the watered-down, pro-Southern versions of the play proved more in touch with the general public's tastes as the decade continued and opposition to slavery threatened to destroy the Union. To be sure, antislavery versions of *Uncle Tom's Cabin* ran in Boston and Philadelphia, but what happened when the play opened in Baltimore was more representative of late antebellum versions. To make the production acceptable to the audience, John E. Owens, a comedian who managed the theater, adapted and softened the Aiken version. Owens ordered the parts of Legree and George and Liza Harris toned down, and he himself played Uncle Tom as a low-comedy type. "I've raked up all sorts of situations from old farces, and so on— anything to cover up the real drift of the play." [42]

Although *Uncle Tom's Cabin* sparked at least fourteen rebuttal novels contrasting images of happy, fulfilled plantation Negroes to those of destitute, homeless Northern blacks and wretched white "wage slaves," they never got the exposure in the North that the pro-Southern versions of the play had. In 1854, the Conway version opened in San Francisco and played the West Coast for two years. The Bowery Theater in New York offered the play with T. D. "Jim Crow" Rice as Uncle Tom. After its short run, a similar version starring Frank Brower, one of the original Virginia Minstrels, replaced it. As the sectional conflict over slavery grew more ominous, escapist farces and burlesques of *Uncle Tom's Cabin* dominated stage productions of the novel. In the early 1850's, some of these parodies were done as Irish skits, including *Uncle Pat's Cabin* by Henry J. Conway. The parody *Uncle Mike's Cabin* ran at the National Theater only a month before the Aiken version opened there. The rival Bowery Theater later offered *Uncle*

Crochet's Parlour, and similar rebuttals played in New Orleans.[43]

As performers who fancied themselves experts at portraying the plantation and as entertainers who burlesqued theatrical
hits and topical events, minstrels quickly made *Uncle Tom's
Cabin* part of their shows. With such parodies as "Uncle Dad's
Cabin," "Uncle Tom and His Cabin," and "Aunt Dinah's
Cabin," they soon topped all others in the extent of their caricatures and their public exposure. As early as 1853, Christy's Minstrels billed Part III of their show "Life Among the Happy,"
a clear takeoff on "Life Among the Lowly," the novel's sub-
title. Beginning in the spring of 1854, Christy and Wood's
Minstrels topped their bill with an extremely popular burlesque
"opera" of *Uncle Tom's Cabin* that set the tone for many of the
minstrel versions of the play that followed it. In this version,
Tom apparently was not even sold, and although Eva was one
of the characters, her father and Simon Legree were not. The
first scene, which featured Tom's return to Chloe from a camp
meeting, concluded with his "description of free darkies and his
preference for Old Kentuck." In the next scene, played before a
tableau of Liza's cabin, George serenaded Liza, after which
Eva somehow appeared and sang several songs. Then, in the
third scene, Eva lectured Topsy, they each sang, and finally
George and Liza were married by "jumping the broom." The
last scene featured "Eva's Farewell" and concluded with the
"Grand Characteristic Dance, 'Pop Goes the Weazle.' " Christy
and Wood portrayed none of the cruelty or suffering of slavery
as they reduced *Uncle Tom's Cabin* to just another grouping of
plantation songs and dances loosely connected by a weak plot,
which differed from the standard plantation closing act only in
name.[44]

Consistent with the completely proplantation position that
they had taken by this time, minstrels generally retitled *Uncle*

Tom's Cabin "Happy Uncle Tom" and followed the Christy pattern of emasculating the story. Frank Brower and Sam Sanford, both prominent minstrels, virtually made their careers playing the title role. Beginning in the fall of 1854, Brower got top billing with Wood's Minstrels in New York as "Happy Uncle Tom," an act he regularly repeated at least until 1865 in New York and Philadelphia with some of the most popular minstrel troupes.[45] Wherever he played, Brower's act always featured his Uncle Tom jig dance and ridiculous dialogue:

> We wur cakes.
> What kind ob cakes wur we?
> Jist black cakes.
> What kind ob cake is Little Eva?
> Angel Cake!
> An Massa St. Clair
> An eclair.[46]

An 1863 text of his skit, picturing Uncle Tom as hard of hearing, simply revolved around repetition, misunderstanding, and Tom's stupidity. In it, Tom was just a decrepit, near-deaf old man who understood little about the world, but who was invigorated by the sound of banjo music to which he compulsively danced.[47] In itself this portrait of a dim-witted, dancing darky was common in minstrel playlets. But this was Uncle Tom—paragon of spirituality, morality, and humanity. Few would have wept for this Uncle Tom—except from laughing too hard.

Sam Sanford, who reportedly began performing "Happy Uncle Tom" in Philadelphia in late 1853 and continued it into the Civil War, gave it a similar interpretation. "I did a piece," Sanford later recalled, "called 'Rebuke to Uncle Tom' in which I tried to depict slave life as I knew it, and as it actually existed at the time. I took in $11,000 in nine weeks." He also sold manuscript copies of "Sanford's Southern Version of *Uncle Tom's Cabin*" to other minstrel troupes, which gave it even wider distribution. Like Brower's, Sanford's version, which did not even include Eva, focused entirely on happy plantation images.

> Oh, white folks, we'll have you to know
> Dis am not de version of Mrs. Stowe;
> Wid her de Darks am all unlucky
> But we am de boys from Old Kentucky.
>
> Den hand de Banjo down to play
> We'll make it ring both night and day
> And we care not what de white folks say,
> Dey can't get us to run away.[48]

"Happy Uncle Tom's" great popularity with Northern audiences prompted many other minstrel companies to perform what were probably similar versions. In the spring and summer of 1854, for example, Campbell's Minstrels performed "The Plantation, Life Among the Happy." Perham's Burlesque Opera House contributed "Happy Uncle Breve, or Life in Old Kentucky," which included the following numbers: "Opening Chorus—Let's Be Gay," "Happy Are We, Darkies So Gay," "Happy Uncle Breve is Getting Old," "Old Uncle Ned," "Uncle Breve Tells About the Good Time He Had on the Old Plantation," and closing with "Old Plantation and a Virginny Jig." In 1858, Wood's Minstrels concluded their show with a tableau of Southern life, which depicted Negroes loading cotton on the Mississippi levee and lying in the mid-day sun, blacks at work on a tobacco plantation, a "merry group dancing and feasting" at a Christmas Eve Festival, a corn-husking contest, Uncle Tom kneeling before Eva with St. Clare and Topsy standing nearby to hear her "sacred words," and, finally, the sun rising over an equestrian statue of George Washington—with "Veneration and Patriotism." [49] Wood's had reduced *Uncle Tom's Cabin* to only one of a series of plantation scenes placed within the highest possible national sanction—the shadow of Washington. To put Uncle Tom in "his place," minstrels used the same process they used for blacks in general. They selected certain aspects of the novel and used them in conjunction with their other material to present a simplified caricature of a contented plantation Negro. Clearly, minstrels tried to demonstrate, the old folks at home had no problems.

At the same time that they lampooned her novel, Sam Sanford and other minstrels personally vilified Mrs. Stowe. One black character, for example, complained that he had run away from his plantation because of her but arrived in New York City to find that she had gotten rich and gone to England. "Oh, Aunt Harriet Beecha Stowe," he asked, "how could you leave de country and starve poor darkies so?" Shunned by abolitionists, lonely, and unable to support himself, he lamented not having taken Uncle Tom's advice to "be true unto your masta, and nebber run away." After recalling how "kind and gentle" his master and mistress were, he resolved to return to the plantation. Besides charging that Mrs. Stowe selfishly took "care of number one," minstrels used their black characters to lecture her in much the same way that the literary answers to her novel did:

> But don't come back, Aunt Harriet; in England
>   make a fuss,
> Go talk against your country, put money in your
>   puss;
> And when us happy darkies you pity in your
>   prayer,
> Oh, don't forget de WHITE SLAVES dat's starvin'
>   ober dar! [50]

97

Negroes in Antebellum Minstrelsy

Purging the antislavery content from *Uncle Tom's Cabin* and attacking Mrs. Stowe were only the most obvious indications of the way in which minstrelsy refashioned its portrayals of Negroes after the mid-1850's. On stage, minstrelsy repeatedly acted out images which illustrated that there was no need to fight a war over slavery, no need to accept Negroes as equals in the North, and no need to feel guilty for contradictions between slavery and the American Creed. Fulfillment for blacks, minstrels demonstrated, came only within the subordinate roles of the plantation; blacks needed supervision, and they got it in a benevolent atmosphere of a loving extended family. For them, the fundamental American equation had to be altered; if blacks were to enjoy the American rights to Life and Happiness, they could not have their Liberty. The benevolent subordination of the romanticized plantation allowed blacks to reach the highest level they could achieve and purified the mythic fantasy world that whites needed. In the first decade of minstrelsy, white Americans had gotten a brief glimpse, though itself quite limited, of the complexity and humanity of the black man and a clearer look at the consequences of their own egalitarianism if extended to black Americans. Faced with challenges to their own status and values, they rejected these images for simplified caricatures that rationalized white subordination of blacks and provided the molds into which blacks were forced—on stage and off.

NOTES

[1] For example, see Elias Howe, *Ethiopian Glee Book #3, Christy Minstrels* (Boston, 1849) which had eight positive and eight negative references to slavery; a similar pattern is found in *Buckley's Song Book for the Parlour* (New York, 1855); E. P. Christy, *Christy's Plantation Melodies #2* (New York, 1851); Charles White, *White's New Book of Plantation*

Melodies (Philadelphia, 1849); *White's Serenaders' Songs* (New York, 1851); Matt Campbell, *Wood's New Plantation Melodies* (New York, 1855); among others. Sterling Brown, *Negro Poetry and Drama* (Washington, D.C., 1937), pp. 86, 106, noted the presence of a "mournful note" of the "slave's sentimental plaint" in early minstrelsy, but other scholars have missed it.

² For a detailed description of minstrelsy's physical caricature of blacks see Cecil Patterson, "A Different Drum: The Image of the Negro in Nineteenth Century Popular Song Books," unpublished doctoral dissertation, University of Pennsylvania, 1961, pp. 45–85; for the specific examples cited here, see *Christy's Plantation Melodies #2* (New York, 1851), pp. 57–58; Charles Fox, *Sable Songster* (New York, 1859), p. 36; "Going Ober De Mountain," *Deacon Snowball's Songster* (New York, 1843), n.p.; Charles White, *Policy Players* (New York, 1863); "Dis Nigger'd Like To Marry," *Ethiopian Glee Book #4* (Boston, 1850), p. 228; Virginia Serenaders, "Lubly Fan Will You Come Out?" n.p., 1844, sheet music, HTC.

³ See programs and playbills for Ethiopian Serenaders, Campbell's Minstrels, Ordway Aeolians, and The New Orleans Serenaders, in HTC and NYLC.

⁴ Leon Litwack, *North of Slavery* (Chicago, 1961) is the best study of the treatment and actions of Northern Negroes before the Civil War; see especially, chapter 3, "The Politics of Repression." A superb study of early American attitudes toward blacks is Winthrop Jordan, *White Over Black: American Attitudes Toward the Negro, 1550–1812* (Chapel Hill, N.C., 1968); for other discussions of nineteenth-century white Americans beliefs about Negroes, see Eric Foner, *Free Soil, Free Labor, Free Men* (New York, 1970), George M. Fredrickson, *The Black Image in the White Mind* (New York, 1971), James Rawley, *Race and Politics* (New York, 1969), and Forrest Wood, *Black Scare* (Berkeley, 1968).

⁵ "Virginia Sam," *Jim Along Josey Roarer* (Philadelphia, n.d. [1830's]), n.p.; Virginia Minstrels, "Dandy Jim, From Caroline," New York, 1844, sheet music, HTC, and virtually every other early minstrel troupe; "Good Looking Cuff," *Negro Melodies No. 2* (Philadelphia, 1864 [reprint of early songs]), pp. 12–13; "Dandy Broadway Swell," *De Susannah and Thick Lip Melodist* (New York, 1855), n.p. and *Wood's New Plantation Melodies* (New York, 1855), p. 51; Ethiopian Serenaders, "De Colored Fancy Ball," New York, 1848, sheet music, HTC,

and *Wood's Minstrel Songs* (New York, 1855), pp. 27–28; Dan Bryant, "Aristocratic Darkey," *Bryant's Essence of Old Virginny* (New York, 1857), pp. 9–10; for a discussion of minstrelsy's treatment of social change after the Civil War, when it became a major minstrel concern, see chapter 6.

⁶ Charles White, *Charley White's Ethiopian Joke Book* (New York, 1855), pp. 35, 36, 60; *Fox's Ethiopian Comicalities* (New York, 1859), p. 37; "One and Twenty," *De Sable Harmonist* (Philadelphia, 1850), pp. 1–3; "What Shall This Darkey Do?" *Old Uncle Ned Songster* (Philadelphia, n.d.[1850's]), pp. 89–90; "O Walk Along Gumbo, Sound Your Horn," *Thick Lip*, pp. 17–18.

⁷ "The Devil and the Lawyer," *Negro Forget Me Not Songster* (Philadelphia, n.d.[1840's?]), pp. 109–11; Charles White, *Joke Book*, pp. 12, 36–37, 54–55; Edward F. Dixey, "Necessary Consequences," *Dixey's Essence of Burnt Cork* (Philadelphia, 1859), pp. 36–37; White, *Joke Book*, p. 34.

⁸ Virginia Serenaders, Worcester, Massachusetts, 1843, program, HTC; similar claims were on many other early minstrel programs, playbills, and posters.

⁹ "Nigga's Heart Am Bery Gay," *Negro Melodist* (Cincinnati, n.d. [1850?], pp. 47–48; Stewart McCauley, "The Shanghai Crow," *Songs Of Kunkel's Nightingale Opera Troupe* (Baltimore, 1854), p. 49. Slave parties were extremely common in minstrelsy and in Afro-American folk tradition; for examples of the latter, see Langston Hughes and Arna Bontemps, eds., *The Book of Negro Folklore* (New York, 1966), p. 509; Richard Dorson, *American Negro Folktales* (New York, 1967), p. 136.

¹⁰ White, "We'll All Make a Laugh," *New Book of Plantation Melodies*, p. 12; Charles White, "Whar Is The Spot," *White's Illustrated Songster* (New York, 1848), p. 12; E. P. Christy, "Oh, Come Darkies, Come," *Plantation Songster #1* (New York, 1851), p. 55; and many others.

¹¹ As a defense mechanism, Afro-Americans learned to put on a false face that let whites believe their caricatures of blacks were accurate characterizations, while black people created their own culture "behind the veil." But this meant that Afro-American culture was channeled into areas that coincided with whites' stereotypes of blacks, into the physical not the intellectual, the verbal not the literate, the lighthearted not the serious. Minstrelsy reveals that process at work.

For a discussion of the channeling of Afro-American culture and black people's creative response, see Roger Abrahams, *Positively Black* (Englewood Cliffs, N.J., 1970); for a sample of "John and Old Master stories, see: Dorson, *American Negro Folktales*, pp. 124–70.

[12] "Come Back Wid De Brass Tacks," *Black Diamond Songster* (Philadelphia, 1840), p. 21; representative of the many minstrel versions of the party is Christy, *Plantation #1*, p. 48; of black folk versions, Dorson, *Negro*, pp. 136–37; "Old Cuff in de Mornin'," *Ethiopian #3*, p. 122; "Hop de Dooden Do," *World of New Negro Song* (Philadelphia, 1856), pp. 62–63; "Sich a Gitten' Up Stairs," *Thick Lip*, pp. 12–14, and Charles White, *Serenader*, p. 70.

[13] Christy, "Way Down in Cairo," *Plantation #1*, p. 11; "De Long Island Nigger," *Negro Melodies No. 2*, n.p.

[14] "Walk Along John," *Thick Lip*, pp. 19–20; "Jasper Jack," *Negro Melodies No. 2*, pp. 11–12, *Thick Lip*, pp. 91–93, *Sable*, pp. 2–3, among others.

[15] Christy, "Old Ned," *Plantation #2*, pp. 21–22; "Carolina," *Thick Lip*, pp. 7–9; Nightingale Serenaders, "De Banks ob de Ohio," n.p., 1846, sheet music, HTC, and in White, *New Illustrated Melodeon* (N.Y., 1848), p. 16., and E. P. Christy, *Christy's Plantation Melodies #5* (New York, 1851), p. 38; "The Weeping Willow," *Christy and Wood's New Songster* (New York, 1854), p. 13; Ordway Aeolians, "Farewell Old Home," Boston, 1853, sheet music, HTC.

[16] Patterson, pp. 70–71.

[17] Stephen Foster, "Old Uncle Ned," N.Y., 1848, sheet music, HTC, was performed by almost every minstrel company, among them: Sable Harmonists, n.p., 1848, sheet music, HTC; Howe, *Ethiopian #3*, pp. 116–117, Christy, *Plantation #1*, pp. 36–38. Among the many imitations were: "Night Funeral of a Slave," *Old Uncle Ned Songster* (Philadelphia, 185–?), pp. 119–20, and *Bryant's Virginny*, pp. 20–21.

[18] Christy, "Massa'a in the Cold Ground," *Plantation #2*, pp. 8–9, and many other minstrels; Ordway's Aeolians, "Farewell Old Home," Boston, 1853, sheet music, HTC; George Christy, "Massa's Death," *Christy and White's Ethiopian Melodies* (Philadelphia, 1854), pp. 57–58.

[19] New Orleans Serenaders, "Aunt Dinah Roe," n.p., 1850, sheet music, HTC; White, *Serenader*, pp. 83–84; *Ned Songster*, pp. 117–18; Matt Campbell, *Wood's Minstrel Songs* (New York, 1855), p. 58.

[20] White, "We'll All Make A Laugh," *New Book of Plantation Melodies*, p. 12. In its first decade minstrelsy presented virtually every argument abolitionists used. They did it piecemeal, however, within a generally favorable portrayal of the plantation. Unlike antislaverites, minstrels did not use Christianity in their shows, probably to avoid charges of sacrilege. This meant they did not present religious objections to slavery. For abolitionists' attacks, see Theodore Dwight Weld, *American Slavery As It is* (New York, 1968, Arno Press ed.); for antislavery songsters, see William Wells Brown, *Antislavery Harp* (Boston, 1851); George Washington Clark, *The Liberty Minstrel* (New York, 1844) and *Harp of Freedom* (New York, 1856); fugitive slaves' views are synthesized in Charles H. Nichols, *Many Thousand Gone* (Bloomington, Ind., 1969, paperback ed.).

[21] Virginia Serenaders, "Lucy Neal," New York, 1844, sheet music, and many other early minstrels; Congo Melodists, "Lucy Neal," n.p., 1844, "Rose ob Alabama," n.p., n.d., sheet music, HTC; Howe, "Think ob Me," *Ethiopian #4*, pp. 208–9; "Dilly Burn," *Pop Goes the Weasel Songster* (Philadelphia, 1855), pp. 167–68.

[22] "Oppossum Up a Gum Tree," *Negro Melodies #2*, pp. 68–69; Harmoneons, "My Lucy and Me," Boston, n.d., Campbell Minstrels, "Lovely Nell," n.p., 1848, sheet music HTC; "Dinah Clare," *Thick Lip*, pp. 33–35; "Rosa Moon," *New Negro Band Songster* (Philadelphia, 185–?), p. 232.

[23] Charles White, "Goodbye Linda Lub," *New Book of Plantation Melodies*, p. 31.

[24] "Massa Is a Stingy Man," *Negro Melodist*, pp. 18–20.

[25] White, "Dinner Horn," *Illustrated*, p. 19; Howe, "De Dinner," *Ethiopian #4*, p. 222; "Niggers of de Wild Goose Nation," *Thick Lip*, pp. 11–12; "De Original Jim Crow," *Negro Melodies No. 2*, pp. 5–7; Campbell's Minstrels, "Darkey's Lament," n.p. 1848, sheet music, HTC; "De Mississippi Bank," *Sable Harmonist*, p. 17, and *Thick Lip*, pp. 20–21.

[26] "Walk Jawbone," *Snowball's*, n.p., and Howe, *Ethiopian #4*, pp. 216–17; "Ring De Hoop and Blow de Horn," *Negro Melodies No. 3* (Philadelphia, 1864 [reprint of early songs]), pp. 17–19.

[27] "Harper's Negro Medley," *Jim Along Josey*, n.p.; "Such A Dancing of the Niggers," *Lucy Neale's Nigga Warbler* (Philadelphia, n.d. [early 1840's]), n.p.

[28] "A New Jim Along Josey," *Jim Along Josey*, n.p.

[29] Christy Minstrels, "Uncle Gabriel the Negro General," New

York, 1846, sheet music, HTC; Christy Minstrels, New York, 1847, program, NYLC; White, "De Nigger General," *New Book of Plantation Melodies, pp.* 52–53; "Uncle Gabriel, Darkey General," *New Negro Band Songster*, pp. 130–31.

³⁰ "Jolly Raftsman," *Negro Melodies No. 3*, p. 53; White, *New*, p. 49; "Jolly Darky," *Ethiopian #3*, p. 135; White, "Sally Weaver," *New Book of Plantation Melodies*, pp. 9–10; White, "Dinah, Why Don't You Hush?" *Serenader*, p. 40.

³¹ James D. Hart, *The Popular Book* (Berkeley, 1963, paperback ed.), pp. 85–105; David Grimsted, *Melodrama Unveiled* (Chicago, 1968), p. 182.

³² White, "Ole Mass Is Going To Town," *New Book of Plantation Melodies*, p. 22; Christy, "Ring, Ring de Banjo," *Plantation Songster #1*, p. 13; "Massa's Old Plantation," *Old Plantation Songster* (Philadelphia, 184–?), pp. 150–51.

³³ White, "My Old Virginia Home, *Serenader*, p. 67; "Mary Bloom," and "Old River Farm," *Weasel*, pp. 199–200; Sam Sanford, "The Returned Fugitive," *Popular Ethiopian Melodies* (Philadelphia, 1856), p. 46; "Sweep Song," *Bryant's Virginny*, pp. 37–38.

³⁴ For a discussion of these issues, see: Foner, *Free Soil . . .* , Fredrickson, *The Black Image . . .* , Litwack, *North of Slavery*, Rawley, *Race and Politics*, and Wood, *Black Scare*.

³⁵ Foner, *Free Soil . . .* , 263–67; Rawley, *Race and Politics*, p. 167.

³⁶ Rawley, *Race and Politics*, pp. 14–15.

³⁷ John Crandall has found a remarkably similar pattern in the children's literature of the period. Before 1850, it contained the full range of arguments against slavery, but after that date, they were replaced by appeals for compromise and preservation of the Union. Crandall concluded that faced with a choice or reform *or* order, the writers of children's literature chose order: John Crandall, "Patriotism and Humanitarian Reform in Children's Literature, 1825–1860," *American Quarterly*, XXI (Spring 1969), 3–23.

³⁸ Harriet Beecher Stowe, *Uncle Tom's Cabin* (New York, 1963, Washington Square Edition); for an analysis of the novel in the context of plantation literature and the sectional conflict, see William R. Taylor, *Cavalier and Yankee* (New York, 1963, paperback ed.), pp. 127, 138–40, 280, 287–94.

³⁹ Harry Birdoff, *America's Greatest Hit: Uncle Tom's Cabin* (New

York, 1947), pp. 70–72; *Liberator*, Mar. 26, 1852, Sept. 3, 1853, quoted in *Ibid.*, p. 77; Birdoff, *America's Greatest Hit*, p. 84.

[40] *Ibid.*, pp. 88–91.

[41] *Liberator*, Dec. 16, 1853, quoted in *Ibid.*, p. 88; Birdoff, *America's Greatest Hit*, pp. 96–97, 101.

[42] *Ibid.*, pp. 104, 109–11, 112–14.

[43] Sterling Brown, *Negro Poetry and Drama*, pp. 21–23; Taylor, *Cavalier and Yankee* pp. 292–94; Birdoff, *America's Greatest Hit*, pp. 102, 121; James H. Dorman, Jr., *Theater in the Ante Bellum South* (Chapel Hill, N.C., 1967), pp. 278–80.

[44] George D. Odell, *Annals of the New York Stage*, 15 vols. (New York, 1927–1949), Vol. VI, pp. 325–27; Christy and Wood's Minstrels, New York, June 2, 1854, program, HTC.

[45] Wood's Minstrels, New York, 1859, program, HTC; Sanford's Opera House, Philadelphia, 1859, programs and playbills, HTC; Morris Brothers, Pell, and Trowbridge Minstrels, Boston, June 6, 1859, Mar. 26, 1860, playbills, HTC.

[46] Birdoff, *America's Greatest Hits*, p. 141.

[47] Frank Brower, *Black Diamond Songster* (New York, 1863), pp. 5–8.

[48] "Interview with Sam Sanford," Boston *Globe*, Oct. 28, 1882, clipping, Boston Public Library; Sanford's Opera House, Philadelphia, Oct. 1860, Jan. 1861, Feb. 1861, Aug. 15, 1861, programs and playbills, HTC.

[49] Campbell's Minstrels, New York, Mar. 13, Mar. 27, Apr. 3, May 18, May 24, July 26, 1854, programs and playbills, HTC; Perham's Burlesque Opera House, New York, 1855, program, HTC; Wood's Minstrels, New York, Dec. 1858, program and playbill, HTC. Such minstrelized versions of *Uncle Tom's Cabin* continued throughout the nineteenth century, adding large casts of singers and dancers and honeycombing the nation as "Tommer" companies.

[50] "Aunt Harriet Beecha Stowe," *Weasel*, pp. 210–11; Sanford, "Aunty Sarah Rowe," *Melodies*, pp. 36–37; Dixey, "Take Care of Number One," *Essence*, pp. 64–65.

4 Minstrels Fight the Civil War

On the eve of the Civil War, George Christy, the minstrel who first converted *Uncle Tom's Cabin* into "Happy Uncle Tom," took his minstrel show to the South. Although his conscious purpose undoubtedly was to make money, at least symbolically he was carrying Northern minstrelsy's proplantation message to calm Southerners' agitated feelings. Christy, however, took his "compromise Unionism" to Charleston, the hotbed of secessionism. And he tried to open his show on December 20, 1860, South Carolina's "Independence Day." As one of the few visible Northern targets in the state, the Christy Minstrels, like Fort Sumter, soon found themselves under siege. But when the troupe's manager assured the audience that the minstrels had absolutely no sympathy for the Northern cause, they were able to put on their show without interruption. After the performance, the company, still fearing for its safety, quietly slipped back to the North. Other Northern minstrel troupes, in slave states from Maryland to Louisiana, also quickly retreated when a similar fate befell them.[1]

But minstrels could not escape the impact of the Civil War as easily as they could flee from irate Confederates. Between 1861 and 1865, the war completely dominated the minstrel show, even though the inane laughter, slapstick comedy, and sentimental romance of earlier years remained standard minstrel features.[2] Like many other Northerners, minstrels went into the war as buoyantly optimistic nationalists expecting to quickly achieve their goal of "The Constitution as it is, The Union as it was." They patriotically rallied public support for the national government and then awaited the kind of reconciliation that had preserved the Union in 1850. But instead, they and their audiences had to face a long, frustrating Civil War that profoundly affected every aspect of American life, including the minstrel show, which as always reflected changes in public moods, concerns, and desires. Although their nationalism never waned, minstrels quickly took on a much more somber tone in response to the unprecedented suffering and anguish. Then, after 1863, when the horrendous scope of the carnage and the economic burdens of the war hit the homefront and minstrels saw all hopes of compromise lost, they strikingly increased their criticism of Northern society and lashed out at the people they felt were responsible. After emancipation and the use of Negro troops became part of the Union war effort, minstrels were even forced to reconsider their position on blacks. How they coped with these problems reflects the impact of the Civil War on Northern public opinion.

As dedicated nationalists, minstrels and their audiences unequivocally supported the Union. Since the 1830's they had boasted of national destiny, advocated expansion, and offered to defend the national honor against the British, the French, or both if necessary. They had gloried in the easy victories of the

Mexican War and had looked forward to other conquests—to Texas, Oregon, Cuba, and the day when "de Yankee boys will hab de flag ob almost ebery nation." [3] They had patriotically punned that the United States would inevitably outlive all others because "it's got the best Constitution." And taking great pride in the American flag, they had bragged that wherever it waved it made tyrants tremble because it represented a country of free men united into a "young Giant of might" that opposed all oppression. "And may we forever with one heart and head," one song concluded, "stand up for our Flag and our laws." [4] With this nationalistic heritage, they approached secession and the outbreak of the Civil War.

Confronted with the national crisis, minstrelsy first marshaled the country's historical and patriotic heritage in flag-waving support of the Union. In the fall of 1860 and in early 1861 Sanford's Minstrels in Philadelphia, for example, featured lavish nationalistic tableau of American history, including "The Pilgrim Fathers," "The Signing of the Declaration of Independence," "Washington Preserving the Union," and "Washington and the Constitution" with the "Star Spangled Banner" played as accompaniment. Minstrel nationalists centered their Unionist litany on George Washington, the "Father and Preserver of the country," and to much lesser degree on the men who had given their lives to win independence from England. Just as these men had willingly fought and died for their country, minstrels preached, all good Americans must be prepared to make similar sacrifices in order to "prove ourselves worthy of the noble Washington." [5] Minstrels made Andrew Jackson second only to Washington as a nationalistic model in this crisis because he himself had stood against Southern secessionists only thirty years before!

> If I was President in these times, I know what I would do.
> I'd do as Andrew Jackson did, Stand by the Union too.

By 1862 such patriotic Unionism pervaded minstrelsy. If Americans did not preserve the Union, warned minstrels and many other Unionists, all the glory of the American past and all the promise of the future would be lost. "One country and one flag," Bryant's Minstrels and many others exclaimed. A Christy Minstrel effectively summed up this torrent of nationalistic rhetoric:

> Strike! Strike! the blot from treason's hand
> For God, for fame, for liberty,
> For Union and our native land.[6]

Throughout the war, even in the years when they had little to boast about, minstrels selectively reported war news that would anger, encourage, or stimulate their audiences to further commitment to the Union. At the outset, they denounced the assassination plot against Lincoln, lashed out at Secretary of Treasury Floyd for "stealing" $32,000,000 for the Confederacy, and condemned Maryland mobs for attacking Massachusetts volunteers. When Union forces finally won their first major victory at Fort Donelson, minstrels eagerly anticipated an early end to the war. "We've gone easy on you so far," they gloated to the rebels, "but we'll now whip you soundly." They had to wait longer than they expected, however, before they had other triumphs to celebrate. Although they hailed the battle of the Monitor and Merrimac, they had to admit that the war had not gone too well. Better times would come, they tried to assure the public and themselves, with new military leaders.[7] After the victories of 1863, they exuberantly praised Union generals, and one enthusiastic minstrel even predicted that U. S. Grant would be the next president:

> He dug a trench at Vicksburg, As sure as you're alive
> He'll dig one more round the White House door in 1865.

> Here's a health to the pet of the Yankee nation,
> The next overseer of Sam's plantation.[8]

Even during militarily trying times, minstrels remained as bellicosely antiforeign as they had been since the 1830's. Europeans, especially the English, they charged, had aggravated, if not instigated, the threat to the American republic.

> John Bull he tried a row to make.
> He tried this Union for to break.

When England protested Union Captain Wilkes's seizure of two Confederate diplomats from a British ship, a minstrel responded by boasting that "we've beat them twice before and if they're not careful we'll take Canada." Their thoughts of manifest destiny also turned to Mexico, as they warned Louis Napoleon:

> So take advice friend Louey,
> Keep away from Mexico,
> For the doctrine we will carry out,
> Was taught by Old Monroe.

Only a friendly visit of the Russian fleet to America made minstrels deviate from their anti-European sentiments in anticipation of an alliance between "the Yankee Doodle Eagle and Russian Rugged Bear." [9]

Before 1863 minstrels directed surprisingly few diatribes at Confederates. They still hoped for a compromise or an early Union victory that would bring quick restoration of prewar conditions. Furthermore, they were not yet confronted with the unprecedented casualties of subsequent years. For these reasons, they were less concerned with fixing blame for the war than with rallying nationalistic sentiment in favor of speedy reunification. But, on occasion, their anti-Confederate attacks could be extremely vicious, especially when directed at Confederate President Jefferson Davis. In 1862, for example, a minstrel charged that the devil had made Davis king of the Southern Confederacy in exchange for his soul, a debt the singer hoped would soon be collected so Davis would go where he belonged. More commonly, minstrels pictured themselves as the agents of retribution. Using a Union army marching song, several minstrels threatened to hang Jeff Davis. But others conjured up more imaginative curses:

> I want musketeers to smite him, rattlesnakes to bite him,
> I want his trees to not bear and his head to have no hair,
> I want bunions like onions to grow on his feet,
> I want Dr. Timblety to drug him and John Heeman to plug him.[10]

But no amount of patriotic rhetoric and nationalistic optimism could change the fact that the war produced more strife than reconciliation, more casualties than victories, and more anguish than glory. With every casualty list, the public's frustration, anxiety, and despair mounted. Even the victories, when they finally came, were rendered somewhat hollow by the greatest cost in human lives that Americans had ever borne. Since nearly every member of the audience had a close friend or relative serving in the military, minstrels poured out a torrent of maudlin sentimental songs that grew in direct proportion to the merciless increase in anguish. From the decision to enlist and the departure scene, through the soldiers in battle and the anxious relatives waiting at home, to the wounds, the deaths, and the tears, minstrels portrayed every facet of the war's torment. They were trapped in a tragic dilemma. To save the American national family, individual families had to be sacrificed. In this predicament, the minstrel show provided an outlet for personal suffering which gave the heartrending losses a broader social meaning by linking them with nationalism and sharing them with the public. One typical singer assured the audience of his patriotism even as he cried for his friends:

> I love my country, while I weep
> I pray her sons may all things dare
> But still the memory will not sleep
> That I have dear friends fighting there.[11]

The widespread and intense pain Northerners had to endure caused minstrels to shift their tearjerkers about broken families and unrequited love from plantation blacks to the suffering of Northern white women. During the war, a flood of emotional minstrel songs lamented the wounds suffered by the mushrooming "invalid corps," bemoaned the deaths of the less fortunate, and sobbed about the torment of the women left behind to wait, worry, and mourn. The single most popular sentimental song of the war, "Weeping, Sad, and Lonely," also called "When This Cruel War Is Over," centered on the anguish of waiting. The song, which sold over a million copies of sheet music and was reportedly so depressing that some generals would not let their troops sing it, opened by recalling how gallant the female singer's young man had looked in his uniform when he went off to war, but it quickly switched to the somber tone of the chorus:

> Weeping, Sad, and Lonely, Hopes and Fears how vain!
> When this cruel war is over, Praying that we meet again!

After describing a tormented nightmare of her valiant lover dying from battle wounds while calling in vain for a last caress from her, the song still cast the young woman as a model patriot who, despite her personal suffering, urged her lover to fight on, "to let all nations see, How we love the starry banner, Emblem of the free." [12].

Even more than young love nipped in the bud, minstrelsy's sentimental war songs dwelt on the emotionally moving images of the mother-son relationship. What had been a trickle of such songs after the Mexican War gushed into a torrential deluge during the Civil War. "Dear Mother, I'll Come Home Again," "Just Before the Battle, Mother," "Just After the Battle, Mother," "Break It Gently to My Mother," "Is That Mother Bending O'er Me?" and many other such songs flooded the stage. They described reluctant mothers sending their boys off to fight for their country and then sitting at home to wait, worry, and fret. Paralleling this theme, others focused on young men going into battle thinking of God, country, home, and, most of all, mother. Many of these songs depicted young soldiers longing for their mothers to comfort them as they lay wounded and dying on the battlefield.[13] In the most frequently performed song of this type, "Mother I've Come Home to Die," the singer pleaded with his mother to hold and comfort him before his death. In the sequel "My Boy, How Can I See You Die?" his mother elegized:

> With breaking heart, I bade you go, my boy
> And weeping, breathed a sad goodbye;
> You told me that you'd soon return
> You have, but oh, you've come to die.[14]

Like the antebellum minstrel songs that had focused on the slave family, these wartime sentimental songs portrayed tragic images of the destruction of strong family bonds, a central human theme. But unlike the plantation songs, these focused on young white lovers or on white mothers and their sons, not on husbands and wives. In these songs, minstrels ignored not only blacks but also adult white men. According to minstrels, fathers did not worry about or mourn for their sons and did not even go to war! In minstrelsy, young men left lovers or more often, sisters and mothers for a war that pitted brother against brother. Like minstrel Negroes, young white boys could properly feel and express tender emotions, but grown white men could not do it without losing their masculinity. The man's world was the world of the head, not the heart, of business and politics, not the home and the family. When men failed in their province, the very heart of the social fabric was destroyed. The bearer of matters of the heart, the women—mother, sister, and lover—suffered and mourned. Minstrels and other popular singers gave her a chance to cry openly while assuring her that she made her sacrifice for a noble cause.

Until 1863 the government's only stated objective had been the restoration of the Union, a cause that minstrels and their audiences wholeheartedly supported. But in 1863 Lincoln made emancipation and military participation of blacks part of the Union war effort, largely because of persistent pressure from black men, white abolitionists, and Radical Republicans, but also because of military necessity. Although these decisions strengthened the Union cause by giving it added moral depth at home and in England and by adding badly needed troops to the Union forces, they also disillusioned minstrels who saw the original reason for the war corrupted, all possibility of compromise destroyed, and only the gloomy prospect of an interminable war ahead.

Reflecting their mounting frustration with the long grueling war fought for causes they did not believe in, minstrels, after 1862, lashed out at what they saw as a conspiracy between "traitors in de Souf and hot heads in de Norf" who wanted to destroy the Union. Why talk about Garibaldi uniting Italy, one of the Christy Minstrels asked, when America had the likes of Henry Ward Beecher, Horace Greeley, Wendell Phillips, and W. L. Yancey "trying to make any number of countries of these United States?" If they could have their way, minstrels knew what they would do with the troublemakers:

> I'd send the abolitionists into de Atlantic Ocean,
> Send de darkey to Africa, just where dey ought to go
> And skeedaddle all de rebels into de Gulf of Mexico.[15]

Although minstrels attacked both "extremes," they directed their greatest attention and their sharpest invective at the abolitionists. The apparent presidential shift to abolitionist goals in 1863 allowed minstrels to unleash a pent-up torrent of antiabolitionist abuse that had reached a fever pitch in the late 1850's but had quieted in the nationalistic unity of the early war years. Minstrels had previously vilified all abolitionists as self-serving hypocrites who only pretended to be the Negro's friend so they could use him to gain power for themselves, even if it meant provoking a sectional conflict that might destroy the Union.[16]

"To go in for de Union," one of Hooley's minstrels succinctly observed during the war, "ain't nigger abolition." [17] Leaving no doubt about where they stood, minstrels sought to discredit abolitionists by charging that blacks had been content in their places until these agitators put "de debbel in de nigger's head." More ominously, minstrels claimed that abolitionists kept trying to turn Negroes white by scrubbing them with soap, using sandpaper on them, and even whitewashing them. Echoing proslavery apologists, minstrels used their blackfaced characters to claim that black people only wanted to see the war end, to forget equality, and to return to the good old days:

> I don't like to see folks in de Norf cut such foolish figures
> And get the country in dis fuss all about de niggers.
> I don't like abolitionists, to please a foolish whim,
> Shove poor white folks out of work and put de niggers in.

Again like Southern propagandists, minstrels reminded the abolitionists that they should "mind dere poor white folks at home" instead of making trouble on the happy plantations.[18]

The minstrels' principal villain, as he had been before the war, was Horace Greeley, the "great hero," whom they "praised" for bravely fighting all the important battles, but only in the pages of his *Tribune*. They charged Greeley with favoring blacks over whites, with saying that "white is de same as black," and with having a black "pet" who wanted to succeed Abe Lincoln as president. They told a story about a Negro hiding in a crate of eggs to avoid paying a railroad fare. When he was discovered rising out of the packing straw, a conductor raced down the street calling for Greeley because he knew that Greeley would pay lots of money for a box of eggs that hatched "niggers." An unusually scurrilous minstrel song suggested that Greeley and Wendell Phillips should each marry a monkey because that was "the nearest thing to a nigger." Unconcerned with consistency, minstrels branded him a "nigger lover," while at the same time also claiming that he hypocritically used Negroes during the war for his own ends and afterwards would say "no niggers need apply." [19]

Although minstrels felt President Lincoln had moved into the Radical Republican-Abolitionist camp (they made no distinctions within or among these groups), except for a few jibes at "abe-o-lition," they made few direct attacks on Lincoln or the national government. But while other Northern popular songs praised Lincoln,[20] minstrels rarely mentioned him. They had increasingly come to identify him with the forces that kept the Union apart and the war raging. Yet he was still the president and therefore to nationalistic minstrels was above criticism. To vent their dissatisfaction with the course of the war, they had to be content with their diatribes against abolitionists and their apparent support of General George McClellan for president. In 1864, the editor of the New York *Clipper* praised minstrels for doing good service in behalf of the Union and "that sterling patriot Little Mac." In Ohio and Pennsylvania, he complained, "abolitionists and radicals" had tried to prevent some minstrels from performing on the grounds that they were "sent from New York to manufacture public sentiment for McClellan." [21] Since McClellan's Unionism and his commitment to a compromise based on a return to prewar conditions embodied minstrelsy's fundamental positions, many of them may have supported him. But whatever their wishes for a change, they had to face the reality of an increasingly bloody, seemingly endless war.

The mounting horror of the war that was striking down young soldiers in their prime and devastating their families at home forced minstrels to take a harder, more critical look at the Northern society for which the sacrifices were being made. Beginning during the war, the emphasis of minstrelsy began to shift from romantic fantasy to social criticism, from Southern plantations to Northern cities, from blacks to whites. Reflecting their egalitarian orientation, minstrels focused first on the glaring gap between rich and poor. They lambasted corrupt businessmen, who seemed to minstrels to be prolonging the war in order to make more money for themselves. The fighting would not end, one minstrel cynically charged, until the "Army contractors' pockets are full." Others effectively contrasted images of rich war profiteers "fattening themselves on the blood of the land" to those of gallant soldiers fighting and dying for the Union with inadequate and defective supplies, including guns that failed in battle. Minstrels also charged that politicians shared in this "blood money":

> Shoddy contracts all de go, and money fur de same;
> And if you're a politician, you're sure to git de game.
> No matter what the job is either shoddy or a ram
> For all you've got to do is, charge the bill to Uncle Sam. [22]

Combining these indictments with their bitter attacks on abolitionists, minstrels forcefully argued that the original war goals had been corrupted by self-seeking Northerners who extended the war for their selfish ends while the general public suffered.

Predictably, minstrels detested the discriminatory draft law which offered the wealthy easy exemptions while compelling the poor to fight and die in the tarnished cause. Minstrels patriotically denounced the draft evaders who fled to Canada refusing to defend "our firesides and flag" and warned them not to return once they had turned their backs on their country. But they also sympathized with those who opposed the inequitable draft law and the order to fight and die in what increasingly seemed like a war to help blacks. Although they shared many of the deep frustrations and anxieties that erupted in the New York City anti-Negro, antidraft riot, they did not feature it in their shows. They were caught between dedication to the Union and their deep disillusionment with the new national priorities and with Northern graft and corruption. Their solution was to ignore the people who did not comply with the draft but did not leave the country and to focus their angry attacks against the system of exemptions and substitutes. If the bribes offered the draft doctors were sufficient, minstrels complained, exemptions could be obtained for being too small, too fat, too tall, or even for having red hair. Senator Charles Sumner was exempt, one of Hooley's Minstrels jibed, even though he loved the war and had "nigger on the brain." And if a person had $300, all he had to do was buy a substitute, a system that fundamentally conflicted with minstrels' egalitarianism. Combining their dislike of the draft law with their antiwar-profiteering campaign, minstrels indicted "Substitute Brokers" for preying on naïve, patriotic young men by persuading them to "join" the army while the amoral broker sold them as substitutes to the rich and also collected their enlistment bounty.[23]

Minstrels Fight the Civil War

By 1864 everything seemed to be going wrong. From its noble beginning as a glorious crusade in the spirit of Washington, the Founding Fathers, and Andrew Jackson, the war seemed reduced to a tawdry, bloody struggle, exacting a great price in lives, morale, and principles. And minstrels knew that many more casualties and much more anguish and suffering would be needed to preserve the Union. Although they disliked the extended war goals, they realized after Lincoln's re-election that they were irreversible and that the war would end only when "Jeff Davis was beaten." Why not, then, use Negroes to fight and let them do the suffering? If darkies want their freedom, one minstrel put it, they should be drafted and fight for it.[24]

When blacks flocked to join the Union army, thus relieving some of the burden on whites, minstrels again expressed racial ambivalence. Although they completely opposed emancipation at first, and were at best ambivalent about it, minstrels, both as nationalists and egalitarians, had to admit that blacks were earning their freedom by fighting and dying for the Union and the American Creed. Furthermore, as the frustrating war dragged on and minstrels equated defeating secession with reuniting the nation, they became increasingly vindictive against the South, gloating over each victory and delighting in the news of Sherman burning his way across the Confederacy. With blacks a secondary issue, and a conveniently distant one at that, minstrels could favor emancipation because it removed a blot against American ideals, rewarded Negro war allies, and punished the South. But at the same time, they never accorded blacks a "place" in the North or a position as the equals of whites. Minstrels supported emancipation only because of practical and emotional decisions emerging out of the war experience, decisions based on what was best for white Northerners, not on a deeply felt concern for blacks.

"There's no disunion among the niggers," Eph Horn observed for all minstrels. Although they found him lacking in many ways, minstrels consistently praised the ex-slave's loyalty to the Union:

> My massa he turned traitor, so I thought I'd
> better come
> Up where they go for Union, our good old Union
> strong.

Many of minstrelsy's black Unionists willingly joined the army to fight for the cause:

> We'll join togeder hand in hand to drive secession from de
> land.
> I'll fight like de debel as hard as I can.

Minstrels even used the abolitionist Henry Clay Work's "Babylon's Fallen" to portray the power of their new black allies. The dark clouds coming from the South, the singer assured the audience, were black men fighting for Uncle Sam, the lightning in the canebrake was from their bayonets, and the thunder was the sound of their shooting. They even captured the singer's ex-master, a "kernel" in the rebel army, who had run when he saw Union forces approaching. "Babylon is fallen!" the singer shouted anticipating victory, "Babylon is fallen!" One of Buckley's Serenaders reported that "ebery cullered mudder's son" would join the army, make the rebels "ride de rail," and hang Jeff Davis. When these black soldiers hit the South, he boasted, "Dey'll think John Brown am coming down to make anudder raid." [25] What could be more terrifying to secessionists, after all, than vindictive black insurrectionists rising up, taking their masters prisoners, and fighting like John Brown?

In the context of blacks fighting for the Union, minstrels' ideological opposition to slavery again found expression in the shows. As they had done until the mid-1850's, minstrels con-

demned the destruction of black families, the theft of black
women by white men, the long hours blacks had to work without pay, and the brutal and senseless beatings they had to endure.[26] Such criticisms were, however, infrequent during the
war and lacked the vitality and emotional impact they had had
fifteen years earlier. Minstrels now channeled all their emotional energy into their accounts of white people's suffering and
into justifying the war effort. Even though black people suffered greatly from the fighting, minstrels did not include them
in their sentimental songs about the anguish of the war. To
them, Negroes were merely pawns in the struggle for Union.

Throughout the war, minstrels, with few exceptions, continued to portray blacks as happy and contented inferiors. The
genius of minstrelsy was that, unlike the vitriolic anti-Negro
propaganda that bluntly advocated repression of blacks, minstrelsy phrased racial subordination in terms of benevolent pa-
ternalism. While Negrophobes tried to scare whites into openly
putting aside the American Creed and forcing Negroes to be an
inferior caste, minstrels took threatening images of blacks and
softened them into those of good-natured children or at the
very worst of ludicrous incompetents who required supervision
for their own good. Thus, whites who listened to minstrels
could actually take pride in racial subordination as a *fulfillment*
of the American Creed.

The contrast between Negrophobes and minstrels was
strikingly evident in the way each responded to the issue of
Negro soldiers. Led by the "Copperheads," Northern racial
demagogues denounced black troops from the beginning, arguing that this would be the first step to Negro equality and that
armed black men would rape and plunder whites. These demagogues even manufactured incidents of alleged antiwhite violence committed by black troops, which gained wide circulation
in the Democratic press. Yet, despite their scurrilous campaign,

they failed to win broad public support.[27] Minstrels, on the other hand, reduced the threat by laughing at black soldiers. Even while the war still raged, the same minstrels that described the determination of Negroes to fight and die for their country revealed their ambivalence toward black troops by commonly portraying negative images of them. In fact, the most popular minstrel feature that involved Negro troops, "Black Brigade" sometimes called "Greeley's Brigade," presented only ludicrous images of cowardly incompetents. In the song, the "Black Brigade" vowed to join the Union army and to fight the South, but only "'by word ob mouth." "To fight for death and glory," they laughed, "Am quite anudder story." [28] Other minstrel material also portrayed Negro troops unwilling to fight or running from battle. In one such joke, Sambo explained how he had been at the Battle of Bull Run and in New York on the same night. When his commander told the soldiers to strike for their country and their homes, he recounted, "some struck for der country, but dis chile he struck for home." [29]

Even when not called on to fight, minstrel blacks often proved to be laughable soldiers. Beginning during the war with "Raw Recruits" and reaching full development in the 1870's, minstrels created a series of popular farces centered on blacks who were ludicrously inept at "playing soldier." Like children who imitate without understanding, these uniformed blacks captured part of the form of the military but none of the substance. Besides exploiting the comic potential inherent in the contrasting images of strict military discipline and of disorderly slapstick versions of military "know-nothings," these skits also gave minstrels a chance to lampoon the very idea of Negroes as soldiers.[30] Minstrelsy's military "komical koons" could not perform even the most basic maneuver or obey the simplest military command. When the black troops received the order to

4.   This sheet music cover mocks Negro soldiers as bewildered incompetents, except for the drummer who is in "his place" as a musician.

Bryant's Minstrels, "Raw Recruits," New York, 1862, Harvard Theatre Collection.

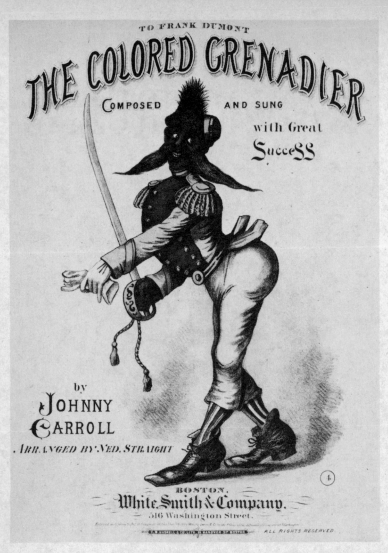

TO FRANK DUMONT

THE COLORED GRENADIER

COMPOSED AND SUNG

with Great
Success

by
JOHNNY
CARROLL
ARRANGED BY NED. STRAIGHT.

BOSTON,
White, Smith & Company.
516 Washington Street.

5.   Portrayals of Negro soldiers as dandies perpetuated the early "Zip Coon" image that ridiculed ludicrous free Negroes and effete white fops.
Johnny Carroll, "The Colored Grenadier," Boston, 1879, Harvard Theatre Collection.

6. This early image of the dandy persisted throughout the history of minstrelsy.

*George Washington Dixon, "Zip Coon," New York, n.d. [1830's].
Harvard Theatre Collection.*

"Fall In," several of them jumped into a nearby lake. When "Eyes Right" was given, a black soldier replied, "I'se right too," and "At Trail Arms!" produced a group raggedly walking off dragging their guns in the dirt. After their black officers deluged the "Gentlemen Coons" with overblown rhetoric praising their drill and marching skills, they tried to get their men to fall in. But only confusion resulted. "Take dat musket out of dat coon's eye," an officer snapped, while soldiers hit each other in the face and on the feet with their muskets. After the troop finally managed to form into ragtag ranks, it marched right into its own officers, pushing them off the stage in a chaotic ending.[31]

The way minstrels reduced black soldiers to silly dandies in uniform was an extension of their antebellum argument that Northern Negroes were inevitably inept fools or absurd imitators of the worst in whites. Whether "Charles Augustus," "Dandy Pete," or the "Gay Cavalier," these characters spent their entire lives cultivating appearances, manners, and speech that they never really mastered and that, to minstrels, were not worth mastering. Wearing false moustaches, brass stick pins, gaudy, bright clothing, and other such "luxuries," these dandies pranced and strutted to the delight of girls like "Manda Jane Lucinda Snow." The unproductive way blacks lived when unsupervised, minstrels suggested, was in a real sense not their fault. When Billy Birch observed that "money am de ruination of all de colored folks," he used money as a symbol of the freedom that minstrels sought to convince themselves and their audiences that blacks could not sucessfully cope with.[32]

"Now if dey set de niggers free," as a minstrel crudely but succinctly phrased one of the central questions left unanswered by the Union's crushing military victory, "Whar is dey gwine to send em?" [33] As long as the war had lasted, minstrels and their audiences did not have to try and answer the question.

Focused on the Union cause, they could retain their ambivalence about freedmen. They could welcome black troops to fight against the Confederacy in the South, but also portray them as cowards, Northern dandies, and slapstick fools. They could concede that blacks were earning something and that slavery was wrong, but still never concede Negroes a "place" in Northern society. But with victory in sight and abolition of slavery a certain result of the war, the federal government had to establish new definitions of the position of Negroes in America, and minstrels had to work out new unofficial models of black subordinates. In 1864, one minstrel predicted that after the war slavery and the slave driver would be gone; the black man would not have to work without pay; no one could sell his wife or babies; he could have his own cabin; and he would remain in the South to hoe cotton not only because he preferred it, but also "case it's natur." With the evils of slavery purged, minstrels and their audiences could happily relegate the black man to the South where, they wanted to believe, he "naturally" belonged. Thus, well before it actually evolved in the South, a minstrel foresaw the tenant-farmer system as an ideal solution to the position of blacks in America. It kept blacks as voluntary subordinates, allowed whites to "tend to business, makin' boats and buildin' railroads," and left blacks "raising the crops." [34]

To reaffirm that Negroes belonged in the South as "wards" of whites, minstrels ridiculed any suggestion of equality for blacks. "Let him vote," a minstrel warned as early as 1863, "and he's what you call a mighty sassy chile." As with Negro soldiers, minstrels voiced mocking contempt for the very idea that blacks might hold political office. They laughed at Horace Greeley's "pet" wanting to succeed Lincoln and jokingly forecast, in 1863, that "a moke will be applying for a Senate seat." During Reconstruction, when Negroes actually sat in both houses of Congress, minstrels dismissed them as ignorant pawns in a Radical Republican-Abolitionist power grab. One minstrel whitewasher promised his fiancée he would give up his profession, run for the Senate, and take a seat "tween [Charles] Sumner and Old [Wendell] Phillips." Another minstrel character, an innocent dupe carrying a trunk he called his "freedman's bureau," reported that his last job had been with the "Loosana" legislature. "Jist after the lexion was ober," he explained, "a fellow came to me and says, Jube you're lected." But he had no idea what that meant and was finally arrested for stealing a chair when he tried to "take his seat." [35]

Minstrels used this same derogatory tone throughout their burlesques of Reconstruction topics, which included: "Civil Rights Bill, or Uncivil William," "The Black and Tan Convention," "The Impeachers, or Scenes in Congress," "The Carpetbaggers," and "Scenes in the Freedmen's Bureau." "We've heard of the 'Freedman's Bureau' and of Freedman's Washstands too; /Still no one offers us poor mokes a job of work to do," complained a minstrel character resurrecting the charge that abolitionists and their Radical Republican successors selfishly exploited blacks and then turned their backs on them. Minstrels also portrayed the frustrations of a dedicated Northern schoolteacher who went South "on a philanthropic errand" to uplift Negroes. After patiently trying everything she knew to teach them, she became so exasperated with her black students' carefree attitudes, frivolous behavior, and hopeless ignorance, that she finally hollered, "What Fools! What Fools!" and left. [36] Even sincere Northern "do-gooders," minstrels contended, ultimately had to admit that it was hopeless to try to lift blacks out of their "proper place" as subordinates to whites in the South.

After attacking the idea of Negro equality and satirizing Reconstruction, minstrels began, in 1877, to invoke the emotional family-oriented images, that they had used in various forms for decades, to urge the great American family to pull itself back together after its fratricidal splintering. The "treasonous rebels" of earlier years now became "true and brave soldiers" who had fought like heroes for the South. And with similar determination, minstrels asserted, they would now stand by the nation "through thick and thin."

> Should a foreign foe insult us, Right eager for
>   the fray
> It's hand to hand with Dixie's band, We'd march
>   in Blue and Gray.

Minstrels also used sentimentalism in their reunification efforts by portraying families that had lost sons to both sides. Wearing blue and gray arm bands for the two brothers he lost, a singer praised them both. "Each fought for what he deemed was right and fell with sword in hand." Minstrel mothers, who had given sons to both armies, urged that all Americans come together with honor and mutual respect.[37] Abolition of slavery and the, at least tacit, agreement that Negroes would be left to Southern whites removed the issues that had torn the nation apart. Finally, minstrels had the accommodation with the South that they had sought for so long. And they got it on the racial terms that they had formulated twenty years earlier.

As it did to many other areas of American life, the Civil War profoundly affected the direction of minstrelsy's development. Although the mythic images of the idealized plantation remained a minstrel fixture that they took to virtually every corner of the nation long before Joel Chandler Harris, Thomas Nelson Page, Thomas Dixon, and others had popularized it in fiction, social commentary about the problems of white Americans outside the South replaced "Negro Subjects" as the focus of minstrelsy. Similarly, the emphasis on large-scale, nationwide organization that grew out of the war also had a great impact on minstrelsy. These trends developed fully only in the post-bellum decades, but they were products of the Civil War.

NOTES

[1] W. Stanley Hoole, *The Antebellum Charleston Theatre* (Birmingham, Ala., 1946), p. 63; M. B. Leavitt, *Fifty Years of Theatrical Management* (New York, 1912), p. 30.

[2] Although minstrelsy existed in the Confederacy during the war, it was overwhelmingly concentrated in the same Northern areas in which it had been centered before the war.

[3] Virginia Minstrels, "Jim Crow Polka," New York, 1846, sheet music, HTC; Charley White, *New Illustrated Melodeon* (New York, 1848), pp. 22, 32, 38, 41, 59; *New Negro Forget-Me-Not Songster* (Cincinnati, 1848), pp. 106–7; Charley White, "General Taylor," *New Ethiopian Song Book* (New York, 1850), p. 30; Elias Howe, "Success to Oregon," *Ethiopian Glee Book #3, Christy Minstrels* (Boston, 1849), p. 131; Charles White, "Old Gray Goose," *White's Serenaders Song Book* (New York, 1851), p. 55; Matt Campbell, "Rosy Anna," *Wood's Minstrels Songs* (New York, 1855), p. 52.

[4] Charles Fox, *Fox's Ethiopian Comicalities* (New York, 1859), p. 41; Stewart McCauley, "Hurrah for the Flag of the Free," *Songs of Kunkels' Nightingale Opera Troupe* (Baltimore, 1854), p. 13.

[5] Sanford's Opera House, Philadelphia, Oct. 1860, Apr. 1861, playbills, HTC; the New York *Clipper* regularly reported such fare after the spring of 1861; *Bob Hart's Plantation Songster* (New York, 1862), pp. 6–7, 23, 30–31; *Charley Fox's Minstrel Companion* (Philadelphia, 1863), p. 30.

[6] Bob Hart, "Git Up and Git," p. 15; E. B. Christy, "Our Union None Can Sever," *Christy's New Songster and Black Joker* (New York, 1863), pp. 70–71; "Yankee Doodle," *Hooley's Opera House Songster* (New York, 1863), pp. 62–63; Bryant's Minstrels, "Raw Recruits," New York, 1862, sheet music, HTC; Carncross and Dixey's Minstrels, Philadelphia, June 11, 1862, playbill, HTC; "Or Any Other Man," *Frank Converse's Old Cremona Songster and Banjo Melodist* (New York,

1863), p. 32; "Our Native Land," *Christy's Bones and Banjo Melodist* (New York, n.d. [mid-1860's?]), pp. 37–38; for a discussion of general Northern reaction to secession, see Kenneth Stampp, *And the War Came: The North and the Secession Crisis 1860–61* (Baton Rouge, 1950).

⁷ Hart, "Come, Jeff, Come," pp. 11, 17; Skiff and Gaylord's Minstrels, "Capture of Fort Donelson," n.p., n.d., program, HTC; Newcomb's Minstrels, "Running the Blockade," Cincinnati, Jan. 22, 1863, poster, HTC; Canterbury Music Hall Minstrels, n.p., May 11, 1863, program, HTC; Sam Leon's Minstrels, n.p., n.d., program, HTC; G. D. Odell, *Annals of the New York Stage*, 15 vols. (New York, 1927–1949), Vol. VI, p. 595; E. B. Christy, "Better Times Are Coming," *New*, n.p.

⁸ Frank Brower, "The Men of the Day," *Black Diamond Songster* (New York, 1863), pp. 17–18; "Halt, Boys, Halt," *Gems of Minstrelsy* (New York, 1867), pp. 67–68; "Uncle Sam Grant," Hooley's, pp. 69–70, and many other troupes; Frank Converse, "Or Any Other Man," p. 32; "We Will Have The Union Still," *Carncross and Dixey's Melodies* (Philadelphia, 1865), pp. 54–55; Eph Horn, "Gin'ral Butler" and "Walk Along John," *Eph Horn's Own Songster* (New York, 1864), pp. 7–8, 18–19.

⁹ Converse, "Pop Goes the Nigger," pp. 33–34; Fox, "Cork It Up and Stop It," *Companion*, p. 16; E. B. Christy, "Raw Recruits," *New Songster and Black Joker*, pp. 42–43, and Dan Bryant, *Bryant's New Songster* (New York, 1864), p. 50; "Away Goes Cuffee," *Ibid.*, p. 48; Harry Pell, "The Union Volunteer, or a Word to England," *Harry Pell's Ebony Songster* (New York, 1864), pp. 25–26; S. S. Purdy, "Louey Napolean," *Paul Pry Songster* (New York, 1865), pp. 54–55; *Gems*, p. 48.

¹⁰ Hart, "Jeff Davis Dream," p. 14; Charles Fox, "To De Army We Belong," "Jeff Davis Lament," *Companion*, pp. 9, 22; Bryant, "Away Goes Cuffee," *New Songster*, p. 49; Pell, "Bad Luck to Ould Jefferson Davis," pp. 18–19; Morris Brothers, Pell, and Trowbridge Minstrels, "We'll Hang Jeff Davis," n.p., June 13, 1865, playbill, HTC; this song was, of course, often sung by Union troops; Fox, "The Deplorable Effects of Secession," *Companion*, p. 34.

¹¹ "Oh, Let Me Shed One Silent Tear," *The People's New Songster* (New York, 1864), pp. 22–23; for a discussion of Civil War popular songs, see Willard A. Heaps, *The Singing Sixties* (Norman, Okla., 1960); for more examples of these songs, see Heaps, Chapter 6.

¹² Heaps, *The Singing Sixties*, pp. 224–25; Wood's Minstrels, "When This Cruel War is Over," New York, 1863, sheet music, HTC; this song was in virtually every minstrel songster of these years. For a general discussion of the music popular in the Confederacy, see Richard Harwell, *Confederate Music* (Chapel Hill, 1950).

¹³ Bryant, "Tell Me Mother, Can I Go?" "Our Boy is a Warrior Now," *Bryant's New Songster*, pp. 8–9, 44; "Just Before the Battle, Mother," "He's Watching O'er Thy Mother," "I Am Lonely Since My Mother Died," *People's*, pp. 5, 9, 11; Bryant, "My Mother's Grave," *Bryant's New Songster*, p. 59; "Rock Me To Sleep Mother," *People's*, p. 23; "Is That Mother Bending O'er Me?" *Buckley's Melodist* (Boston, 1864); Bryant, "Mother Kissed Me In My Dream," *New*, p. 19, *People's*, p. 7; Buckley's Serenaders, "Break It Gently to My Mother," Boston, 1863, sheet music, HTC.

¹⁴ Most minstrels performed this song regularly; for examples, see *Gems*, p. 34, *People's*, p. 8, Duprez and Green's Minstrels, New York *Clipper*, April 2, 1864; for a readily available text, see: Heaps, *The Singing Sixties*, pp. 249–50; "My Boy How Can I See You Die," *Gems*, pp. 41–42.

¹⁵ E. B. Christy, "Canaan," "Dat's What's de Matter," "Uncle Sam's Cooks," *New Songster and Black Joker*, pp. 38–39, 17–20, 6–7; "Saucy Sam," *Carncross and Dixey's Minstrel Melodies*, pp. 43–44; "Pompey Snow's Philosophy," *Hooley's*, pp. 19–20.

¹⁶ "Old Dan Tucker," *Deacon Snowball's Negro Melodies* (New York, 1843), and *The Negro Melodist* (Cincinnati, 185 ?), p. 17; "Away Down South," *Kunkel's*, p. 38, "There's Nothing Like It," "Dat's So," *Buckley's Ethiopian Melodies #4* (New York, 1857), pp. 21–22, 53–54; Bryant, "Working On The Railroad," *Bryant's Essence of Old Virginny* (New York, 1857); "Aunt Harriet Beecha Stowe," *Pop Goes the Weasel Songster* (Philadelphia, 1853?), pp. 210–11, and Sam Sanford, *Popular Ethiopian Melodies* (Philadelphia, 1856), pp. 36–37; Edward F. Dixey, "Take Care of Number One," *Dixey's Essence of Burnt Cork* (Philadelphia, 1859), pp. 64–65; *Charley White's Ethiopian Joke Book* (New York, 1855), pp. 40–41, 62; Matt Campbell, "Lubly Rosa," *Wood's New Plantation Melodies* (New York, 1855), pp. 30–31; "Eggs Hatch Niggers," *Dixey's Essence of Burnt Cork*, pp. 58–61.

¹⁷ "Get Back," *Hooley's*, pp. 30–31.

¹⁸ "Contraband's Adventure," "Dat's My Philosophy," "Saucy Sam," *Hooley's*, pp. 9, 11–12, 40–44; Frank Dumont, "The Younger

Generation in Minstrelsy," New York *Clipper*, March 27, 191 ?, clipping, NYLC; Purdy, "Topsey's Doctrine," pp. 29–30.

[19] Fox, "Nancy Bell," *Companion*, p. 40; Bryant's Minstrels, "How Are You Greenbacks," New York, 1863, sheet music, HTC; and most other companies; "The World's Topsy Turvey," *Carncross and Dixey's Minstrel Melodies*, p. 37; Purdy, "Horace Greeley's Pet," pp. 20–21; "Eggs Hatch Niggers," *George Christy's Essence of Old Kentucky* (New York, 1864), n.p.; "Yankee Doodle," "The Nigger May Apply," *Hooley's*, pp. 63, 10–11.

[20] Heaps, *The Singing Sixties*, p. 315.

[21] New York *Clipper*, n.d. [1864], clipping, HTC; typical of minstrelsy's songs praising McClellan and compromise, were: Fox, "Banjo Solo," *Companion*, p. 44; Frank Converse, "Oh, Yes 'Tis So," p. 52; "We Will Have the Union Still," *Carncross and Dixey's Minstrel Melodies*, pp. 54–55; for popular songs about McClellan, see Heaps, *The Singing Sixties*, p. 295.

[22] Bryant's Minstrels, "How Are You Greenbacks?" New York, 1863, sheet music, HTC, and many other troupes; Morris Brothers, Pell, and Trowbridge Minstrels, "Satire on War Experiences," reported in New York *Clipper*, Jan. 1863; Fox, "The Volunteer," *Companion*, p. 29; Frank Brower, "The Port Royal Contraband," "I Wish I had a Fat Contract," pp. 9, 67–68; Converse, "Shoddy Contracts," "Shoddy," pp. 15–16, 45–46.

[23] Purdy, "Skedaddlers," pp. 14–15; "Get Out of de Draft," *Carncross and Dixey's Minstrel Melodies*, pp. 46–47; Hooley's Minstrels, Brooklyn, n.d. [1863?], playbill, HTC; "The Invalid Corps," *Buckley's Melodist*, pp. 77–78; "Wait Till You Get It," *The People's New Songster* (New York, 1864), p. 6; "He's Gone to the Arms of Abraham," *Carncross and Dixey's Minstrel Melodies*, pp. 22–23; "The Substitute Broker," *Negro Melodies No. 1* (Philadelphia, 1864), pp. 51–52.

[24] Pell, "The Slippery Nigger," pp. 34–35.

[25] Horn, "Lean and Scraggy," pp. 16–17. For the roles of Negroes in the war, see Dudley Cornish, *The Sable Arm* (New York, 1966) and Benjamin Quarles, *The Negro in the Civil War* (Boston, 1953); Hart, "Happy Contraband," "Dat's What's De Matter," pp. 5, 27–30; Brower, "Filibuster Sam," pp. 8–9; Fox, "To Battle in de War," *Companion*, p. 35; Converse, "Fightin' in de War," pp. 68–69; "Babylon Is Fallen," *Carncross and Dixey's Minstrel Melodies*, pp. 59–60; "I'm One of the Black Brigade," *Buckley's Melodist*, p. 109.

²⁶ "White Wash Army," *Billy Birch's Ethiopian Melodist* (New York, 1862), pp. 17–18; "Song of the Contraband," *Companion*, p. 36; Converse, "De History of de Banjo," pp. 53–54; "Sarah Bell," *Gems*, pp. 72–73.

²⁷ For a discussion of the Negrophobes' reaction to the Civil War and Reconstruction, especially their political rhetoric, see Forrest Wood, *Black Scare* (Berkeley, 1968).

²⁸ The song was regularly performed by most leading minstrel companies, including: Buckley's Serenaders in Boston, Bryant's, Wood's, and Campbell's in New York, Carncross and Dixey's in Philadelphia, and the traveling Sharpley's Minstrels; see programs and playbills in HTC and NYLC; for a conveniently available text, see Hans Nathan, *Dan Emmett and the Rise of Early Negro Minstrelsy* (Norman, Okla. 1962), pp. 390–93.

²⁹ "Jumbo's Courage," *Negro Melodist #1*, pp. 10–11, 62; Fox, "Lean and Scraggy," *Companion*, p. 45; Converse, "Send de Sogers Down," pp. 47–48.

³⁰ Bryant's Minstrels, "Raw Recruits," New York, 1862, sheet music, HTC; many other minstrel troupes also performed this routine; "Shine On," *Big Pound Cake Songster* (New York, 1878), p. 23; Clinton De Witt, "Gentleman Coon's Parade," *Bones: His Gags and Stump Speeches* (New York, 1879), pp. 1–6; Andrew Leavitt, *The Deserters* (New York, 187–?).

³¹ *Minstrel Gags and End Men's Hand-book* (New York, 1875), p. 84; John Arnold, *Obeying Orders: Ethiopian Military Sketches* (Chicago, 1874).

³² George Christy, "Charles Augustus," *Kentucky*, pp. 15–16; Converse, "Dandy Pete," pp. 40–41; Hart, "Gay Cavalier," p. 44; Carncross, "Sammy Blue," p. 45; "Manda Jane Lucinda Snow," *Negro Melodies No. 1*, pp. 34–35; Birch, "High, Low, Jack," pp. 33–34.

³³ Converse, "I Can't Help Dat," pp. 50–51.

³⁴ *Ibid.*

³⁵ Birch, "High, Low, Jack," pp. 33–34; Purdy, "Horace Greeley's Pet," pp. 21–22; George Christy, "Election Day," *Bones*, p. 14; Charlie Petergill's Minstrels, "The Rival Congressmen," Boston, 1866, playbill, HTC; "Sally Strong and I," *Great American Song and Dance Songster* (New York, 1870), pp. 52–53; "Policy Jake," *Ned Turner's Bones and Tambourine Songster* (New York, 1869), p. 50; Phil H. Mowery, *The Musical Servant* (New York, 1875). "Moke" was an eth-

nic slur that minstrels frequently applied to blacks. Although most likely a derivative of "smoke," it may have originated with the word "mocha" as contended in Harold Wentworth and Stuart Flexner (eds.), *Dictionary of American Slang* (New York, 1967), p. 341.

[36] G. D. Odell, *Annals of the New York Stage*, Vol. VIII, pp. 349–50, 393; New York *Clipper*, May 30, 1868; Brooklyn Minstrels, n.p., Nov. 14, 1870, program, HTC: Dougherty, Wild Barne, and Mac's Minstrels, n.p., n.d., program, HTC; "Happy Little Flip Flops," *Pound Cake*, p. 45; F. Stanton, *The Select School* (Clyde, Ohio, 1883).

[37] William Delehantey, "The Blue and the Gray," *I Hope I Don't Intrude* (New York, 1877), p. 65; "Friends that Stand By Us," *Queen and West's Popular Songster* (New York, 1878?), p. 28; Al Field, "We Fought in the Same Campaign," *Al G. Field and Co.'s Minstrel Songster* (New York, 1890), p. 7; "A Knot of Blue and Gray," *Thatcher, Primrose, West Latest Songster* (New York, 1885?), n.p.; William West's Minstrels, "The Blue and the Gray, or a Mother's Gift to Her Country," New York, 1900, sheet music, HTC.

5 The Grand Transformation: Minstrelsy after the Civil War

In the late nineteenth century, the minstrel show underwent a fundamental reorganization. Like other institutions, minstrelsy felt the general effects of the powerful new developments which were profoundly altering the quality of American life: the completion of a national transportation system, the emergence of national businesses demanding standardization and uniformity, the development of more sophisticated marketing and promotional techniques, the westward population shift, the influx of immigrants, and the accelerated growth of the size and influence of cities. But minstrelsy faced new problems of its own. Most immediately, minstrels lost their virtual monopoly on popular stage entertainment. Variety shows, purified of their earlier off-color image, offered an even broader entertainment kaleidoscope than minstrelsy and began to win acceptance as wholesome family outings. Lavishly produced musical comedies, featuring partially undraped women and truly spectacular staging, became common after the stupendous success of "The Black Crook," which in 1866–67 ran 472 consecutive performances in New York and thereafter toured the country for years. Furthermore, white minstrels were even challenged in the area of their supposed expertise when black people became minstrels and earned reputations as the authentic "delineators of Negro life." [1]

Minstrels responded to these challenges in the decades after the Civil War by making substantial changes in their format and repertoire. To broaden their audience base and to reach new markets, troupes traveled widely. To enhance their appeal, they increased the size of their companies, expanded their olios, added new speciality features, staged much more lavish production numbers, and featured more "refined" acts—guaranteed to offend no one. And to avoid black competition, they even moved away from "Negro Subjects." In the process, minstrelsy almost completely transformed itself. It went from small troupes concentrating on portrayals of Negroes to huge companies staging lavish extravaganzas and virtually ignoring blacks, from resident troupes with a Northeastern, urban base to truly national traveling companies whose greatest strength was in the Midwest and South. In many ways, the changes in minstrel form reflect the basic restructuring of American society in the late nineteenth century.

Many of the "new" postwar changes in minstrelsy were actually expansions of previous practices. By 1861, for example, Duprez and Green's Minstrels had developed many of the techniques that became standard after the war. They traveled to every city and town they could reach, pioneered in using uniforms for the minstrel parade, and were the first to use four endmen in one show and to stress numbers as important attractions in themselves. "THE MOST COMPLETE AND LARGEST MINSTREL TROUPE IN THE WORLD," their pictorial billboards (also a first) proclaimed, "UNEQUALLED AND INCOMPARABLE, DOUBLE

TROUPE AND BRASS BAND, TWENTY PERFORMERS." [2] But it was over a decade before the Duprez innovations became common. Minstrelsy, like other American institutions, evolved slowly through discernible stages.

To stimulate public interest in their traditional shows, minstrels employed many of the promotional techniques pioneered by P. T. Barnum. Drawing attention to themselves in every conceivable manner, they increased the size and elaborateness of their newspaper advertisements and the visual impact of their colorful posters and playbills. To get free "plugs," they did benefits, serenaded newspaper offices, got local clubs to sponsor performances, used local people in their shows, and began to offer door prizes. Beginning in 1856, for example, Sam Sharpley exhibited prizes in a local jewelry store and then had a drawing in his minstrel theater to select the winners. Other troupes gave away watches, rings, and sewing machines as well as toys for Christmas. Such practices were widespread enough so that one New York group jokingly offered such "rare articles" as a small multiplication table, one hundred tickets to a buffalo hunt in Idaho, and a picture of an alderman done in brandy and watercolors. [3]

But since improved promotional efforts were not enough to meet the growing competition, minstrels expanded their antebellum practice of assimilating successful features from other entertainment forms, beginning with Barnum's freaks. In 1850, Campbell's Minstrels had offered a ten-foot, three-inch African giant, "alias a Barnum humbug," at no extra cost. George Christy had responded with a twelve-foot African, "the largest man in the world." And in 1857, Charley White's Minstrels had advertised a "company of Dancing Turkeys and Singing Cats" newly arrived from Paris, "who will go through their performances in the style of the Ravels." Such attractions did not lose their appeal after the war. In 1870, a minstrel troupe advertised an eight-foot, two-inch Chinese Giant. The California Minstrels went to great lengths to explain that their "African dwarf" was genuine and truly exotic, having been captured by Henry Stanley, the explorer, in the "Ujiji Islands." Postwar specialty acts also included other unusual people. One minstrel strongman had a 309-pound stone broken on his chest with sledgehammers and then got up to bend "an immense bar of iron across his arm with a single blow." Years later, a champion wrestler and weight lifter, August Schmidt, who also posed as "Roman statuary," challenged all comers to contests in feats of strength and wrestling. And, in the supreme achievement of this sort, Lester and Allen's Big Minstrels and Cornet Band signed none other than John L. Sullivan to appear with their troupe "in poses representing ancient and modern statuary." [4]

Minstrels and other males had posed as statuary (dressed in tights) even before the mid-1840's without attracting too much attention. But by 1847, sex had become part of professional American stage entertainment when female models had begun posing in revealing tights. Their big audiences, one New York newspaper complained, were "bald and grey headed men, armed with prodigious opera glasses and pocket telescopes." In February 1848, for example, the Hall of Novelty had presented "a young lady of faultless form" portraying Power's "Greek Slave," a widely known nude sculpture. But such displays of women's bodies had been restricted to disreputable variety halls and saloons until 1869, when Lydia Thompson's British Blondes made a spectacular debut in the United States. Although they nominally performed burlesques of famous plays, their principal attraction was the display of their "lower limbs," in the short togas they wore to play classical male roles. Unlike the earlier "statuary," this troupe gained a great deal of favorable publicity and was respectable enough to play in New York's Niblo's Garden, where the "Black Crook," with its own prominent display of women's legs, had its earlier triumphant run.[5]

Combining women in tights, minstrelsy, vaudeville, and burlesque, M. B. Leavitt, in 1870, created Madame Rentz's Female Minstrels. The all-woman cast, prominently displaying their legs and bodies through snuggly fitting tights, performed the basic minstrel show supplemented with special attractions of their own. "In San Francisco, we had advertised that we were going to put on the can-can," recalled John E. Henshaw, who began his acting career as a prop boy with the troupe. "Mabel Santley did this number and when the music came to the dum-de-dum, she raised her foot just about twelve inches; whereupon the entire audience hollored 'Whooooo! ' It set them crazy." By 1871, the troupe's success had spawned at least eleven female minstrel companies, one of which directly revealed the impact of Lydia Thompson, by performing in white-face with blonde wigs. Although some of these troupes occasionally argued that women's abilities at portraying Negro characters were as great as men's and cited Harriet Beecher Stowe as proof, most of the time the groups stressed the unique attributes that only women had:

TWELVE SYMMETRICAL FEMALE FORMS

A bevy of beauty,	the octroon
the blonde,	the quadroon
the brunette,	the mulatto
and the	

BEAUTIFUL CREOLES

The promise of a revealing glimpse at scantily clad women was the principal appeal of female minstrels. "The main thing is shape," a female minstrel admitted when discussing the requirements for the job. "All they have to do is to put on their costumes and let the jays look at them. . . . We give a tough show, draw tough houses, and have a tough time." [6]

The Grand Transformation

Although nominally minstrels and actually performing many features of the standard show, these female minstrel troupes were really the forerunners of the "girlie show." But except for a rare male troupe like Skiff and Gaylord's, which in the spring of 1872 featured Mlle. Zitella, whose principal attraction was that she wore a "dress rather too low cut in the neck for her posturing and acrobatic act," the mainstream of minstrelsy remained all-male. Since minstrelsy's principal competition came from the variety shows that billed themselves as perfectly respectable family entertainment, minstrels re-emphasized their earlier claims to propriety.

REFINED AND ARTISTIC MINSTREL ENTERTAINMENT . . . IN-TRODUCING NOVELTIES, NEW AND ORIGINAL SENSATIONAL SPE-CIALTIES. Nothing to offend. FUN WITHOUT VULGARITY. Heads of families can bring WIVES AND DAUGHTERS without fear of having their ears offended by COARSE AND VULGAR WITTICISMS!

In the 1870's and 1880's, as they toured the heartland of America, the large minstrel companies lived up to these promises and successfully appealed to families by offering them "clean, bright, amusement," where they could enjoy good wholesome fun together. Only a few years earlier proper society would have looked with "holy horror" at a lady attending a minstrel performance, the editor of the *Clipper* observed in 1879, "but now, and very properly too, our fair ones turn out in numbers second to none." [7]

Minstrel audiences could, however, look forward to beautiful female figures, though fully dressed, promenading across minstrel stages and even flirting with the audience. But these were only illusions created by the female impersonator, who emerged in the postwar period as minstrelsy's most important new speciality role. Precisely when and how this feature began in America is uncertain, but it evolved out of minstrels portraying pretty plantation yellow girls. "Lucy Long," a song of coquettish flirtation, was most often identified as the source of the "prima donna" or "wench" role, as it was called.[8] Although he may not have been the first to perform it, George Christy made the song and the role famous. By 1849, he claimed to be the "Original Lucy Long," and on playbills and sheet music of the late 1840's he and other male minstrels were frequently pictured as well-dressed, even elegant, females dancing with male-attired partners.[9] Since minstrel companies at that time were still small, female impersonation was only one of many roles such men performed. But in the 1860's as the companies grew markedly in size and as performers became much more specialized, the prima donna emerged as a major featured role.

Unlike the low-comedy female role, the "Funny Old Gal," which was played by a burly comedian clad in tawdry, mismatched clothes and large "valise" shoes, the prima donna role was played seriously by an elegantly dressed performer in "a very delicate manner." Some of these men, actress Olive Logan observed, were "marvelously well fitted by nature for it, having well-defined soprano voices, plump shoulders, beardless faces, and tiny hands and feet." Perhaps the clearest illustration of the nature of the prima donna role was the songs they performed. With fluttering eyelashes and hearts, they flirted behind fans and forced beaux to steal kisses.

> We girls would ne'er give kisses; Don't treat
>   the matter light;
> I love my Charley dearly, For in my heart I
>   feel it;
> But if he asks for a kiss, I'll make him try
>   to steal it.[10]

They also played sweet young things in their first love affair and were regularly featured as ingenues in burlesques of popu-

7. This sheet music cover demonstrates how prominently the Christy Minstrels featured George Christy's graceful portrayals of charming yellow girls as part of their romantic appeal.

Christy's Melodies, Boston, 1844,
Harvard Theatre Collection.

lar plays and operas, the latter perhaps having provided minstrelsy with the title "prima donna."

Francis Leon, who billed himself simply as "Leon" or "The Only Leon," did more than any other man to establish the prima donna as a major minstrel role. Having begun his minstrel career in 1858 at the age of fourteen as a female impersonator, Leon quickly rose to stardom as a beautifully costumed specialist. With his partner, Edwin Kelly, he formed his own troupe in 1864. In the next five years, it created a sensation with its musically serious, lavishly produced burlesque operas, featuring Leon as the heroine. Although Kelly and Leon's Minstrels did not provide a diverse enough show to survive as an independent troupe, they demonstrated Leon's drawing power as a serious female impersonator. By 1873 the prima donna role was so well established, primarily because of Leon, that the *Clipper* observed that "no well-organized troupe could be without one." By 1882, Leon was the highest paid minstrel performer and one of the most praised.[11]

"Leon is the best male female actor known to the stage," the editor of the *Clipper* observed in 1870, while arguing that Leon's act was perfectly reputable. "He does it with such dignity, modesty, and refinement that it is truly art." Like the sculptors, painters, and poets who created sensitive, artistic images of women, the editor argued, Leon did not burlesque women. He exalted them with his voice, his dancing, and his refinement. "He is more womanly in his by-play and mannerisms," another reviewer noted, "than the most charming female imaginable." He was so convincing as an "actress" that many men refused to believe he was a man. "Heaps of boys in my locality," a Rochester, New-York, critic wrote, "don't believe yet it's a man in spite of my saying it was." Leon was enchanting enough, the writer continued, "to make a fool of a man if he wasn't sure."[12]

8. Francis Leon, the most famous minstrel female impersonator, in two of his typical costumes.

Harvard Theatre Collection.

Leon himself took great pride in successfully capturing the essence of femininity. A reporter who visited Leon's dressing room in 1881 found his closet full of women's clothing and his dressing table covered with "powder, paint, and perfume." "With real feminine pride," Leon explained that he did not wear "costumes." He wore only authentic women's clothing, from the $200 dress he had worn that evening to his lace-trimmed petticoats. He boasted of over 300 dresses (some cost-

ing $400), expensive jewelry, and all the other necessary accou-
trements. Besides his outfits, he also prided himself on his
dancing, singing, and good taste. His ballet dancing, he
claimed, was "the real thing, not a burlesque. I took lessons of a
good · teacher and for seven years practiced my dancing for
hours every day." He also claimed that in his youth he had
studied voice with Errani, the person who had taught Clara
Louise Kellogg, a famous opera singer. Above all else, he
proudly asserted that he did nothing offensive or vulgar.[13]

    Female impersonators excited more interest than any other
minstrel specialist. Besides reviewers regularly describing in detail what they wore, newspapers printed several lengthy discussions with prima donnas, especially Leon, when interviews
with other minstrels rarely appeared. Other than the general
novelty of impersonators and the inherent curiosity they must
have aroused, it is difficult to account precisely for their great
popularity. Men in the audience probably were titillated by the
alluring stage characters whom they were momentarily drawn
to, and they probably got equal pleasure from mocking and
laughing at them. Women were probably intrigued by the im-
peccable grace and femininity of the beautiful illusionists who,
unlike the female minstrels, posed no real sexual challenges.
Furthermore, prima donnas provided women with lavish pre-
views of the latest fashions.[14] At a time when anxiety about
social roles was intense, the female impersonator, who actually
changed roles, fascinated the public. As a model of properly
"giddy" femininity, he could reassure men that women were in
their places while at the same time showing women how to
behave without competing with them. Thus, in some ways, he
functioned like the blackface "fool" who educated audiences
while also reassuring them that he was their inferior. Neither
man nor woman, the female impersonator threatened no one.
Whatever the secrets of his success, the impersonator gave min-

strelsy a novelty to counter the variety show's diverse appeal and a feminine role to offset some of the attraction of the "girlie" show without sacrificing minstrelsy's respectability. But adding a new feature, even an extremely popular one, was not enough to meet the ever-mounting competition.

In the late 1870's, J. H. Haverly, the greatest minstrel entrepeneur, completely transformed the minstrel show in order to meet the new challenges. Other forms of entertainment—variety, drama, opera, and equestrians—he observed in 1878, had all "increased and enlarged their dimensions until their proportions and attractive qualities have appeared unlimited." But minstrelsy, he continued, had not substantially changed from what it had been twenty years before. It had not grown with the nation and was not appealing to the country's expansive spirit of large, indeed unbounded growth, development, and improvement. The colossal scale of physical products exhibited at the national centennial celebration, he concluded, had not been reflected in minstrelsy as it had been in other entertainment forms. Thus, he resolved to create a minstrel troupe "that for extraordinary excellence, merit, and magnitude will astonish and satisfy the most exacting amusement seeker in the world." [15]

Haverly himself was evidence that minstrelsy had already undergone significant changes reflecting trends in society at large. Unlike earlier troupe owners, Haverly was *not* a performer. He was a professional manager and promoter with great ambition, an uncanny ability to sense public taste, and a flamboyant flair for advertising and producing. With a finger on the public's pulse and a great eye for talent, he assembled a large, talented company, produced a well-organized, diverse show free of vulgarity, and brought it to the American people. From its inception, Haverly's minstrel troupe was a traveling company that played throughout the nation. He made minstrelsy truly national and incredibly profitable. Like other successful gilded age entrepreneurs, Haverly set out to build an empire. Financed and paid for by his minstrels, it included at its height in late 1881 three theaters in New York City and one each in Brooklyn, Chicago, and San Francisco, two large white and the largest black minstrel troupes, four touring comedy theater groups, three mining and milling companies, and numerous stock investments, which ultimately proved his downfall. By the end of 1877, the wildly speculating Haverly was reportedly $104,000 in debt, but he refused to declare bankruptcy. Instead, in typical Haverly fashion he took vigorous, creative action, which reshaped minstrelsy.[16]

"FORTY—40—COUNT 'EM—40—FORTY—HAVERLY'S UNITED MASTODON MINSTRELS," trumpeted his posters, playbills, and newspaper ads. Haverly had consolidated four companies into one troupe of forty minstrels, which he ballyhooed with a torrent of promotion unrivaled even by P. T. Barnum. "Forty is a magical and historical number," one ad explained. "In the time of Noah it rained forty days and nights. The Children of Israel wandered forty years in the wilderness. Haverly's famous forty are just as important."[17] When others ran newspaper ads of perhaps two-column inches, he bought five-by-seven inch ads and filled them with quotes lauding his company. And his promotion only began with the printed page. Led by a brass band, dressed in shining silk hats, frock coats, and lavender trousers, his forty minstrels paraded two abreast strung out in as long a line as possible through every town they entered. In 1878, the Mastodons added a drum corps, which paraded through one part of town while the brass band toured another. After maximizing their exposure, the two units joined together to complete the crowd-gathering march to the theater. Moreover, the troupe's manager, Charles Frohman, later an important theatrical entrepreneur, carried an iron safe three feet high with "Haverly's Mastodon Minstrels" painted in large gilt letters on the side. Whenever the company entered a town, he prominently displayed it with the luggage in the hotel lobby so every one would think the troupe was rich, even though the safe was usually empty.[18]

Besides conveying a general aura of success and glamor, Haverly consistently stressed the size and grandeur of his company. In 1879, for example, the curtain went up for a performance of the Mastodons in Chicago, and the audience saw nineteen men seated in front of a curtain decorated with a female figure of "Dance"; then it rose to reveal more men in front of a curtain portraying "Music"; when that went up, there were even more men in front of a curtain with "Art" on it; it too rose to reveal still more men against a backdrop depicting Haverly's New York and Chicago theaters. By using the series of dramatic openings, each incrementally building and enhancing the impression that there was a huge number of performers on stage, Haverly ingeniously made his large troupe seem even larger.[19]

Combining his sense for the visually dramatic with his willingness to invest large sums of money, Haverly also created dazzling extravaganzas. "The attention of the public is respectfully called to the magnificent scene representing a Turkish Barbaric Palace in Silver and Gold," an 1880 program boasted of the first part finale. The skit opened with a body of Turkish soldiers descending a mountain and passing in review, followed by a "grand transformation" into the King's palace with dancing contests. It concluded with a "realistic Tableaux" including "Base-Ball," "The Strong Defending the Weak," "United We Stand," and "The Dying Athlete." Obviously consistency in content was irrelevant. The grandeur of a Turkish palace, nationalism, and baseball each appealed to the public, so Haverly simply combined them in one lavish production. After an extensive olio, the program closed with "PEA-TEA-BAR-NONE'S KOLLOSAL CIRKUSS, MUSEUM, MENAGERIE AND KAYNE'S KICKA- DROME KAVALKADE." This parody of Barnum's circus opened with an "Equestrian Kavalkade and Karaven—Glittering Pageant—Magnificent Costumes—Gorgeous Effects"—and in- cluded bareback riders, clowns, tumblers, tightrope walkers, and "trained elephants"—the elephants played by Denman Thompson and Barry Maxwell.[20]

In his lavish productions, Haverly made the conspicuous consumption of the rich available to ordinary citizens at least for the duration of the show, just as vaudeville promoters later did with their opulent "palaces." Haverly and other minstrels thus regularly boasted about the high cost of their productions. The black satin embroidered dress worn by the princess in "The Princess of Madagascar," for example, supposedly cost $500, not counting her elaborate jewelry and gold embroidered tights with rich ostrich plumes; and the king's brocade tights and plush gold robe were reportedly "assessed at $1500." [21] Coupling such claims with the great impact that his productions made everywhere, Haverly convinced the public that there had never before been a minstrel troupe like his. And he was right. He had in essence created a new form—a gigantic composite of the most attractive features in popular entertainment, expertly packaged and promoted, grandly produced, purged of anything that might be offensive, and available wherever people would pay to see it.[22]

After Haverly showed the way, it was only a matter of time until other minstrel troupes increased their personnel, ex- panded the scale and elegance of their productions, and became permanent national traveling companies. These large touring troupes were a necessity in the late nineteenth century. Not only had population spread, transportation strikingly improved, and competition in urban markets markedly increased, but the great cost of mounting the lavish production numbers necessitated long runs, which were impossible for resident companies because their regular audiences would tire of the same spectacles. By traveling and playing either one-nighters or limited runs in large cities, minstrels made each night an opening night; the material and the sets were always new to the audience. But this also meant that they had to make their material acceptable to everyone—the farmer in Iowa and the New York b'hoy. They had to homogenize their shows, which meant the disappearance of raucous material. In the economically fluctuating decades of the 1870's and 1880's, large companies, with their great drawing power and larger resources, had a much better chance to survive. Many small troupes collapsed. In 1877, the Brooklyn *Eagle*, commenting on this trend to consolidation, reported only twelve recognized minstrel companies in the whole country, in contrast to the sixty that had existed only ten years earlier. In 1881, there were at least thirteen major traveling troupes, and in some extremely prosperous years there were more. But the small marginal companies simply found it much harder to survive when troupes like Haverly's honeycombed the nation, playing in small towns while en route to cities.[23] Like other late nineteenth-century businesses, minstrelsy reflected the trends toward concentration and standardization.

In the winter of 1883–84, Haverly bought the San Francisco Minstrels and absorbed their personnel into his company. What might seem just another routine business venture for the Haverly empire actually symbolized the final demise of minstrelsy as it had been known for its first forty years. The San Francisco Minstrels were much more than just another minstrel troupe. The last resident minstrels in New York, they had performed the traditional minstrel show there for nineteen years beginning in May 1865. With excellent performers in each of the speciality roles, the company starred Charley

Backus and Billy Birch, the greatest minstrel comedians of their day, and based its appeal on the Birch-Backus farce that invariably closed their shows. Occasionally accused of too many "broad" jokes, or too much off-color material, they relied on rollicking, earthy humor.[24] They drew their farce topics from popular fads and fancies: the British Blondes, velocipeds, French operettas, Wild West shows, politics, the cancan, or anything else their audiences were interested in. But whatever the subject, it was their raucous comedy that drew the crowds. In 1879–80, when they departed from their formula to stage musically serious parodies of Gilbert and Sullivan, business declined. But after they returned to their usual romps, it picked up again.[25]

Since the San Francisco Minstrels were considered unrivaled masters of the freewheeling, spontaneous ad lib, it is especially difficult to recapture their performances. But anyone familiar with the madcap antics of the Marx Brothers can imagine what a Birch-Backus skit must have been like. In 1880, these zany, unpredictable comedians performed one of their greatest farces, "Pleasant Companions." Set in an asylum for sleepwalkers, the skit had a cast that was hilarious in itself. Roaming the stage were: Tobias Elect, a politician who incessantly spouted flag-waving Fourth of July rhetoric and threw firecrackers; Romeo Bazan, a compulsive lover who constantly gushed drippingly romantic speeches; Abigail, a kleptomaniac who tried to steal everything in sight, including the other characters' clothing; and Reuben Canine, a "Canine Hydrophobia patient," who imagined he had been bitten by a mad dog. Played by the hulking Charley Backus, Reuben prowled the stage, barking, snarling, attacking, and even biting the other patients. Into this incredible menagerie crept Zeb Doolittle, a burglar played by Billy Birch. As a thief among sleepwalkers, the almost rotund Zeb tried to commit his robbery without awakening any of the cast, all of whom roamed the stage at the same time acting out their various obsessions. Deluged with Tobias's nationalistic rhetoric and deafened by his firecrackers, Zeb was wooed and kissed by Romeo and had his clothes and valuables stolen by Abigail. Finally, the growling, snarling Backus pounced on him, biting and howling like a giant, rabid dog. The skit closed with all the characters wildly chasing each other around the stage.[26]

By 1875, the San Francisco Minstrel troupe was the only resident minstrel company in the city that had once abounded with them. Faced with stiff competition from other entertainment forms, especially variety houses, it had managed to hold its own by lowering prices. But it also had to face the major traveling minstrel shows that regularly played New York as part of their national tours. Since these increasingly refined and opulent shows had great drawing power during their short runs, the San Francisco Minstrels constantly had to struggle against different, lavishly produced minstrel opponents. Its own material was too tailored for New York b'hoys for it to become a successful traveling troupe, and it was too firmly entrenched in the city to try.

In 1883 the San Francisco Minstrels faced a battle for survival, and they had to do it without Charley Backus, who had died in June. In November when the Mastodons came to town, the symbolic conflict between the new and the old styles of minstrelsy was fought out in the entertainment capital of the country. Even though the San Francisco Minstrels had added "The Only Leon" to their cast, the troupe still relied heavily on its rollicking comedy in contrast to Haverly's extravagant productions and refinements. After "torturing an audience with laughter," Billy Birch reportedly challenged it to go see the Mastodons and compare the two companies. Whether that occurred or not, the Mastodons won the competiton. Haverly bought the rights to the San Francisco Minstrels and, except for Birch and Leon, absorbed most of them into the Mastodons.[27] For the first time since minstrelsy began there forty years before, New York was without a resident minstrel troupe. An era of minstrelsy had ended. The large, refined traveling company, which heavily relied on lavish inoffensive productions, thereafter dominated minstrelsy.

The various companies led by the song-and-dance team of George Primrose and Billy West took the last step in the evolution of minstrel form. After they and others had left Haverly in 1877 over a salary dispute, they fielded their own minstrel company. By 1879 they were so successful that their pictures and short biographies appeared on the front page of the *Clipper*, a spot usually reserved for leading actors and actresses. But even at that high point of recognition, their show did not differ significantly from Haverly's.[28]

Then, in 1881, Sam Hague's touring British minstrels provided Primrose and West with their "gimmick." Conscious that Englishmen were unconvincing as Negroes and generally lacked the comedy skills Americans liked, Hague had only his endmen in blackface and promised that the troupe would do absolutely no low comedy. In fact, it did little comedy of any sort. Furthering the image of refinement, the performers in the first part appeared in full evening dress, with their vests trimmed in gold braid and boutonnieres in their lapels. The company, which had a much larger orchestra than American minstrels, also stressed musical and vocal precision. Almost totally lacking in comedy, the *Clipper* reviewer observed, "the first part was more like a high class ballad or operatic concert than a minstrel show." [29]

Capitalizing on Hague's success, Primrose and West soon promised that their show, without sacrificing the "true essence of fun," would have the "refinement and genuine artistic excellence which proved such a delightful innovation when in-

9. Minstrelsy in its elegant final stage.

*Thatcher, Primrose, and West's Minstrels, n.p., n.d. [1800's], program,
Harvard Theatre Collection.*

troduced in this country by Sam Hague's British Minstrels." [30] Surpassing both Hague and Haverly, they lavishly costumed the entire show, not just the production numbers, and often performed without blackface. "We were looking for novelty," George Thatcher recalled of these innovative years with Primrose and West, "and for a change tried white minstrelsy" and put the cast in "Shakespearian costumes." One of their shows, for example, opened with the cast, wearing no blackface makeup, dressed in the "court dress of the fops and beaux of the early nineteenth century." The singers and musicians wore blue satin coats, cream-colored satin vests, with blue satin knee breeches, silk stockings to match the vest, black patent leather low-cut shoes, and white wigs. The stars wore "Louis XI court dress": white satin coats, vests, breeches, silk stockings, low-cut white satin shoes with diamond buckles, lace collars, and white wigs. [31] When Milt Barlow left the troupe in 1882, his Negro characters went with him. Even while he was there, the company rarely did any plantation material, but after he was gone, the entire show was as "white" as the first part. Concentrating on refined singing and dancing and inoffensive material, they focused on lavish productions of current fads. Lawn tennis, baseball, bicycle riding, yacht racing, polo on skates, and fox hunting furnished them with subjects for their balletlike dances and their light musical comedy skits. This approach brought Primrose and West such success that they were known as "The Millionaires of Minstrelsy." But they brought minstrelsy to a stage where it was distinguished from other entertainment only by its name. [32]

"They have refined all the fun out of it," lamented Lew Dockstader, a minstrel comedian who almost single-handedly continued the Birch-Backus tradition. "Minstrelsy in silk stockings, set in square cuts and bag wigs," he observed with his usual flair, "is about as palatable as an amusement as a salad of pine shavings and sawdust with a little salmon, lobster, or chicken. . . . What is really good is killed by the surround-ings." [33] Although men like Dockstader kept minstrelsy alive and distinct as a form well into the twentieth century, it was only a matter of time until vaudeville and musical comedy ab-sorbed what was left of minstrelsy—the blackface act.

As it underwent such fundamental changes, mistrelsy be-came nostalgic about its own past. As early as 1857, in fact, Christy and Wood's Minstrels "in answer to many requests" devoted one night a week to a first part composed of songs of the "olden time." In 1859, Sam Sanford's troupe concluded with "Virginia Minstrels" because so many of their patrons wanted to see "the old style as originally presented . . . when minstrelsy was in its infancy." Twelve years later, Sanford again offered the old style of minstrelsy, "delineating the legiti-mate plantation festivities as distinguished from the pseudo-operatic style now so much in vogue." In 1881 Dan Emmett, one of the original Virginia Minstrels, traveled with Leavitt's Gigantean Minstrels as part of an old-time quintet, including Sam Sanford, now himself an object of nostalgia. [34] After 1880, such "histories of minstrelsy" or "Ethiopian Renaissances" be-came common minstrel features, as minstrelsy itself became al-most indistinguishable from its competitors. Like the rest of the nation, the raucous, vital antebellum form had grown larger, slicker, and more concerned with a respectable appearance as it matured. Its original form had become just a quaint relic suit-able only for nostalgia.

NOTES

[1] Douglas Gilbert, *American Vaudevillle* (New York, 1940); Isaac Goldberg, *Tin Pan Alley* (New York, 1930); Albert F. McLean, *Ameri-*

can Vaudeville as Ritual (Lexington, Ky., 1965); Cecil Smith, *Musical Comedy in America* (New York, 1950), pp. 12–22; Irving Zeidman, *The American Burlesque Show* (New York, 1967), pp. 1–51; for the impact of black minstrels, see Chapters 7 and 8.

² "Old Time Minstrelsy," Boston *Herald*, 1893, clipping, HTC; Shorey, Carl, Duprez, and Green's Minstrels, n.p., 1860, clippings, HTC; New York *Clipper*, Nov. 5, 1870; Frank Dumont, "The Younger Generation in Minstrelsy," *Clipper*, March 27, 191 ? clipping, NYLC.

³ New York *Clipper*, Dec. 28, 1861; Primrose and West's Minstrels, Rochester, New York, n.d., clipping, HTC; Sharpley's Minstrels, Lebanon, Pennsylvania, 1856, program, HTC; Frank Davidson, "The Rise, Development, Decline, and Influence of the American Minstrel Show," unpublished doctoral dissertation, New York University, 1952; Wood's Minstrels, New York, Aug. 1862 and 1863, programs, HTC; *Clipper*, Dec. 31, 1864, Jan. 15, 1870; G. D. Odell, *Annals of the New York Stage*, 15 vols. (New York, 1927–49), Vol. VIII, pp. 670–71; *Spirit of the Times*, 1868, clipping, NYLC.

⁴ Campbell's Minstrels, Mobile, Alabama, Feb. 22, 1850, program, NYLC; George Christy's Minstrels, n.p., n.d., program, NYLC; Odell, *Annals of the New York Stage*, Vol. VI, pp. 587–88; *Clipper*, Feb. 26, 1870; California Minstrels, Hooley's Theatre, Chicago, n.d. [1872?], playbill, NYLC; *Clipper*, Mar. 18, 1871; Masonic Temple Minstrels, Williamsburg [?], n.d., program, HTC; San Francisco Minstrels, New York, July 12, 1886, program, NYLC; *Clipper*, June 13, 1885.

⁵ *Spirit of the Times*, Oct. 16, 1843, Nov. 23, 1843; New York *Herald*, Nov. 21, 1844, quoted in Odell, *Annals of the New York Stage* Vol. V. pp. 114–15, 142; *ibid.*, Vol. V, pp. 378–80, 398; Smith, *Musical Comedy* . . . , pp. 30–35; Bernard Sobel, *A Pictorial History of Burlesque* (New York, 1956), pp. 14–24.

⁶ M. B. Leavitt, *Fifty Years of Theatrical Management* (New York, 1912), p. 38; John E. Henshaw quoted in Sobel, *A Pictorial History* . . . , pp. 45–46; *Clipper*, Jan. and Feb. 1871; Female Christy Minstrels, n.p., n.d. [1870's], program, HTC; *Clipper*, Jan. 15, 1876; "In Torn Tights," n.p., n.d., clipping, HTC.

⁷ *Clipper*, Apr. 20, 1872, Cool White's Broadway Minstrels, Patterson, New Jersey, May 23, 1866, program, HTC; on vaudeville, see

Gilbert, *American Vaudeville,* and McLean, *American Vaudeville as Ritual; Clipper,* Oct. 18, 1879.

[8] Olive Logan, "The Ancestry of Brudder Bones," *Harper's,* Vol. LVIII, 698, said the first female impersonator was Barney Williams, who left minstrelsy after introducing "Lucy Long" in the 1840's; *Clipper,* Nov. 1, 1873, identified George Christy as the first wench; Joe Laurie, Jr., *Show Biz from Vaudeville to Video* (New York, 1951), p. 88, observes that "In America we date the female impersonator from our minstrel shows," but gives no other information.

[9] Christy Minstrels, New York, 1849, programs, HTC; see also Campbell Minstrels and the Harmonians' sheet music, HTC; Odell, *Annals of the New York Stage,* Vol. V, p. 396.

[10] Logan, "The Ancestry of Brudder Bones," pp. 698–99; "Stolen Kisses Are the Sweetest," *Charles H. Duprez's Famous Songster* (New York, 1880), p. 38.

[11] T. Allston Brown, *History of the American Stage* (New York, 1870), pp. 216–17; Odell, *Annals of the New York Stage,* Vol. VIII, pp. 220, 351–52, 392; see Kelly and Leon's Minstrels' programs, HTC; Edward L. Rice, *Monarchs of Minstrelsy* (New York, 1911), pp. 143–44; "How Burnt Cork Pays," Boston, 1882, clipping, Boston Public Library; *Clipper,* Sept. 21, 1873.

[12] *Clipper,* May 28, 1870, Nov. 25, 1871, Nov. 23, 1872, Jan. 13, 1873, May 16, 1874.

[13] *Ibid.,* Dec. 31, 1881, June 2, 1883, Oct. 21, 1882; Kelly and Leon's Minstrels' Brochure, Chicago *Times-Herald,* Aug. 12, 1900, HTC; "Leon the Lovely," *Cleveland Press,* Dec. 2, 1881, reprinted in *Clipper,* Dec. 31, 1881.

[14] *Clipper,* Jan. 21, 1871; Joe Laurie, Jr., *Vaudeville* (New York, 1953), p. 91, pointed out some of these factors, especially women's interest in fashions, to explain the popularity of female impersonators.

[15] Haverly's United Mastodon Minstrels, n.p., 1878, playbill, HTC.

[16] *Clipper,* Dec. 24, 1881; Chicago *Times,* March 6, 1879, reprinted in Haverly's Minstrels, n.p., May 31, 1880, program, HTC.

[17] *Virginia City Enterprise,* Aug. 21, 1879, quoted in an ad in *Clipper,* Sept. 6, 1879.

[18] Daniel Frohman, *Charles Frohman Manager and Man* (New York, 1916), pp. 46–47, 49, 52–53.

[19] Chicago *Times*, Mar. 16, 1879, reprinted in Haverly's Minstrels, n.p., May 31, 1880, program, HTC.

[20] Haverly's United Mastodon Minstrels, Jersey City, New Jersey, Jan. 3, 1880, and Providence Opera House, March 1880, programs, NYLC.

[21] Haverly's Mastodon Minstrels, n.p., 1883, clipping, NYLC.

[22] By mid-1885, Haverly had to sell his minstrels because of disastrous stock investments. After that, he was only sporadically involved with minstrels. In 1905, he died penniless. Marion S. Revett, *A Minstrel Town* (New York, 1955), pp. 34–36, sketches his career; also see obituaries, Oct. 1905, clippings, NYLC.

[23] Brooklyn *Eagle*, Jan. 14, 1877, clipping, HTC; *New York Daily Mirror*, Nov. 5, 1881, date picked at random during touring season; *Clipper*, Nov. 19, 1881. Similar developments took place in drama when companies toured with one play as Combination Companies. See Glenn Hughes, *A History of the American Theater* (New York, 1951), pp. 206–7.

[24] For information on these and other performers, see Rice, *Monarchs* . . . , especially, pp. 68–71; *Clipper*, June 10, 1871; *Spirit of the Times*, Oct. 25, 1884; New York *Tribune*, Feb. 5, 1884, clipping, HTC.

[25] Odell, *Annals of the New York Stage*, Vol. VIII, pp. 495, 535; for subjects of their farces, see San Francisco Minstrels, New York City, playbills and programs, NYLC and HTC; Odell, Vol. X, pp. 485–86.

[26] San Francisco Minstrels, New York City, Nov. 1880, program, NYLC; Frank Dumont, *Pleasant Companions* (New York, 1880); *Spirit of the Times*, Nov. 1880, clipping, NYLC.

[27] Odell, *Annals of the New York Stage*, Vol. XII, pp. 142–43, 338–39; *Spirit of the Times*, Nov. 24, 1883; New York *Tribune*, Feb. 5, 1884, clipping, HTC; Odell, Vol. XII, p. 473.

[28] Thatcher, Primrose, and West, n.p., May 14, 1888, clipping, Boston Public Library; *Clipper*, Jan. 11, 1879; for information on the content of their shows, see programs and playbills, HTC and NYLC.

[29] *Clipper*, Mar. 26, 1881, May 14, 1881, Sept. 17, 1881.

[30] *Ibid.*, Aug. 18, 1883.

[31] "Interview with George Thatcher," n.p., Mar. 11, 1906, clipping, HTC; *Clipper*, Aug. 13, 1887.

[32] Thatcher, Primrose, and West, 1885–86, programs, NYLC;

The Grand Transformation

Primrose and West, Rochester, New York, n.d., clipping, NYLC; *Clipper*, Feb. 16, 1884; "How Burnt Cork Pays," Boston, 1882 clipping, Boston Public Library.

[33] "Dockstaders Ideas," n.p., July 1893, clipping, HTC.

[34] Christy and Wood's Minstrels, New York, 1857, playbill, HTC; Sanford's Opera Troupe, Philadelphia, 1859, program, HTC; *Clipper*, Jan. 14, 1871, Feb. 8, 1873, July 16, 1881; Leavitt's Gigantean Minstrels, n.p., Aug. 27, 1881, Sept. and Nov. 1881, Dec. 1882, programs, NYLC, HTC.

6 Social Commentary in Late Nineteenth-Century White Minstrelsy

After the Civil War, the content of minstrelsy changed as pervasively and fundamentally as its form did. Faced with basic changes in American society as well as with increased entertainment competition that included large numbers of black minstrels who made the plantation their specialty, white minstrels devoted much less attention to Southern Negroes and much more to national developments.[1] Minstrels had begun to look more critically at life in the Northern states during the sectional crisis of the late 1850's. But more than anything else it was the Civil War experience—the jarring contrasts between war profiteering and corruption and national idealism and sacrifice—that made white minstrels strikingly expand the range and depth of their social commentary. This became the primary concern of white minstrelsy in the late nineteenth century when immigration, urbanization, and modernization forced the American public to undergo fundamental institutional, social, and moral changes.

Social Commentary in White Minstrelsy

In their own informal, perhaps unconscious way, minstrels tried to help their audiences cope with their deepest concerns, anxieties, and needs. But since minstrels, like most other people, did not really understand the complex forces that were transforming their lives, they focused their criticism and explanations on only the most superficial features and the most striking evidence of these changes. In the short run, this oversimplification allowed minstrel audiences to feel that they understood what was happening to them and to their country. Minstrelsy's simplified ethnic caricatures made the nation's diverse immigrants seem comprehensible to native white Americans. Similarly, its attacks on cities as the causes, not the evidence, of social and moral decay gave audiences convenient, though inappropriate, targets for public dissatisfaction and anxiety. In the long run, minstrelsy implanted these stereotypes in American popular thought. As decades passed and conditions grew steadily worse and more uncontrollable, minstrels intensified their criticisms. They also became increasingly frustrated with their inability to offer any solutions. Ultimately, they took refuge in sentimental nostalgia.

When minstrels shifted away from Negro topics, they did not, however, automatically discard their blackface. From the beginning of minstrelsy, one of the functions of the blackface had been to give the minstrel a position similar to the classical fool. Set apart from the society, believed to be mentally inferior and immature, black characters could express serious criticism without compelling the listener to take them seriously. Through the antics and opinions of these characters, audiences could laugh at some of their own difficulties and anxieties while being assured that someone was more ignorant and worse off than they.[2] The blackface that was originally such an eye-catching novelty became, after the war, little more in most cases than a familiar stage convention. The use of Negro dialect was what

indicated to the audience that minstrels were portraying Negroes, usually the ludicrous low-comedy types that peopled
minstrel farces and provided both the targets and the vehicles
for minstrelsy's social criticism. The absence of dialect, on the
other hand, permitted blackface characters to sing of their blue-
eyed, blond-haired lovers without provoking any protests or to
use Irish and German dialects to portray immigrant groups.

Before the Civil War, minstrels ranged widely in their
social commentary. They lampooned other entertainment, from
Barnum to Jennie "Leather-lungs" Lind, and joked about the
telegraphic cable to England, the world's fair in London, and
country rubes falling in love with Hiram Powers's nude sculpture "The Greek Slave." Through their ignorant black characters, they "explained" natural phenomena like gravity and elec-
tricity. They sympathetically conveyed both the high hopes
and the bitter disappointments produced by the California gold
rush; and they made light of some of the cults and fads of the
day—Millerites, spirit-rapping, "free-knowledgey" (Phrenol-
ogy), and the Shakers.[3]

Aside from slavery and the abolitionists, however, the only
serious subject they extensively treated before the war was the
women's rights movement, which they consistently ridiculed
and condemned. Some performers, like Eph Horn, specialized
in parodying women's rights, and the "Women's Rights Lecture" became one of the standard stump speeches. Besides the
typical malaprops, non sequiturs, and convoluted verbiage,
these stump speakers hammered at the same point:

> When woman's rights is stirred a bit
> De first reform she bitches on
> Is how she can wid least delay
> Just draw a pair ob britches on.

The alleged desire of women to wear pants, and thereby symbolically reject their traditional subservient role, was the minstrels' greatest concern. Predictably, they ridiculed bloomers and any suggestion of equality for women. Mocking women's demand to participate in politics and to "direct the ship of state," minstrels often punned about women loving "parties" and being "vessels."

> Jim, I tink de ladies oughter vote.
>
> No. Mr. Johnson, ladies am supposed to care berry
> little about polytick, and yet de majority ob em am
>   strongly tached to parties.

If women had equal rights, minstrels argued, they would be "lowered" from their exalted moral position until they would lose their femininity and act like rowdy men.

> I'll run and fight and gouge and bite and
>   tumble in de mud
> Till all de ground for miles around am
>   kivered wid my blood.

Women, like Negroes, provided one of the few stable "inferiors" that assured white men of their status. Since women's rights seemed to be challenging that, minstrels lashed out against the movement almost as strongly as they attacked Negroes who threatened white male superiority. After the war, when minstrels increasingly turned to social and moral problems, women's challenge to men's traditional role became part of a broader critique of the general decay of social values.[4] Before the war it was a deeply disturbing topical issue, closely linked to the Negro's threat to proper social order. But throughout the nineteenth century, minstrels never varied from their complete condemnation of women's rights.

In the 1850's minstrels began to take note of America's human diversity, a subject that became a major post-Civil War theme. Besides making extensive use of the frontier lore and characters, they occasionally portrayed other native white American folk types: "Sam Simple" the Yankee, "Sam Patch the Jumpin' Man," and "Mose the B'howery B'hoy." But only Mose got more than slight coverage and that only in the mid-1850's.[5] After the mid-1850's the grave questions about slavery and blacks that seriously threatened the nation dampened the buoyant optimism expressed in these white folk types. Furthermore, based as they were on regional folklore, they could not serve as unifying symbols that transcended sectionalism. Thus, they virtually disappeared from the popular stage before the Civil War.

But the most exotic native American, the Indian, who also first came to minstrels' attention in the antebellum years, interested them until about 1880. Over these decades, minstrelsy's portrayals of Indians sharply changed, revealing the public's fluctuating attitudes toward them. Traditionally, white attitudes toward Indians have been characterized by ambivalence. As natural products of America, Indians were viewed as a noble, honorable, fiercely independent people— traits white Americans liked to believe all native Americans had.[6] But as occupants of the land "destined" for white Americans, they were viewed as barbaric pagans, blocking the fulfillment of the American mission. Vacillation between these views typified white attitudes during the nineteenth century.

Although minstrels treated Indians only sporadically before the Civil War, they consistently followed in the idealized footsteps of James Fenimore Cooper's Red Noblemen of Nature and the heroic Sagamore in the popular play *Metamora*. Despite a few negative comments, such as "it was great fun when Tecumseh was shot," [7] minstrels usually presented Indians as innocents in any idyllic American setting that white men had destroyed. The "Indian Hunter," for example, portrayed an Indian pleading with the white man to let him return to his Western home, to his valiant chieftain father, who had resisted the "insolent conquerors," and to his dark-eyed maid whose "fawn's heart was as pure as snow." Again, minstrels invoked the familiar themes of the idealized home and family threatened by "progress." Why had the white man come to take the Indian's land, the hunter asked, when he had abundant riches of his own? "Why should he come to harm one who never harmed him?" Minstrels completed their tragic images by describing gallant warriors giving their lives to defend their wigwams and their way of life.[8]

Caught up in the turbulence of modernization, antebellum white Americans grasped for symbols of an idealized, romantic past. Since Indians were not at that time a threat or an obstacle to whites, while plantation blacks (not yet fully romanticized) were, in fact, threatening the existence of the Union, the minstrels cast Indians as representatives of a more innocent time and place that had been destroyed by modernization. In mourning for them, the audiences could mourn for their own lost simplicity and for a heroic American past.

In 1865 Bryant's Minstrels enjoyed great success with a long run of "The Live Injin," a typical minstrel farce, except that it centered on an Indian. In the skit, a young lover hired a black servant, Pete, to smuggle notes past his girl friend's interfering father. But when Pete tried it disguised as a woman, his skirt was pulled off and the father chased him away. Deciding that he needed a completely different approach, he masqueraded as an "injin." After several comic Indian songs and dances, he was possessed by his role, went on a rampage, and scalped all the other cast members. This "innocent," heavily slapstick farce signaled a striking change in minstrelsy's portrayals of Indians. Even in lighthearted comedies like this one, the central minstrel image of the Indian shifted from the noble red man to the vicious scalper. Thus, in 1870, when Duprez and Benedict's Minstrels featured an account of their transcontinental railroad trip, they concluded with a railroad explosion after which the "festive red man" rushed in and scalped his "pale(?) faced brother." [9]

After the Civil War, Indians again stood in the way of American expansion. Throughout the 1870's Indian wars raged mercilessly as white Americans, again invoking their "manifest destiny," moved Westward, literally destroying the red man in the process. In this decade, minstrels devoted a good deal of attention to Indians by regularly portraying them in farces, the featured spot in the show. Performed around the nation by many troupes, these skits were consistently, even violently, anti-Indian. In 1872–73 "Life on the Indian Frontier, or The Comanches" had successful runs performed by different troupes in at least San Francisco, Philadelphia, and Chicago. Set in a frontier town, the skit opened with Indians and whites eating and drinking together. But as the Indians drank more and more, they became increasingly belligerent and threatening, and the villagers retreated. Only the help of the army averted "the attempted Wholesale Murder" of the townspeople by the Indians. The skit concluded with the "downfall of the Savages," underscoring the message that whites should not mix with or trust Indians. [10]

That same year, Schoolcraft and Coes, in a vicious skit, "The Three Chiefs," attacked Indian treaties as too lenient and generous. The minstrels' treaty with Chief Black Foot provided that the government supply every male Indian with rifles, revolvers, and 1,000 rounds of ammunition on the condition he agreed to kill no more than three white people a year or steal no more than two horses every six months. The whole tribe was to get roast beef, plum pudding, custard pie, and ice cream if they committed no more than one massacre and burned down no more than one town a week. Despite this generosity, Black Foot became a renegade, and a $3,000 reward was put on his head. When a Negro deputy, disguising himself as Black Foot, attempted to turn himself in to collect the reward, he was recognized, and the skit ended with people yelling "kill the nigger" and firing guns in a general chase scene.[11]

"WARPATH, SCALPING KNIVES, TOMAHAWKS, Or Adventures in the Black Hills," the San Francisco Minstrels titled their skit about General "Muster." The minstrels evidently portrayed all of the soldiers being killed, because the minstrel playing Muster later appeared as "Crawling Lizzard," and other military men later played other roles. The synopsis, too, indicated that Muster and his men went to the Black Hills and unsuccessfully met the Sioux Nation. "Get your scalps insured," it warned. The Sioux were "a strange tribe. No mercy. Retreat cut off." The scene then shifted to a battle between Ned Buntline, "a noted Indian slayer," and Crawling Lizzard. With the woods burning and all seemingly lost, Pond Lilly, a lovely Indian maiden played by Ricardo the prima donna, emerged out of nowhere to lead the backswoodsman out of danger. Except for the happy ending, this was an unusually morose way for the San Francisco Minstrels to close a show. But once they had decided to do a skit about Custer, they really had no choice. In this period, nationalistic white Americans could not simply laugh about or romanticize Indians, who were the enemies in a bloody war. But they could still accept the convention of the Indian girl who aided and loved a white man.[12]

At least two other farces in this period attacked the notion that Indians were anything other than terrifying. In one, Mr. Bones, wearing warpaint, feathers, and a ring in his nose, was adopted into a tribe, which he persuaded to give up fighting in favor of show business. The Indians hired members of the Nebraska legislature and the governor to appear with them in "Wild Bullalum ob de Wilderness," the governor acting as one chief and Bones as the other. They may not have made money, the skit reported, but they did get "lots of scalps worth $100 a piece on the reservation." [13] "Noble Savage," first performed by Duprez and Benedict in 1874 in Providence, Rhode Island, lampooned a tenderfoot writer's romanticized image of Indians. In the skit, a suitor had to bring a real Indian to his prospective father-in-law in order to win his daughter's hand. Rather than actually go West, the suitor hired a black man to impersonate an Indian. When the bogus Indian appeared before the father-in-law, who had been writing romantic novels about the Indian as a noble savage, the father-in-law took one look at him, was terrified, and fled in panic, screaming for someone to "shoot the savage." Like Dan Bryant's "Injin," this black imitator got carried away with the role and went on a scalping binge.[14] This skit explicitly stated minstrelsy's message about Indians in the 1870's: only from the secure armchair did the Indian seem to be a nobleman of nature; in the real world, he was a frightening, vicious enemy.

Minstrels had come full circle from their views of only twenty years before. By the 1870's, caricatures of darkies, in their idyllic plantation homes, served minstrels as romantic symbols of stability, simplicity, and order. Furthermore, minstrel darkies were contented subordinates. Even on stage, minstrels could not portray Indians as content to be the white man's subordinates, either because they in fact violently resisted subordination or because white Americans wanted to believe their country produced only brave, independent people who would rather die than become anyone's subordinates. To fulfill their roles, Indians had to die, either as cruel enemies or as tragic victims—there was literally no "place" for them within white American society.

Social Commentary in White Minstrelsy

In 1877, Bret Harte and Mark Twain wrote a play based on Harte's poem about the "heathen chinee." On opening night in New York, Twain explained their purpose to the audience. "The Chinaman is getting to be a pretty frequent figure in the United States," Twain observed, "and is going to be a great political problem and we thought it well for you to see him on the stage before you had to deal with that problem." [15] Although he was wrong about the scope of the "Chinese problem," Twain explicitly stated one of the most important functions of minstrelsy's presentations of ethnic characters. Although on the surface they just sang songs and told jokes about peculiar people, minstrels actually provided their audiences with one of the only bases that many of them had for understanding America's increasing ethnic diversity. [16]

Minstrels delighted in the strange-looking and -sounding immigrants who arrived in America in the mid-nineteenth century and provided unusual material for their shows. As entertainers, minstrels tried to create vivid stage characters, recognizable and amusing types. To do this, they used the technique of the caricaturing cartoonist. That is, they selected highly visible traits unique to a group and then constructed their characterization, really caricatures, around them. [17] Asians had odd-sounding languages, bizarre diets, and wore pigtails; Germans spoke "Dutch," drank lager beer, and ate sauerkraut and sausage; and Irishmen had brogues, drank whisky, partied, and fought. Exaggerating these ethnic "peculiarities" and minimizing or ignoring their commonplace features, minstrels and their vaudeville successors molded distinct ethnic caricatures, each of which sharply contrasted to all the others. Furthermore, since minstrels presented them as if they were adequate representations of these groups, these caricatures made America's human heterogeneity and complexity seem comprehensible and psychologically manageable to members of the audience. Although the minstrels only intended to entertain their public and to increase their own popularity, what they did in the process was to embed ethnic stereotypes in their audiences' minds.

Minstrelsy's most exotic foreigners were the Asians. Although they were rarely seen in most of the country in the mid-nineteenth century, the California gold rush brought white Americans, including minstrels, in contact with the Chinese. Different from Americans in race, language, and culture, the Chinese quickly became a part of the minstrels' array of minor curiosities. Although they referred to the Chinese only occasionally, minstrels consistently presented them as totally alien. They concentrated on the strange sound of their language, their odd clothing, and their reported preference for exotic foods: "Ching ring, chow wow, ricken chicken, a chew/Chinaman loves big bow wow and little puppies too." [18] They did "Burlesque Chinese Dances," mocked the sounds of the language with their "Ching, chang, chung," and were obsessed with the notion that Chinese ate cats and "Bow-wow soup, roasted bow-wow, and bow-wow pie." In the 1870's, Bret Harte's popular poem "The Heathen Chinee," and Dennis Kearny's vehemently anti-Chinese political campaigns in California produced a mild revival of minstrel interest. But except for the ethnic slur, probably inspired by Kearny, "He's no more suited to it [the job] than a chinaman for the Presidency," minstrelsy's portrayals remained unchanged. [19] Even though minstrels never devoted much attention to the Chinese, the way they caricatured them reveals how this process worked at its simplest level. As a new and different group caught the public's eye, minstrels selected a few of their most visible and distinctive features for inclusion in the shows, and when interest in them did not develop further, minstrelsy's treatment remained superficial and laughable.

The dramatic news of Commodore Perry opening up Japan to the United States, coupled with the establishment of a

Japanese Embassy in America in 1860, made the Japanese greater public sensations in the Northeast, where minstrelsy was concentrated, than the Chinese ever were. In fact, minstrelsy figured in the initial contacts between the United States and Japan. After the Japanese had entertained Perry and his crew with a Kabuki performance, members of the American crew staged a minstrel show for their Japanese hosts. If this was the end of Japanese interest in minstrelsy, it was just the beginning of minstrelsy's involvement with the Japanese.

"Everybody expects to make a pile by the advent of the 'outside barbarians,' " the editor of the New York *Clipper* observed after the arrival of the Japanese diplomats in June 1860. By that time, George Christy already had incorporated the "Japanese Treaty" into his show with a skit featuring characters like "Simnobudgenokamia," "More Hoecakeawake Moonshee," and "Princess Ko-ket." As a further enticement for audiences, Christy boasted that several members of the Japanese Embassy would attend the "Grand Japanese Matinee" to be held every Saturday afternoon "for the accomodation of ladies and children." [20] Following their familiar pattern, minstrels capitalized on an eye-catching group, treated them humorously, and even offered them as curiosities for the audience to gawk at.

Minstrel portrayals of the "jap-oh-knees" peaked between 1865 and 1867 when a troupe of Imperial Japanese Acrobats toured in America. Billing themselves as "The Flying Black Japs," at least eight major minstrel companies performed take-offs on this new sensation. [21]

BALANCING, JUGGLING, TOP SPINNING, AND ENCHANTED LAD-
DERS, HAM-SANDWICH-CELLAR-KITCHEN and his beautiful son
ALL WRONG . . .

"will appear assisted by eleven or eight other 'japs'," Carncross and Dixey boasted in typical fashion in 1865. [22] Although they did not use real Japanese in their shows, minstrels actually attempted spectacular acrobatics. Several, in fact, injured themselves when they fell over thirty feet while performing these gyrations. Yet, the principal attraction remained racial, not gymnastic. Kelly and Leon's large advertisement in the *Clipper* simply announced:

The original burst of interest in these exotics of the Orient subsided until Gilbert and Sullivan's *Mikado* again brought the Japanese into public attention. In the mid-1880's J. H. Haverly presented a "Colossal Japanese Show" including jugglers, tumblers, necromancers, from "the court theatre of his Imperial Majesty the Mikado of Japan." Haverly evidently had hired an actual Japanese troupe. The playbills and posters advertised what appeared to be authentic Japanese names and showed pictures of Oriental acrobats.[24] Other than this extravaganza, minstrelsy limited its treatments of the Japanese in the 1880's to their extremely popular burlesques of the *Mikado*. In 1885, for example, Thatcher, Primrose, and West advertised the 138th consecutive performance of the *Black Mikado*, which ran well into 1886. The political commentary at the heart of some of these burlesques was revealed by the cast that Carncross's Minstrels used: "Alvin Blackberry," a "smart Coon, chairman of the Ward Committee"; "Whatdoyousay," a Japanese "Black and Tan"; "Grover Tycoon Cleveland," the big Fly Coon from Washington"; a Japanese "no account"; and "as a special curiosity," a few honest New York Aldermen. Another company added "Boodle Taker," a Japanese alderman, to the same political cast.[25]

Social Commentary in White Minstrelsy

By the 1880's minstrels were not really interested in the Japanese themselves. They were just burlesquing a popular musical and condemning political corruption in America. As they had with the Chinese, minstrels presented the Japanese only as a curiosity and only when some unusual event focused public attention on them. Minstrels never pretended to portray Asians' feelings, attitudes, or motives. For minstrels, Asians were just strange, passing fancies, like Barnum's curiosities. Contrary to Twain's prediction, nineteenth-century white Americans did not have to come to grips with the nature of Asians and their place in America.

Since both the Irish and the Germans made a permanent place for themselves in America, they earned a similar position in the minstrel show. Minstrelsy's treatment of the Germans, which became frequent only after 1860, was consistently more favorable than that it accorded any other group. Although minstrels created comic characterizations of them, they portrayed Germans as practical, hard-working people. Usually played for good-natured comedy, robust German women and burly men, speaking "Dutch" dialects, indulged their immense appetites for sauerkraut, sausage, cheese, pretzels, and beer. Although men frequented lager beer saloons, sometimes drank too much, or ran up tabs they could not pay, they were never rowdy or obnoxious as the minstrel Irish often were. German women were usually built like the "Radish Girl," who was "butty as a shack horse," but, despite their tendency to overeat, they were good, solid, practical women. Minstrels joked about German courtship only because of the characters' hefty physiques and even heftier appetites:

> Vonce dere lifed a dailor's darter
> Und a vellar vot loofed her very much;
> Dat vellar used to take her up to Shon's Woods
> Und dreat her do everding fine,

> Lager bier, und pretzels, blenty of Limburger Cheese,
> Good bologny sausage and Rhine Wine.

Except for the abundance of odd foods, minstrels presented German courting as very proper, indeed almost a model. Unlike many of the frivolous fashion butterflies whom minstrels condemned, German women did not waste their money on senseless fads or flirt their lives away. They always demanded that suitors ask their fathers for permission to court and to marry them; they did not make expensive demands on their wooers; they got married after a proper, if somewhat comical, courtship; and they were efficient homemakers. Even when poor and living in a shanty, a German would always "give you shelter mit something to eat,/Un not from his door turn you into de street." [26]

Minstrels also testified that Germans had earned themselves a place in America by valiantly fighting for the Union. One such character, a shoemaker, enlisted with General "Sigel's" forces to "schlauch dem tam Secession volks," even though he did not want to give up his sauerkraut, "switzer kase," and beer for army salt pork. And, minstrels asserted, Germans also paid the brutal costs of the war along with the native Americans. Many died, and others like "Shonny" had his legs blown off. But despite such sacrifices and the good lives they led, Germans still suffered discrimination. Know-Nothings who attacked Germans, Frank Converse charged in 1863, did not even know the difference between good and bad people. And thirteen years later, Sam Devere, a German minstrel who, like Luke Schoolcraft and other Germans, performed a good deal of German material, had one of his characters say he hated to complain about America, but he had been harassed wherever he went and whatever he did by "loafers" who should "be dead for making fun of the Dutchman." [27]

Reflecting their bias in favor of the industrious Germans, minstrels contrasted German successes in America to Irish failures. One song, for example, compared a German to an Irish woman. Although Biddy, who had been in America for five years, was still a complete failure, Hans, who had come to America without a cent only two years before, already owned his own home, a sausage and bakery shop, and was worth $2,000. Hard work and a keen business sense had paid off for him. But Biddy, with her lackadaisical manner, did not realize that she could not succeed selling flat beer and stale food. After he purchased her business, Hans quickly converted Biddy's failure into another of his successes.[28] To minstrels, as to many other Americans, all Germans were like Hans. Because they fit so well into white American values and world-view, Germans seemed model immigrants. Thus, from the beginning, minstrels portrayed them as positively as they could any group while still playing for laughs and emphasizing group peculiarities.

If Germans were the favorite immigrants in the minstrel show, the Irish were the most numerous. In the 1840's prejudice and discrimination against the Irish in America were rampant, principally because the Irish were a rapidly growing cheap labor force that drove wages down, but also because they were Catholics, who natives feared were Papal agents sent to corrupt the American democratic experiment. Although the earliest minstrel portrayals of the Irish were less vitriolic than most of the anti-Irish rhetoric, they reflected some of these feelings. As early as 1843, minstrels attacked "Paddy" as "de biggest fool dat eber walk" because he did not know how to do anything right. When he got political rights, minstrels charged, he just sold his vote to the highest bidder. In 1848, they condemned the Irish for rioting in Philadelphia and killing both blacks and "natives" in violent raids supposedly led by priests.

Minstrels also complained that the city officials offered a re-
ward to find the people who had burned a Catholic church:
"But to cotch dem [Irishmen] dat killed freedom's sons,/De
state couldn't find no law nor funds." [29] In the 1840's minstrels
also began to describe the Irish as heavy-drinking, free-swing-
ing brawlers. But minstrelsy's tone in much of this was light,
not sinister or threatening. Even the fights were brotherly
brawls gleefully enjoyed by all, much like the last dance at a
party—a happy, if violent, closing formula. [30] This light tone
made these songs the antithesis of the somber temperance songs
on the same theme and of the menacing "razor-toting nigger"
songs of later years. But they still presented unfavorable, stereotyped images of Irish men and of nagging and/or brawling
Irish women.

But in subsequent years, the large number of Irishmen
who became minstrel stars, including Dan Bryant, George
Christy, Matt Campbell, Billy Emerson, and a host of others,
broadened and softened these negative images of the Irish.
Beginning in the 1850's, when minstrelsy was still concentrated
in the Eastern cities where the heavy proportions of Irish population must have comprised part of the ministrel audience, minstrels began to portray more favorable images of the Irish. A
collection of the Sable Harmonists' songs published in about
1850, for example, contained six Irish songs by John Collins.
Except that he used Irish names like "Molly Malone" and "Katy
O'Conner" and referred to St. Patrick's birthday, his songs
were indistinguishable from typical romantic and sentimental
ballads of the period. Later in the decade, Collins sang of the
beauties of Ireland and his sorrow at leaving it, concluding with
a prayer that Erin become a free nation. The Irish, Collins asserted in song, differed only in name; they too were romantic
lovers and freedom-loving patriots. In 1859, Matt Peel, also an
Irish minstrel, added another favorable dimension by singing

Social Commentary in White Minstrelsy

that although Paddy was poor and had only a small shabby house, "no king in his palace" was prouder than he was when at home with the family he loved "more than gold." [31]

Complexity and humanity in portraying the Irish became common only in the 1870's, when an Irishman, Edward Harrigan, left minstrelsy for the variety theater and traded his blackface for his more natural Irish brogue. Called both the "American Dickens" and the "American Gilbert and Sullivan," Harrigan and his partner, Tony Hart, began with a short Irish skit in 1873. Within five years they had developed a series of full-length plays portraying ethnic life in New York City. Concentrating on common people and on the vitality of their cultures, the team won unprecedented success by weaving an intricate web of ethnic life and conflict with the Irish at the center and blacks, Germans, and Italians intertwined around them.[32]

Although his German and black characters were important, Harrigan's greatest achievement was his presentation of the Irish point of view. Through his major character Dan Mulligan, who came to America in 1848, fought in the Civil War, bought a grocery store, and became a successful local politician, Harrigan portrayed the complexity of the Irish—and their humanity. His Irishmen were laughed at, but they were also laughed with; they were drinkers and brawlers, but they were also hard workers; they engaged in political graft, but at the same time worked for their people. Harrigan also praised the strong Irish sense of group identity and their flourishing social organizations; he applauded their bravery during the Civil War, lamented the human anthills they had to live in, and denounced the discrimination they had to endure. In short, he presented a full panorama of Irish life.

Although greatly influenced by Harrigan and Hart's portrayal of the Irish, minstrels could never present characters with the complexity, depth, and humanity that Harrigan achieved.

The forms they worked in differed too greatly. Harrigan and Hart had a resident theatrical company in New York that presented full-length plays to a heavily ethnic, working-class audience. Although not strictly speaking an exclusively ethnic theater, like Yiddish theater that was meaningless to people who did not understand Yiddish, Harrigan and Hart's shows were in-group experiences. Because of this and because full-length plays allowed, almost required, depth of characterization, they presented relatively complex, multifaceted characters and plots that unfolded throughout the series of plays. Since minstrels, on the other hand, traveled extensively to the heartland of white America, they did not usually have an ethnic audience and could not build up a consistent clientele with whom they could develop continuities. Furthermore, minstrelsy as a form had its roots in caricature, not characterization, and it required diversity: short, self-contained acts, lavish production numbers, and slapstick farces. None of these allowed the in-depth characterization or the presentation of different perspectives on the same subject that were necessary to capture humanity. Minstrels could easily *diversify* their portrayals of groups but could not easily capture human complexity. Consequently, when they borrowed from Harrigan and Hart, they took individual pieces, not the complex network of interrelated characters and events.

Although some minstrels did not acknowledge their debt to him, Harrigan's presence overshadowed minstrelsy's portrayals of the Irish after the mid-1870's. While continuing to sing of Irishmen drinking and fighting, as Harrigan himself did, minstrels greatly diversified their images of the Irish. Drawing on both Harrigan's description of Irish problems and on the vogue for temperance songs, several minstrels sang of Irish parents lamenting the ill effects of drinking and city life on their children. "Since Terry First Joined the Gang" and "Since Dennis Took to Drink," Irish parents complained, they both used slang, had no jobs, got into trouble, talked back to their parents, and even ended up in jail.[33] Like so many other parents, minstrels pointed out, the Irish too worried about their children facing the city's many temptations and vices. Such concerns were never expressed by minstrelsy's Northern Negro characters, who were living embodiments of vice and folly at their most absurd. In great contrast to their diverse portrayals of both the Germans and the Irish, minstrels presented blacks in only a few stereotyped roles: as contented subordinates on the plantation, as ignorant low-comedy fools, and as ludicrous, pretentious incompetents. Whites needed these fixed images of blacks to reassure them about their own positions. Since they did not use the Irish in this way, minstrels had much greater flexibility in portraying them.

Again following Harrigan, minstrels praised Irish social clubs, policemen, and politicians as representatives of their community. The politicians threw parties for the people, held office in their name, and gave everyone a "fair shake." When there were no jobs, they properly "made them up." Minstrel characters also rejoiced in the dignity all Irishmen gained when John L. Sullivan became heavyweight boxing champion. Irishmen of all sorts worshiped him, minstrels sang, and even lined up to shake the "hand that shook the hand of Sullivan." [34] Minstrels also protested the discrimination the Irish suffered despite their commitment to America. "No Irish Need Apply," minstrels complained, was what honest Irishmen heard when they looked for work. But when America wanted soldiers, it "never said no Irish need apply." The Irish, moreover, had contributed generals, soldiers, statesman, and poets to America. Although minstrel Irish expressed the hope that Ireland would be free, they did not reject America. They merely longed for their homeland to be free from British tyranny, a desire Americans fully understood.[35]

By the 1880's, minstrelsy's images of the Irish had become quite varied and diverse. Unlike the Germans, who had gotten favorable treatment from the beginning, the minstrel Irish went from simple, negative caricatures to a more diversified treatment than that given any other group, even the Germans. Since this so sharply contrasted to their treatment of blacks, it is important to undertand why it happened. Certainly Harrigan's great success, which caused minstrels to incorporate some of his features, was a major factor. But this is an insufficient explanation. Minstrels, after all, could have borrowed selectively and maintained their simple negative images. To be sure, the substantial numbers of Irishmen who became minstrels played an important part in humanizing minstrel portrayals. But when blacks became minstrels, they could make only minor changes in minstrel stereotypes of Negroes. The critical point was that native, white Americans had no deep-seated need to keep the Irish in "their place" or to justify the place they were kept in as they did with blacks. Furthermore, a great many Americans probably had no preconceived image of the Irish, which meant that Harrigan and the Irish minstrels' diverse, humane ideas about the Irish could have great impact. Probably most important of all, the Irish and the Germans were fellow white men, whom white Americans could much more easily accept than they could native-born blacks.

Besides ethnic diversity, minstrels were deeply concerned about the social and moral decay that they saw taking place. To them, cities, where these developments were most obvious, seemed the problem. Although some minstrel songs neutrally described cities, minstrels, like most Americans were overwhelmingly negative toward cities from the time they first noticed them.[36] The only substantial changes in their treatment over time were in the breadth of charges they leveled and in the growing importance urban topics assumed in the shows. As their audience changed, so did their emphasis. In the 1850's, while still based in cities, minstrels limited themselves to attacking the dire living conditions and to lambasting the unproductive and often immoral lives of urban dilettantes; in the 1860's, as they traveled more, they added warnings about "city slickers" preying on new arrivals; and in the financially rocky 1870's and 1880's they also attacked inequities in wealth, which they associated with cities.

Beginning in the 1850's minstrels, speaking to urban audiences, protested a wide range of urban problems: stage coaches that drove too fast and knocked women and babies down, filthy streets that were never cleaned, policemen who demanded bribes, people selling votes and buying wives, manipulating politicians, high taxes, and continual robberies. They frequently complained about the atrociously high rents people had to pay, but what they got for these high prices was even worse—or at least funnier. When moving into a new place, Charlie Fox complained, he and an old lady were asked by the cigar-smoking landlord whether smoke bothered them. Both said it did not, paid their money, and then were told that it was a good thing smoke did not disturb them because the fireplaces smoked so badly that they would be smoked beef in less than two weeks. Fox also said he was changing boardinghouses because the food, which consisted of stewed cat, raw crocodile, monkey's feet, broiled flunkies, and arsenical soups, had hair in it. But at least, he concluded, there was not a single bug in the house. All of them were married and had children.[37]

Minstrels were very seriously disturbed by what seemed a

shocking deterioration of moral values in the city. But they attacked only symptoms, not causes. People no longer attended churches, they lamented.

> Pompey, does you eber attend church?
>
> Why yes, I go a good deal—considerable—almost
> ebery Sunday—occasionally—once in a while—a
> little—not much if any.

And when the city dwellers did go, minstrels complained, "churches built for prayer are where people show off their fashions." [38] Everywhere they looked they saw conventional morality being ignored and families disintegrating. Men put ads in newspapers to meet pretty girls and, what was worse, got answers. Divorce and infidelity seemed to be sharply increasing. One minstrel character's wife "fell to temptation" and deserted him to "live in luxury with her lover." Many husbands became drunkards and adulterers. One drunken man even tried to pick up his own wife on the street, while a number of others boasted of their nightly sexual exploits. [39]

To minstrels, the city's most pernicious effect was its corruption of the young. In Central Park, minstrels complained, there were many wayward young people, often mere boys, who:

> Instead of being home with their mamas
> Are running round smoking penny cigars
> And girls scarcely sixteen years old
> Laughing and chatting with them so bold
> And doing the thing that is not right
> On Central Park on a Sunday night.

Many of the younger generation even showed complete disregard for their aging parents. One old minstrel character, for example, who had loved and cared for his children, found them sending him off to the poorhouse to die alone. "God knows how their father loved them," he lamented, "but they've driven him out into the street." [40]

Perhaps worst of all, young people were obsessed with frivolous and self-indulgent dilettantism like the decadent European aristocrats whom Americans so often condemned.

> Our dandies now have lots of brass, But very little brains,
> Their pants are made to fit so tight, Their legs are like a crane's.
> Our ladies too are like the men, They've got to wearing boots,
> With dresses made of costly silk, Spread out with barrel hoops.

Calculated dishonesty, expensive clothing, lives spent in trivial flirtations, a complete rejection of useful work, a tendency to "obey society not himself": all the best American traits inverted. The very heart of the egalitarian experiment seemed lost. Minstrels continually hammered at these changes by ridiculing the "dandies" and "swells" who epitomized them. Again, ludicrous black characters carried these trends to ridiculous extremes, providing audiences with models of this social inversion at its worst. But minstrels had long presented ludicrous blacks "out of their places." Now they added nondialect characters—their own children. Senseless young women wore hoop skirts, hair pieces, bustles, extravagant silks and satins, and "palpitators to swell their bosoms"; they showed their legs, painted their faces, and shamelessly flirted with strangers; they shirked all work, but read every new romance and sonnet and flocked to lavish balls and parties; and, fancying themselves better than poor people, they forced their parents deeply into debt to maintain their position in the "better set." [41] Minstrels also satirized male dandies, but more often, they portrayed men, even dandies, as victims of demanding females who forced them to live beyond their means. One such "Modern Fast

Young Gentleman" gave lavish parties, had fast horses, several yachts, and many servants to turn poor people away from his gates. Finally, his creditors caught up with him and sent him to prison.[42] Although minstrels attacked both male and female dilettantes, they placed much more blame on the women, who minstrels felt should have forced men to settle down and raise families.

Beginning in the 1860's, as minstrels traveled more widely, they warned their new audiences about the hazards awaiting urban visitors. Again, they commonly blamed women and pictured men as victims. Although they occasionally ridiculed the visitors as "gawks" or "countrymen green as peas" [43] who foolishly squandered their money on women, fashions, drinking, and gambling, they usually pictured them as naïve prey for professional thieves and extortionists. One young farm boy from New Jersey learned of the hardships of the city while he was still on the train. After a young widow asked him to hold her baby and then disappeared, he discovered a note from her telling him that the baby was dead and that she could not afford to bury it.[44] Others were bilked on the train, but most fell victim when they went looking for recreation in the cities. Women picked men up, got them drunk, drugged their wine, and robbed them; some even had male accomplices who "rolled" the victims. One woman, for example, allowed herself to be picked up and then started screaming that she was being molested. After her "date" was arrested, she wrote him a note saying that if he paid her, she would drop the charges and her friends at the police station would release him. Women, too, fell victim to city slickers, especially "old maids" all too willing to trade money for companionship. Rural visitors, minstrels asserted, simply did not know how to cope with the new urban morality, which stressed that the only way to survive was "to be stronger than everybody else—lie, cheat, and steal if necessary." And lest these examples were not enough, minstrels preached directly to their audiences: "Whoever you meet," George Christy warned, "look for their little game." [45]

Besides condemning the living conditions, the social and moral changes, and the hazards of city life, minstrels also associated it with extreme inequities of wealth. During the economically disastrous 1870's and 1880's some minstrels became overtly "antirich man." The wealthy complained of hard times, minstrels claimed, only because they could not get even more money than they already had. "De poor man and his family do all de sufferin." a minstrel charged, "and de rich all de jawin." The rich, another minstrel alleged, "own all the railroads and all of the land, and tell all the people to go and be d——." Employers callously disregarded the welfare of their workers as long as they stayed on the job. Although coal miners labored hard at their dangerous jobs, the "great ones," secure in the warmth of their homes, cared nothing about the danger of the mines even though:

> The very fires their mansions boast
> To cheer themselves and wives
> Mayhap were kindled at the cost
> Of jovial colliers lives.

In 1884, a minstrel complained that businessmen, taking advantage of the economic difficulties, lowered wages and left the workingman's children crying for bread. Another referred to "blood-sucking, thieving employers," while arguing for fair wages. Minstrels also strikingly contrasted the luxurious lives of the rich and the dire fate of orphan children freezing to death in the street while begging for pennies. These songs and speeches constituted a strong indictment of the insensitivity and social irresponsibility of the wealthy. [46]

But like many other Americans in the late nineteenth century, minstrelsy's only remedies were traditional platitudes.[47] In the face of open violence between unions and employers, Bobby Newcomb of the San Francisco Minstrels typically urged: "Let capital shake hands with labor/Let the poor have the bread they earn." After naïvely pleading for this gentlemanly agreement, he concluded by preaching to his audience:

> Remember the poor love their children,
> So give them a smile not a frown.
> Live and let live, be your motto,
> Oh, don't put the poor working man down.[48]

Consistently sympathetic to the poor, who probably sat in their audiences, minstrels still thought only in terms of conventional morality. They reminded their audiences that even thieves and "nymphs of the pave" could mend their ways and urged everyone to "offer a helping hand" to the less fortunate. They incessantly intoned familiar aphorisms extolling nineteenth-century American values: "Always Be Ready When Your Chance Comes," "Pull Hard Against The Stream," "Slow and Steady Wins The Race," "Where There's A Will There's a Way," and many others. They also offered lessons in interpersonal relations and personal morals: "Forgive and Forget, But If You Can't Do Both, At Least Forgive," "Never Hit a Man When He's Down, Boys," "Always Do to Others As You'd Wish to Be Done By," "Put the Brake on When You're Going Down the Hill." [49]

Confronted with what they saw as fundamental decay of their world, minstrels were unable to offer any solution. They made the nation's growing ethnic diversity seem comprehensible by adding more caricatures to the show. They lashed out at the effects of urbanization and industrialism, but they had only moralisms for remedies. Consequently, they became increasingly escapist, wallowing in sentimentalism and nostalgia.

Longing for a simple, secure time when there were no problems, they looked back to an idealized past. In grandfather's day, one minstrel recalled, men were judged by merit, not money; styles were sensible; young men did not ogle girls; married men were faithful; politicians were honest; and there was no war. One hundred years ago, another intoned, farmers did not cut their legs off with mowing machines; there were few divorces; lamps did not explode and kill people; there were no "Turkish harems at Salt Lake"; young women did not lose status if they did a little work; everyone made his own clothes; and everybody was honest.[50]

Even the plantation was not immune from the destructive forces of "progress." After the Civil War, white minstrels concentrated their portrayals of Southern Negroes, a minor but significant portion of the show, on the nostalgic Old Darky. Whether these characters had gone North and then returned or had never left, they found their old plantation gone, destroyed by the war. Aged, weak, and alone, they recalled the happy, carefree prewar days, which further underscored the tragedy of the destruction of the plantation. Since it was gone, however, audiences did not have to hear protests against the more unfortunate aspects of the plantation—like slavery. Yet they could still bask in its warmth through the memories of the Old Darky. They could envy his carefree life of perpetual childhood—singing, dancing, and frolicking. They could even momentarily share his simple world, free of the worries, insecurities, and responsibilities that they had to face. At the same time, they could feel comfortably superior to him and certain that, whatever else changed in their lives, he would always be their subordinate. Through him they could also mourn for lost simplicity, order, and control. Although he certainly did not offer an antidote for their problems, the Old Darky provided a temporary diversion, a reassuring certainty that whites desperately needed and clung to.

NOTES

¹ For a comparison of the ways in which white and black minstrels presented the plantation after the war, see Chapter 8.

² For a discussion of the minstrel as fool, see Constance Rourke, *American Humor*, (New York, 1931, Anchor ed.), pp. 84–85; and Charles Haywood, "Negro Minstrelsy and Shakespearean Burlesque," Bruce Jackson, ed., *Folklore and Society: Essays in Honor of B. A. Botkin* (Hatboro, Pa., 1966), pp. 77–92.

³ "Listen to the Darky Band," *De Susannah and Thick Lip Melodist* (New York, 1850), pp. 18–19; "The Minstrel Band," *Sable Songster* (Philadelphia, 1859), pp. 70–71; Charles White, "Atlantic Steamship," *White's Serenaders Song Book* (New York, 1851), pp. 77; E. P. Christy, "Julius' Trip to the World's Fair," *Plantation Melodies #2* (New York, 1851), pp. 18–19, and *Old Uncle Ned Songster* (Philadelphia, 185–?), pp. 97–98; "Jordan is a Hard Road to Travel," *Wood's New Plantation Melodies* (New York, 1855), pp. 5–6; *Charley White's Ethiopian Joke Book* (New York, 1855), pp. 27, 36, 60; "Billy Barlow," *Bryant's Songs from Dixie Land* (New York, 1861), pp. 15–17; "I'm Off to California," *White's Serenader*, pp. 30–31; *White's Joke Book*, pp. 29, 45; "California Emigrant," *New Negro Band Songster* (Philadelphia, n.d. [185–?]), pp. 241–42; "Going Around the Horn," *Bryant's Dixie*, pp. 32–33; "Around the Horn," *Bob Hart's Plantation Songster* (New York, 1862), p. 6; *White's Serenader*, p. 57; Ordway Aeolians, "The Returned Californian," Boston, 1852, sheet music, HTC; "Joe Bowers," *Bryant's Dixie*, pp. 25–27.

⁴ "Phoebe Anna White," *Songs of Kunkel's Nightingale Opera Troupe* (Baltimore, 1854), pp. 18–19; for Eph Horn's use of women's rights, see programs of Wood's Minstrels, Morris Brothers, Pell and Trowbridge Minstrels, and Buckley's Serenaders, HTC; T. Allston Brown, *History of the American Stage* (New York, 1870); Christy and Wood's Minstrels, "The Bloomer Paraders," May 1857, G. D. Odell, *Annals of the New York Stage*, 15 vols. (New York, 1927–49), Vol. VI, p. 584; Fellows Opera House, New York, July 2, 1851, Odell, Vol. VI, p. 76; *White's Joke Book*, pp. 40–41, 53. For discussions of woman's role as the keeper of morals and the great anxiety about changes in that role, see Ruth Elson, *Guardians of Tradition* (Lincoln, Neb., 1964), pp.

301–12; William R. Taylor, *Cavalier and Yankee* (New York, 1961, Anchor ed.), pp. 141–43; James C. Hart, *The Popular Book* (Berkeley, 1961, paperback ed.), p. 86; Barbara Welter, "The Cult of True Womanhood," *American Quarterly*, XVIII (1966), 151–75.

[5] Charles White, *Sam's Courtship* (New York, 1874 [first performed in 1852]); *White's Joke Book*, p. 46; for more information of Sam Patch, see Richard M. Dorson, "Sam Patch Jumping Hero," *New York Folklore Quarterly*, LXIV (1947), 741–47; for Mose in minstrelsy, see Odell, *Annals of the New York Stage*, Vol. VI, p. 76; Matt Campbell, *Wood's Minstrel Songs* (New York, 1855), p. 25; *White's Serenaders*, pp. 9–10; E. P. Christy, *Plantation Melodies #1; Ned Songster*, pp. 67–68.

[6] Winthrop Jordan, *White over Black* (Chapel Hill, N. C., 1968), pp. 90–91.

[7] "Double Back Action Spring," *Negro Forget Me Not Songster* (Philadelphia, n.d.[1848]), pp. 38–40.

[8] "Indian Hunter," *New Negro Forget Me Not Songster* (Cincinnati, 1848), pp. 128–29, and *Harry Pell's Ebony Songster* (New York, 1864), p. 61; Harmoneons, "Indian Warrior's Grave," Boston, 1850, sheet music, HTC.

[9] Dan Bryant, *The Live Injin* (Chicago, 1874); see Bryant's Minstrels, New York, 1865, programs, HTC; New York *Clipper*, Nov. 5, 1870.

[10] *Clipper*, Sept. 14, 1872, Sept. 21, 1872, Oct. 4, 1873; Simmons, Slocum, and Sweatnam's Minstrels, Philadelphia, 1873, playbill, HTC.

[11] J. C. Stewart, *The Three Chiefs* (New York, 1876).

[12] San Francisco Minstrels, New York City, n.d., program, HTC.

[13] *Minstrels Gags and End Men's Hand-Book* (New York, 1875), pp. 35–36.

[14] Frank Dumont, *Noble Savage* (New York, 1880), first performed Aug. 21, 1874.

[15] Quoted in Arthur H. Quinn, *A History of the American Drama Since the Civil War* (New York, 1943), pp. 110–11.

[16] Robert Merton, *Social Theory and Social Structure* (Glencoe, Ill., 1957), pp. 19–84, clearly distinguishes between manifest and latent functions, basically the difference between stated purposes and practical or objective results.

[17] Milton Gordon, *Assimilation in American Life* (New York, 1964, paperback ed.), pp. 79–81, argues that highly visible (extrinsic)

traits are often more important in perpetuating stereotypes than internal (intrinsic) traits. Minstrelsy certainly supports this view.

[18] "A Chinaman's Tail," *Buckleys' Ethiopian Melodies #4* (New York, 1857), p. 66.

[19] Thomas Carey, *Brudder Gardner's Stump Speeches and Comic Lectures* (New York, 1884), pp. 37–40; New York *Clipper*, Oct. 5, 1878; Campbell's Minstrels, New York, n.d. (1850's), playbill, NYLC; *White's Jokebook*, p. 45; "Heathen Chineee," Luke Schoolcraft, *Shine On Songster* (New York, 1873), "Hong Kong Gong," *Bobby Newcomb's San Francisco Minstrels' Songster* (New York, 1868), pp. 22–23; "Big Long John," *Charles H. Duprez's Famous Songster* (New York, 1880), p. 25.

[20] *Clipper*, June 16, 1860; advertisement for George Christy's Minstrels, n.p., June 21, 1860, clipping, NYLC.

[21] Carncross and Dixey's Minstrels, Campbell's Minstrels, Hooley's Minstrels, Kelly and Leon's Minstrels, Arlington Minstrels, San Francisco Minstrels, George Christy's Minstrels, and La Rue's Minstrels, programs and playbills, HTC, NYLC.

[22] Carncross and Dixey's Minstrels, Philadelphia, 1865, playbill, HTC.

[23] *Clipper*, July 20, 1867, Nov. 17, 1867; Odell, *Annals of the New York Stage*, Vol. VIII, p. 220.

[24] Haverly's American European Original Mastodons, n.p., n.d. [1883?], poster and playbills, NYLC.

[25] Done frequently by Haverly's, McIntyre and Heath's, Carncross', Thatcher, Primrose, and West's Minstrels in 1886, see programs and playbills in HTC and NYLC; Biemiller's Opera House, Sandusky, Ohio, Feb. 4, 1887, program, HTC.

[26] "Der Slate," *Shoofly Don't Bodder Me Songster* (New York, 1871), pp. 78–79; Dan Bryant, "New York City," *Bryant's Essence of Old Virginia* (New York, 1857), p. 12; "The Radish Girl," *Bob Hart's Plantation Songster*, pp. 46–47; "She Shook the Tailor," and "The Schoos Maker's Daughter," *Corporal Jim Songster* (n.p., n.d.[1870's]), pp. 58, 61; "Wake Out Serenade," *The Dockstaders' T'shovel Songster* (New York, 1880), p. 25; "The Dutchman's Shanty," *Bob Hart's*, p. 55.

[27] "I'm Going to Fight Mit Siegal," *Pell's Ebony*, pp. 14–15; "Cruelty to Shonny," *Bob Hart's*, p. 22, and *Bryant's Shoo Fly*, p. 29; "The Difference," *Frank Converse's Old Cremona Songster* (New York, 1863), p. 35; "Look at De Dutchman," *Sam Devere's Combination Songster* (New York, 1876), n.p. This songster had fifteen songs in German

dialect, an unusually large number but typical of Devere and Luke Schoolcraft, both Germans. See also *Sam Devere's Burnt Cork* (New York, 1877), Schoolcraft, *Shine On*.

²⁸ "Ireland versus Germany," *Cool Burgess' Oh Don't Get Weary Children Songster* (New York, 1877), pp. 16–17.

²⁹ For anti-Irish prejudice see Oscar Handlin, *Boston's Immigrants* (Cambridge, Mass., 1941); "Old Paddy Whack," *Deacon Snowball's Negro Melodies* (New York, 1843), pp. 18–19; "Philadelphia Riots" and "De Southwork Rebellion," *Negro Forget Me Not Songster*, pp. 98–101, 101–6.

³⁰ "Lannigan's Ball," *People's New Songster* (New York, 1864), pp. 27–28; "Away Goes Dufee" and "Mr. McLauglin's Party," *Dan Bryant's New Songster* (New York, 1864), pp. 65–66; "Paddy Connor's Wake," *Ned Turner's Bones and Tambourine Songster* (New York, 1869), pp. 59–60.

³¹ "Molly Malone," "The Bowld Soger Roy," "The Birth of St. Patrick," "Widow Machree," "Katy O'Conner," "Croos-Keen Lawn," *De Sable Harmonist* (Philadelphia, n.d. [1850]), pp. 19–27; Charles Fox, "Irish Patriot's Farewell," *Sable Songster* (Philadelphia, 1859), p. 79; Matt Peel, "The Irishman's Shanty," New York, 1859, sheet music, HTC.

³² E. J. Kahn, Jr., *The Merry Partners: The Age and Stage of Harrigan and Hart* (New York, 1955); chapters 3–6 discuss the content of their shows in some detail.

³³ *Johnson and Bruno's Mania Monia Nigs Songster* (New York, 1875), pp. 34, 36; William Delehanty, *I Hope I Don't Intrude* (New York, 1877), n.p.

³⁴ "Alderman Flynn," "Casey's Social Club," and "Are You There Moriarity?" *Haverly's United Mastodon Minstrels Song Book* (Chicago, 1880), pp. 9, 56–57; "Muldoon the Solid Man" [by Harrigan] *Bobby Newcomb's Love Letters and Packet of Poems Songster* (New York, 1880), p. 32; "Moriarity the Dandy M.P.," *Jay Rial's Ideal Uncle Tom's Cabin Song Book* (San Francisco, 1883), p. 8; "Mulligan's Promises" [by Harrigan], *Cool Burgess' I'll Be Gay Songster* (New York, 1880); "Pat Delaney," *Sam Devere's Burnt Cork*, p. 99; Al G. Field, "Let Me Shake the Hand that Shook the Hand of Sullivan," *Field and Co.'s Minstrel Songster* (New York, 1890), pp. 14–15.

³⁵ "No Irish Need Apply," *People's*, pp. 13–14, and *Gems of Minstrelsy* (New York, 1867), pp. 44–45; "Bad Luck to Ould Jefferson

Davis," *Pell's Ebony*, pp. 18–19; "Tom Maguffin," *Queen and West's Popular Songster* (New York, 1878), p. 10; "Tim Flaherty," *Dockstaders'*, n.p.; "Flag of Green," *Gems*, p. 37; "Bold Jack Donahue," *Joe Lang's Old Aunt Jemima Songster* (New York, 1873), pp. 24–25.

[36] For a sampling of negative American reactions to cities, see Glen Blayney, "City Life in American Drama 1825–1860," A. Doyle Wallace, ed., *Studies in Honor of John Wilcox* (Detroit, 1958), pp. 88–129; Elson, *Guardians of Tradition*, pp. 25–35; Richard Hofstader, *Age of Reform* (New York, 1955, Vintage ed.), pp. 23–60; Morton and Lucia White, eds., *The Intellectual Versus the City* (New York, 1964, Mentor ed.). For a sampling of minstrels' neutral descriptions of city life, see "Broadway Song," *Buckley's Song Book for the Parlor* (New York, 1855), n.p.; "Chestnut Street Panorama," *Popular Ethiopian Melodies* (Philadelphia, 1856), pp. 15–16; "Fulton Market Saturday Night," *Ned Turner's Bones*, pp. 46–47; "The Brooklyn Ferry," *Devere's Burnt Cork*, pp. 30–31; "Coney Island," *Haverly's Mastodon Minstrel Songster* (Chicago, n.d.[1880?]), p. 30; "Riding on the Elevated Railroad," *Haverly's United*, p. 11.

[37] "That's So," *World of New Negro Songs* (Philadelphia, 1856), pp. 60–61; "The Broadway Stages," *Frank Converse's Old Cremona Songster*, pp. 27–28; Christy, "Streets of New York," *Kentucky*, pp. 22–23; Bryant, "Odder Side ob Jordan," "New York Times," *Virginia*, pp. 13–14, 41; Charles Fox, *Fox's Ethiopian Comicalities* (New York, 1859), pp. 28–30; Fox, *Sable*, pp. 39–44.

[38] *White's Joke Book*, p. 48; "The Days When This Old Nigger Was Young," *World of Negro Songs*, pp. 74–76; Fox, *Sable*, pp. 37, 39–44.

[39] "Personal in the Herald," *Devere's Burnt Cork*, p. 32; "Divorce," Kelly and Leons Minstrels, *Clipper*, May 4, 1872; "We Never Speak as We Pass By," *Gorton's Original New Orleans Minstrel Songster* (New York, n.d. [1883]), p. 13; "I Do Feel Awfully Loose," *Devere's Burnt Cork*, p. 50; "The Husband's Boot," *Bobby Newcomb's San Francisco Minstrel Songster*, pp. 50–52; "I've Only Been Down to the Club," *Delehanty and Hengler's Song and Dance Book* (New York, 1874), n.p.; "Bobby and His Dear," *Billy Emerson's Nancy Fat Songster* (Washington, D.C., 1880), p. 16.

[40] "Central Park on a Sunday Night," *Christy's Bones*, pp. 44–46; "Out in the Street," *Delehanty and Hengler's*, p. 31; "Poor Old Dad," *Barlow Bros. and Frost's Minstrel Songster* (New York, n.d.[1887]), pp. 22–23.

Social Commentary in White Minstrelsy

⁴¹ "There's Nothing Like It," *Buckley's Ethiopian #4*, pp. 53–55. After 1860, almost every minstrel troupe featured so much material on styles that fashions could be traced through minstrelsy. For examples: "The Style of the Thing," *Gems*, p. 33; "The Shop Gals," *Billy Birch's Ethiopian Melodist* (New York, 1862), pp. 37–38; "Nobody Knows As I Know," *Madame Rentz's Female Minstrel Songster* (New York, 1874), p. 3; "Fearfully and Wonderfully Made," and "Patent Rubber Bustle," *Devere's Burnt Cork*, p. 48; "Nothing to Wear," *Hooley's Opera House Songster* (New York, 1863), pp. 6–7; "A Modern Belle," *World of Negro Song*, pp. 80–81; "The Young Girl of the Period," and "I Wish I'd Been Born a Girl," *Shoofly*, pp. 90–91, 15–17; the latter also in *Thatcher, Primrose, and West's Latest Songster* (New York, n.d. [1885?]), n.p., and *McIntyre and Heath's Scenes in Mississippi Songster* (New York, n.d.[1885]), pp. 32–33.

⁴² "I Wish I Had been Born a Boy," "I Love to be a Swell," *Shoofly*, pp. 18–20, 45; "Curiosity," *Haverly's United*, pp. 35–36; "The Swell at Saratoga," *Devere's Combination*, pp. 46–47; "Captain Jinks of the Horse Marines," *Bryant's Shoofly*, n.p.; "Matinee Brigade," "Sweet Scented Handsome Young Man," *Devere's Burnt Cork*, pp. 15, 34; "Charlie's Curly Hair," *Joe Lang's Old Aunt Jemima Songster*, pp. 35–36; "Modern Fast Young Gentleman," E. B. Christy, *Christy's New Songster and Black Joker* (New York, 1863), pp. 8–9.

⁴³ "Water Cresses," "How the Money Goes," *Christy's Bones*, pp. 53, 63–65; "That's the Kind of Gawk I Am," *Delehanty and Hengler's*, p. 159.

⁴⁴ "Charming Young Widow I Met On the Train," *Bryant's Shoofly*, n.p.; *Christy's Bones*, pp. 66–67.

⁴⁵ "I Really Couldn't Help It," "Jemima Brown," *Billy Emerson's*, pp. 28–30, 37–39; "Old Hats and Rags," "Waiting for the Train," "Under the Gaslight," *Newcomb's San Francisco*, pp. 14–16, 28–29, 61–63; "Soap Fat Man," *Billy Birch's Ethiopian Melodist*, pp. 14–15; "Johnny Stole the Tater Cake," *Ned Turner's*, p. 57; "I Spy Your Little Game," *Christy's Banjo*, pp. 68–69; S. S. Purdy, "The Countryman's Visit," *Paul Pry Songster and Black Joker* (New York, 1865), pp. 11–12.

⁴⁶ Carey, *Brudder Gardner's*, p. 97; "A Dream," *Devere's Combination*, pp. 34–36; "Perished in the Snow," *Haverly's Mastodons*, p. 12; "Down in a Coal Mine," *Joe Lang's*, pp. 66–68; "Little Barefoot," *Ned Turner's*, pp. 13–14; *Bryant's Shoofly*, p. 42.

⁴⁷ For an analysis of the ways diverse Americans attempted to use traditional terms and concepts to cope with the qualitative changes

in their lives, see Robert Wiebe, *The Search For Order* (New York, 1967).

⁴⁸ "Oh, Don't Put the Poor Workingman Down," *Newcomb's Love Letters*, pp. 48–49.

⁴⁹ "Never Too Late to Mend," *ibid.*, p. 59; Delehanty, "Dorkin's Night," *Intrude*, n.p.; "Poor but a Gentleman Still," *Devere's Burnt Cork*, p. 130; "Never Push a Man When He Is Going Down Hill," *Shoofly*, p. 47; "Happy Little Man," *Billy Morris's Songs* (Boston, 1864), pp. 20–22; "It's Not the Miles We Travel," "Pulling Hard Against the Stream," "Where There's a Way," *Shoofly*, pp. 37–38, 54–55, 112; "A Wonderful Wife," *Haverly's Mastodon*, pp. 24–25; "Watermill," *Jay Rial's*, p. 7; "Forget and Forgive," *Gems*, p. 64; "Jonah in de Whale," *Cool Burgess' I'll Be Gay Songster* (New York, n.d.[1880]), p. 50; "The Ballet Girl," *Newcomb's Love Letters*, p. 26; "That's When You Will Know Who's Your Friend," M. H. Foley and C. H. Sheffer, *Big Pound Cake Songster* (New York, 1878), p. 28.

⁵⁰ "My Grandfather," *McIntyre and Heath's*, pp. 30–31; "Grandfather's Cane," *Thatcher, Primrose and West's Latest*, n.p.; "Our Grandfather's Days," *Carncross and Dixey's Minstrel Melodies* (Philadelphia, 1865), 35–36; "One Hundred Years Ago," Bobby Newcomb, *Tambo: His Jokes and Funny Sayings* (New York, n.d. [1882?]), pp. 17–18.

7 Black Men Take the Stage

"A company of real 'cullud pussons' are giving concerts in New Hampshire," the editor of the *Clipper* observed in November 1858, "we do not see why the genuine article should not succeed. Perhaps this is but the starting point for a new era in Ethiopian entertainments." [1] However it was intended, this observation proved prophetic. Although troupes of black minstrels appeared as early as 1855, it was a decade before blacks had established themselves in minstrelsy, their first large-scale entrance into American show business. "The minstrel show at that time was one of the greatest outlets for talented [Negro] musicians and artists," recalled W. C. Handy, who began his own career as a black minstrel in the 1890's. "All the best [black] talent of that generation came down the same drain. The composers, the singers, the musicians, the speakers, the stage performers—the minstrel show got them all." [2]

Emphasizing their authenticity as Negroes and claiming to

195

be ex-slaves, black minstrels became the acknowledged minstrel experts at portraying plantation material. But since they inherited the white-created stereotypes and could make only minor modifications in them, black minstrels in effect added credibility to these images by making it seem that Negroes actually behaved like minstrelsy's black caricatures. This negative aspect of their shows was balanced, perhaps even outweighed, by the fact that black people had their first chance to become entertainers, which not only gave many Negroes a rare opportunity for mobility but also eventually put blacks in a position to modify and then correct these stereotypes.[3] Because black minstrelsy set so many indelible patterns for performers as well as for audiences, for blacks as well as for whites, and because so little is known of these pioneer black entertainers, the history of their struggles to establish themselves as entertainers, managers, and owners demands a careful examination.

Since the colonial period, Negroes had been entertainers, playing and singing music as varied as existed in America. Although most of these performers were slaves who played only locally and were quickly forgotten, Negroes were also active as nonslave professional entertainers. Usually getting only limited exposure, blacks appeared as novelty acts, like "Old Corn Meal" in New Orleans, and as singers of popular songs, like "Picayune Butler"; they wrote, performed, and taught dance band music, like Frank Johnson whose band toured widely in the Northern states in the 1830's and then performed for Queen Victoria during an English tour in 1838; they established a Negro resident theater in New York, which was successful until whites forced it to close and its leading actor, James Hewlitt, to emigrate to England; they composed music, like Richard Milburn who, in 1855, wrote "Listen to the Mockingbird" but did not get credit for it; and they sang and danced in big city saloons, like William Henry "Juba" Lane.[4]

Blacks also performed "serious" music. Called the "Black Swan" and the "African Nightingale" after Jenny Lind, Elizabeth Taylor Greenfield, the most successful of these "classical" performers, made her debut as a soprano in Buffalo, New York, in 1851. She toured the Northern states for three years then traveled to England where her career climaxed in 1854 with a command performance at Buckingham Palace. But after that she had little success in America and retired to teach music. Similarly, the Luca Family—father, mother, and three sons—performed "serious" music throughout the North in the 1850's. In 1853, they performed at a meeting of the Anti-Slavery Society in New York and in the mid-1850's traveled with the Hutchinson Family, famous white antislavery singers. Like most of the other serious black performers, however, their career languished in the late 1850's, and they ceased appearing as a group in 1859. In the crisis years, when minstrels substituted simplified caricatures of happy plantation Negroes for their diverse treatment of slaves, serious black musicians were reduced to local appearances, usually before "Colored Society." Most white Americans were simply unwilling to accept Negroes as creators and performers of cultivated, classical music. The one apparent exception was Thomas Greene Bethune, "Blind Tom," the well-traveled slave whose talent as a pianist was unquestioned. But "Blind Tom" was believed to be an idiot, only able to imitate what he heard. Considered totally lacking in intellect, he was, to audiences, really more a curiosity than an artist, almost like a musically inclined human parrot.[5]

Other than Lane, who starred with white minstrel troupes in 1845 and 1848, after which he emigrated to England, the only black man to play with a white American minstrel company was the dwarf Thomas Dilward, popularly known as "Japanese Tommy." Although he won praise for his violin playing, singing, and dancing, his major attraction was his size, somewhere between twenty-three and thirty-six inches tall. Because he was thought of as a "curious attraction," he could perform with white minstrels when no other black man did. And he played with some of the best. Having begun his minstrel career with George Christy in 1853, perhaps as a counter to Barnum's Tom Thumb, he subsequently played with Dan Bryant's, Woods', Morris Brothers', and Kelly and Leon's Minstrels, as well as with a few black troupes in the 1860's.[6] His career did not, however, signal the opening of minstrelsy to blacks; when that came it was with all-black companies.

Black minstrel troupes began to appear in the mid-1850's: in 1855, one in Philadelphia; in 1857, one touring through Massachusetts and New York and another in Ohio; and in 1858, one in New Hampshire. Although none of these companies survived for long, the one touring New York and Massachusetts, which billed itself as "SEVEN SLAVES just from ALABAMA, who are now EARNING THEIR FREEDOM by giving concerts under the guidance of their Northern friends," anticipated what later became common black minstrel formulas. Realizing that their principal appeal was their authenticity as black men who could perform the "Pure Plantation Melodies and Songs of the Sunny South," they stressed their slave origin in both their advertising and their show. Although they closed their performance with a farce, every other identifiable act was plantation material, including "Root Hog or Die," "The Poor Old Slave," "Darkie's Melody," and "Massa's in the Cold Ground." [7] Both of these elements—the stress on their authenticity as Negroes and slaves and the concentration on plantation subjects— became common in the 1870's when black men established themselves as minstrels.

During the Civil War, black minstrel troupes appeared in

San Francisco in 1862, St. Louis in 1863, and New York, Cincinnati, and Detroit in 1865, but none survived until Brooker and Clayton's Georgia Minstrels, billing themselves as "The Only Simon Pure Negro Troupe in the World," toured successfully throughout the Northeast in 1865–66. Drawing excellent crowds in New England, New Jersey, Pennsylvania, and New York, the Georgia Minstrels established a reputation as first-class minstrels. Reports of their 1865–66 season abounded with assurances that they were excellent performers who drew large, unprecedented audiences.[8] The Northern public, curious about the newly emancipated slaves, flocked to see and learn about them. They had such a great impact that "Georgia Minstrels" thereafter became synonymous with "Colored Minstrels" (whites called themselves Negro or Nigger Minstrels).

As Brooker and Clayton's Georgia Minstrels prospered, reportedly outdrawing *all* other minstrel troupes in March 1866, they faced more and more black competition. In early 1866 "another edition of African rivals" had appeared in Connecticut wearing "the wigs furnished them by nature." In the fall, much more formidable competition emerged when Charles B. Hicks, Brooker and Clayton's original manager, one of its proprietors, and probably one of its performers, began an illustrious career by fielding his own black minstrel troupe. Also, in 1866, a group of ten black minstrels left for a tour of England in a company owned by Sam Hague, a white minstrel dancer from Britain. Hague's Slave Troupe was the forerunner of many white-owned black minstrel companies. Until then, Negroes had evidently owned and run all the black minstrel troupes of the 1860's. But beginning in the early 1870's, whites took over the most successful black troupes and Negroes had to struggle to retain ownership of any companies at all. In 1866, however, the principal importance of the Hague Troupe was that its success in England helped black minstrels establish themselves as entertainers in America, something they devoted considerable attention and ink to in these early years.[9]

Black minstrels tried to legitimize themselves in two ways. In their advertisements, they quoted extensively from favorable reviews stressing that they were at least the equal of whites as minstrels. But realizing that their greatest appeal was their race, they repeatedly stressed that they were "genuine," "real," "bona-fide" Negroes, or as Frank Queen, the editor of the *Clipper*, much less graciously put it, "real nigs." In 1865, Queen sarcastically attacked the very idea of Negroes as entertainers. "Not being so idiotic as Black Tom ["Blind Tom"]," he wrote of a Georgia Minstrel troupe in Detroit, "they are not doing so well as the latter gentleman." [10] Once these troupes became successful and advertised in his paper, however, Queen quickly dropped such denigrating comments. Ironically, even these snide racial slurs helped black minstrels establish their authenticity as Negroes.

To further distinguish themselves from blackfaced whites, most early black minstrels did not use burnt cork, except for the endmen who used it as a comic mask. Perhaps because many whites knew little about Negroes and had mistaken uniformly blackened white minstrels for genuine Afro-Americans, many commentators were astonished that black minstrels actually were of all "hues and complexions from light cream tint down to the darkness visible at Sanford's House [a prominent white minstrel theater]." Callender's Minstrels, another fascinated critic observed, "were mulattoes of a medium shade except two, who were light. . . . The end men were each rendered thoroughly black by burnt cork." In St. Louis, the same performers were perceived to run from light brown to ebony, with several using cork for greater effect. Ten years later, a reviewer still saw fit to remark that the Callender troupe wore no

burnt cork: "the performers had unbleachable complexions." [11]
These and other comments by reviewers stressed that black
minstrels were not uniformly painted imitations; they were the
real thing.

To further pique public curiosity, black minstrels also emphasized their links to the plantation. Brooker and Clayton
boasted that their "Simon Pure Negro" company was "composed of men who during the war were SLAVES IN MACON,
GEORGIA, who, having spent their former life in Bondage . . .
will introduce to their patrons PLANTATION LIFE in all its
phases." Using the same approach, Charles Hicks billed his early
companies: the "Slave Troupe," the "Georgia Slave Brothers,"
and the "Georgia Slave Troupe Minstrels." Many of their patrons doubtless went to see black minstrels for the same reason
as the New York journalist who had a "natural curiosity to see
the original plantation dances, and hear the genuine African
melodies rendered by those who but a short time ago were
deprived of almost all other pastimes." Being "genuine plantation darkies from the South," the Troy, New York *Whig* observed of Brooker and Clayton's troupe, they were "great delineators of genuine darky life in the South, introducing peculiar
music and characteristics of plantation life." [12] Endlessly using
the terms "novelty," "curiosity," "genuine," and "bonafide," reviewers grasped for words to express the unique appeal of these
"authentic" ex-slaves.

Because the notion that blacks were inherently musical was
already deeply embedded in the public's images of Negroes and
because these performers stressed their authenticity, they were
thought of as natural, spontaneous people on exhibit rather
than as professional entertainers. "Being genuine Negroes," one
reviewer succinctly observed in 1865, "they indulge in reality."
Again and again, critics noted that black minstrelsy was not a
show; it was a display of natural impulses, "the music of nature

untrammeled by art or any degree of affectation." "They un-
questionably have the air of doing it for love rather than
money," a New York writer felt.[13] Throughout the country,
regardless of the troupe, and over a span of twenty-five years,
black minstrels were consistently described as "natural" and
"spontaneous" representatives of plantation Negroes. Because
many whites perceived black minstrels as simply being themselves on stage, without artifice, cultivation, or control, black
minstrels' performances greatly enhanced the credibility of
minstrel images of Negroes.

As a result of black minstrels being viewed as authentic
plantation Negroes, many white critics questioned the white
minstrels' qualification to perform Negro, especially plantation,
material. Black minstrels demonstrated to a St. Louis writer
that "there is nothing like the natural thing, and that a negro
can play negro's peculiarities much more satisfactorally than
the white 'artist' who with burnt cork is *at best a base imitator*."
White critics throughout the nation, over decades, echoed the
same opinions. A St. Paul, Minnesota, writer felt that "the efforts of white men in [the] same entertainment must pale before
the genuine fellows, who are naturally negro minstrels." And in
New York in 1880, the *Clipper*, in an unusually strong state-
ment, argued that Haverly's Colored Minstrels depicted plantation life "with greater fidelity than any 'poor white trash' with
corked faces can ever do." [14] Such opinions were one of the
major reasons white minstrels sharply decreased the plantation
material in their shows and moved toward variety. But for the
same reasons, black minstrels found the range of their material
severely limited. "The success of the troupe," a Louisville writer
observed of a black minstrel company, "goes to disprove the
saying that a negro cannot act the nigger." [15] "Acting the
nigger" was precisely what whites expected blacks to do.

Black minstrelsy matured in the 1870's. By early in the decade, several companies regularly toured, primarily in the East

and Midwest; Charles Hicks took a company to Germany; and Hicks and Bob Height, a comedian later compared to Bert Williams, starred with Sam Hague's integrated minstrel troupe in England. Most important of all, shortly after this troupe returned to America in 1872, Charles Callender, a white tavern owner, purchased it and began turning black minstrelsy into big business. With Hicks serving as business manager and Bob Height, Billy Kersands, and Pete Devonear starring as comedians, Callender had the best black minstrel troupe. Extensively advertised and promoted, they toured through the Northeast and Midwest, drawing large crowds and laudatory reviews. As a result of the troupe's talents and of Callender's advertising, the company made such a great impression that "Callender's" joined "Georgia" and "Colored" as words identifying black troupes.[16]

Soon after Callender bought the company, several of the black minstrel stars, including the troupe's best comedians, Billy Kersands and Bob Height, and its finest banjo player, Horace Weston, demanded the money and respect they felt they deserved. When Callender refused, they left to form the nucleus of a rival company. Outraged over Callender's charge that they had been "stolen" from him, as if they were property and/or incapable of planning their own actions, the performers emphatically asserted their independence.

> We are all men under no obligation to anyone, and looking for our best interest in the elevation and maintenance of ourselves and families. We are not blind or insensible to our worth, and honorably proceeded to negotiate for better positions which we have accomplished from our present manager, Mr. Charles White.

Although such shifts in personnel were common in minstrelsy, they almost never prompted public debate. These complaints by blacks against the first white owner of a successful black troupe had racial overtones as well as a firm economic base. Although most of the performers rejoined Callender, evidently after the new troupe collapsed, Bob Height, who was clearly heading for stardom, turned his back on Callender and America by emigrating to Europe.[17]

Despite at least twenty-seven black competitors, the Callender company retained its supremacy during the mid-1870's.[18] Business was so good in late 1874 and early 1875 that Callender formed a second troupe which toured in the Midwest while his major troupe was in the East. As their fame spread, a number of imitators tried to capitalize on the Callender name just as minstrels did with the famous white troupes, and Callender exerted his influence to get the *Clipper* to refuse to mention them. Once a troupe had won this much recognition, it was also much easier for it to enhance its position. Daniel Frohman recalled that, when he was Callender's advance man in 1875, he often competed with his brother Charles, an advance man for a "high-class" comedy show. Although Daniel could always get the advances and credit he needed, Charles could not, because local business men knew how well the black minstrels drew but were skeptical about "dramatic shows." By 1877, the Callender troupe had gained enough stature to be the only black minstrel troupe named on a list of the leading American minstrel companies.[19]

In 1877, a bad year for all minstrels, even the Callender company suffered. In May, they were reportedly "dodging circuses" and "bothered about making their routes ahead." Later that year, they were back to a typical route for a major minstrel company, white or black. They toured through Massachusetts, Rhode Island, New Jersey, Delaware, Pennsylvania, and then headed south to Richmond, Savannah, Charleston, Macon, Atlanta, Montgomery, New Orleans, Houston, and Austin. Early the next year, they played in Chicago, Boston, Brooklyn,

205

Washington, D.C., Baltimore, and towns in between. Perhaps because attendance on this tour was only "fair," Callender, in June 1878, sold the Georgia Minstrels to J. H. Haverly.

Haverly promoted his black minstrels with the same theatrical flair that he had used with his white troupes. He increased the size of the company to as many as one hundred, added new features, and flamboyantly advertised the shows. But most importantly, at the same time that his white troupes were moving away from portraying Southern Negroes, Haverly completely focused his black minstrel shows on plantation material. There was no clearer indication of the differing appeals of white and black minstrels. Instead of the silver and gold Turkish palace that his white minstrels offered, the Haverly Colored Minstrels featured: "THE DARKY AS HE IS AT HOME, DARKY LIFE IN THE CORNFIELD, CANEBRAKE, BARNYARD, AND ON THE LEVEE AND FLATBOAT." [20] At times, Haverly even broke from the traditional opening semicircle and substituted "Southern settings" with the performers spread around the stage in what seemed realistic scenes. In an open field near a Boston theater, he created an entire plantation scene, complete with "overseers, bloodhounds, and darkies at work." It featured over one hundred Negroes appropriately costumed, "indulging in songs, dances [and] antics peculiar to their people." [21]

With its "realistic" portrayal of what whites thought plantations were like, the Haverly Colored Minstrels seemed a departure from the old-style minstrel show. "There is no attempt to burlesque this or that," a Baltimore writer observed, "but what its performers try to do, and succeed in wonderfully, is to give a true idea of the ante-bellum plantation life with a striking realism and wonderful excellence." The troupe's strength, others felt, was the "wholesome and hearty simplicity" of these "genuine sons of Africa." But, as always, no one could express Haverly's message as well as he himself could. He warned the public not to compare his refined white Mastodons to his Colored Minstrels. "The efforts of these much-abused and uneducated sons and daughters of Ethiopia are but the spontaneous outbursts of nature's gifts . . . presented to show what the negroes do, and how they do it, at home on the old plantation." They were, he continued, "natural children of bondage" whose renditions of plantation material were "truthful to nature." [22] In short, Haverly presented the black minstrels not as entertainers but as representatives of the plantation Negro put on exhibit—like animals in a zoo.

The Haverly Colored Minstrels crisscrossed the nation along the same routes that Callender and so many others used. Regardless of where they played, they drew turn-away crowds in both blistering heat and pouring rain. The combination of Haverly's name, his talents for advertising and for mounting productions, and the appeal of the best of the black minstrels portraying the romanticized plantation proved irresistible. After years of success, the high point for the Colored Minstrels came in the summer of 1881, when they followed the Mastodons to England for a triumphant year's tour.

While the Haverly troupe prospered in England, Gustave and Charles Frohman, ex-advance men turned theatrical producers, purchased Callender's new troupe and made plans for the most lavish black minstrel company yet. The new troupe, which retained Callender's name, "naturally" concentrated on "THE ONLY LEGITIMATE PLANTATION MINSTRELSY OF AMERICA—IN ITS PURE NATIVE FORM." Going Haverly even one better, the company promised to use real logs, tree stumps, moss, and a cypress tree to add realism to the plantation opening. Everything about the new company was grand. Each member of the troupe got a light spring overcoat, a black suit, two band suits, and rubber overcoats and boots, each of the garments monogrammed with "C.M." To house them on their tours, they had

10. This poster typifies black minstrelsy's presentation of the plantation as the scene of carefree partying. *Callender's Colored Minstrels, n.p., n.d. [post-1875], Theatre Collection, the New York Public Library at Lincoln Center. Astor, Lenox and Tilden Foundations.*

11. The Old Uncle and Auntie dominated post-Civil War images of the plantation. But even in this happy scene, including the frolicking boy playing the bones, the major characters have animalistic "fangs".

Closeup of # 10.

a "magnificent drawingroom, sleeping and eating car for the exclusive use of the company." Besides "the significant title 'Africa'" painted on the side, the "traveling palace" had a musical stand and seats on the roof so the troupe could perform as the train pulled into each town.[23] Black minstrelsy had clearly become big business.

In contrast to the sophistication of the production, the performers were presented as crude plantation types. In early March, the *Clipper* devoted a full page to an "interview" with one of the black performers in the Callender troupe that was probably just a promotional gimmick for the new company. In an exaggerated minstrel dialect, the heavily caricatured subject of the "interview" tried to prove he was a "rale black Efiopian" by telling of his "foredaddy in Africa" living on a plantation of coconut trees and bananas surrounded by snakes and monkeys and eating all the prisoners he captured. After being caught, he was sent to Louisiana to the "good old plantation," that the Callender troupe would recreate in "de naturallist" show anyone had ever seen. "De darky will be hisself once more and forget that he eber had any trouble," he boasted. The plantation scenes would be so realistic and so happy that old planters from Mississippi would cry for those bygone days, and Northern white men would wish the Almighty had painted them "brack as dese brack fellers up dere dat am making all dis music" and having all that carefree fun.[24] However ludicrous these words now seem this alleged interview with an "authentic darky," who looked forward only to delighting whites with a recreation of carefree plantation days, further indicates how the presence of blacks as minstrels seemed to legitimize these plantation caricatures.

With the news that they had purchased Haverly's Colored Minstrels from a badly overextended Haverly and would merge them with Callender's, the Frohmans' already grand black minstrel production became truly spectacular. In the summer of 1882, when Haverly's troupe landed in New York, Callender's was playing to turn-away crowds in San Francisco, setting up their well-advertised "15,000 mile wedding march" to the "Great Marriage of Minstrelsy." Legitimately ballyhooed as "THE PICK OF THE EARTH'S COLORED TALENT," Callender's Consolidated Colored Minstrels completely overshadowed all other black minstrels. In late 1882, Callender blanketed the country by dividing his troupe into three separate companies. The major one, which retained most of the stars, played in the large cities of the Northeast, the second played smaller towns and cities in the Midwest as the third troupe toured the South.[25]

In the summer and fall of 1883, the Callender troupe indicated its drawing power by virtually monopolizing entertainment in San Francisco, usually a highly competitive market. While other entertainers were failing, they drew so well that Callender sent a second troupe out to surrounding towns and reportedly even offered Billy Emerson, a white San Francisco minstrel idol, an engagement with the black minstrels. Emerson, of course, refused, but the troupe continued to prosper and to add new attractions, including the celebrated Hyer Sisters, Emma and Anna, who had toured with their own Negro Operatic and Dramatic company performing serious plays based on black history. Although they were considered "respectable and refined," the Hyer Sisters, like Alexander Luca of the antebellum singing family, found that minstrelsy provided one of the few consistent salaried outlets for black musical talent. While they were able to star in a production of *Uncle Tom's Cabin* that Callender staged in the San Francisco Opera House, they also had to perform in the regular minstrel show. Emma Hyer and the troupe's band leader were even married on stage before a standing-room-only audience.[26] Nothing about blacks was too personal to be a part of a theater exhibition.

The Callender company continued touring in the 1880's, and Callender himself owned black minstrel companies into the 1890's. After he left the profession, a number of other white theatrical entrepreneurs fielded black minstrel troupes following the Callender-Haverly formula of plantation material, lavish productions, and extensive promotions. These white-owned and -structured shows had the greatest exposure, made the most money, and focused audience expectations on stereotyped images of Negroes. Most of all, they illustrated that when blacks became marketable as entertainers, it was white men who reaped the profits.

Although white-owned companies got the best bookings and dominated black minstrelsy in most ways, a number of black men clearly demonstrated their desire and ability to run their own companies. They simply could not match their white adversaries in influence and capital. The contrasting careers of two of the most successful black owners reveal the range of their experiences and the constant struggle they had to wage to maintain their own companies.

Lew Johnson owned black minstrel troupes for more than twenty-five years after the mid-1860's, primarily because he was tenacious and usually kept his companies away from competition. Marginal in every way, his troupes were small, ranging from six to twenty, with an average of about twelve. They played an endless series of one-nighters in places like Clinton, Iowa; Chippewa Falls, Wisconsin; Duluth, Rochester, and St. Charles, Minnesota; and in many other little towns in the Midwest and West. In 1882, Johnson boasted that his was the first "Colored Minstrel Troupe" to play in the Wyoming, Utah, Idaho, and Montana territories. His companies rarely played in big cities. When he tried to invade the lucrative, but highly competitive, Eastern market in 1886, Johnson found disaster and quickly retreated to the West where he could make good money playing in entertainment-starved areas. Hoping to appeal to current fads, he frequently changed his troupes' names. In 1870, they were Lew Johnson's Plantation Minstrels; in 1875, the Plantation Minstrel Slave Troupe; in 1877, Lew Johnson's Original Tennessee Jubilee Singers; in 1881, simply Lew Johnson's Combination; in 1886, The Black Baby Boy Minstrels, and in 1890, the Refined Colored Minstrels and Electric Brass Band. Through it all, Johnson maintained his ownership of a black minstrel troupe only by remaining in marginal areas where he challenged no one. Forced into rough frontier areas where prejudice and discrimination must have been direct and immediate, mere survival, professional and personal, was a great success.[27]

In contrast to Johnson's marginality, Charles Hicks was at the center of black minstrel action from the beginning. Instrumental in forming the first successful black troupe, Brooker and Clayton's Georgia Minstrels, Hicks ultimately was associated with almost every major black minstrel troupe. Although he was a versatile performer, proficient as a singer, endman, and interlocutor, his intense drive to own his own companies and to make them major attractions was the most fascinating aspect of his career. To do this, he fought anyone who stood in his way, white or black. "This man Hicks," Ike Simond, himself a black minstrel, observed with respect, "was a dangerous man to all outside managers and they all were afraid of him." [28] No other black minstrel and few other black men were so dreaded as business competitors by important white men. And Hicks deserved his reputation.

Between 1866 and 1870 Hicks organized several short-lived troupes of his own. Then, in 1870, he led the first black minstrel troupe to Germany. From there, he went to England to star with Sam Hague's integrated troupe. Besides proving himself as a performer, manager, and owner, he also showed that he was an expert at getting his name in the newspaper. While in England, he wrote letters to the *Clipper* reporting the general entertainment news, with his own exploits always the main feature. After returning from Europe, he managed Callender's Georgia Minstrels, tried to field his own African Minstrels and Georgia Minstrels, and then managed Sprague and Blodgett's Georgia Minstrels.[29] So far, he was neither content to work for others nor able to sustain his own company.

In 1877 he engineered his most spectacular and successful black minstrel venture. In the summer of 1876, J. H. Haverly and Tom Maguire, a successful white San Francisco minstrel promoter, had fielded a black minstrel company in Nevada. Two months later, Hicks had persuaded the black performers to leave the white owners and work for him. Within a month, Hicks's Georgia Minstrels sailed for Australia, safely out of reach of either Haverly or Maguire's influence. During their three years there, Hicks again wrote "reviews" for the *Clipper* boasting of his company's great successes, but he was not content with that. "NOW ON A GRAND TOUR OF THE ENTIRE WORLD— Java, China, Japan, through Suez to England, Ireland, Wales, Scotland, to our Dear Home," boomed an 1878 ad almost an entire page long. Never one to understate his troupe's achievements, Hicks claimed that the company had "visited every city, town, and village in the United States and Canada" before beginning its Australian tour. "THE HEROES OF MONTREAL, SARATOGA, CHICAGO, SAN FRANCISCO AND NOW AUSTRALIA STILL LIVE!" his advertisement concluded with a fine dramatic flair, "PIRATES BEWARE! WE ARE STILL ON THE WAR PATH." Like Haverly, Hicks understood the value of advertising and knew how to write eye-catching copy. He was so expert at getting press notices that he was the only Negro among the 103 men whom M. B. Leavitt in 1912 considered the "best known advance agents during the last fifty years." [30]

"MISSING MAN TURNS UP HOME AGAIN," Hicks advertised upon his return in July 1880. At the same time, he optimistically announced the formation of a new black minstrel company that would sail for Europe that August. But the troupe never materialized and Hicks returned to managing for and playing with others.[31] Sometime in late 1881 or early 1882, while Callender's troupe was doing poor business in western New York, Hicks "took it into his head to take a fly at management." Again dreaming of glory, he persuaded the performers to "rise in mutiny." Forced to withdraw, Callender fled to Chicago where Gustave and Charles Frohman agreed to finance his company as part of their plan to form a mammoth black minstrel troupe. After finalizing the arrangements, Charles Frohman dispatched one of his theatrical managers, Frank Bixby, to get the company back from Hicks. Bixby vigorously attacked his "delicate and difficult" mission, the *Clipper* account reported, and "with the assistance of the various means placed at his disposal," he persuaded the entire company, except Hicks and his partner, Charles Crusoe, to rejoin Callender.[32]

Even Charles Hicks lacked the power to resist the Frohmans. Having defied one of the leading white minstrel owners and persuaded the black minstrels to join him, Hicks could not counteract "the various means" Bixby wielded for the Frohmans. Doubtless Bixby offered the black minstrels more money, but he may also have threatened to "blacklist" them. A year later, in February 1883, when A. D. Sawyer and Tom McIntosh, both black minstrels, tried to field their own black minstrel troupe, they found it impossible to get bookings even though McIntosh was second only to Billy Kersands as a comedian. "Not withstanding the cards issued by the monopoly management," they pleaded for a "fair trial upon their merits." "NO SUCCESS, NO PAY," they begged. But despite their appeals against an evident booking ban and despite Hicks having joined them as business manager, the troupe disappeared.[33] Bixby, then, might well have confronted the bolted black performers with never being able to work for anyone but Hicks. In any case, in the showdown, powerful white men with capital and influence triumphed over a black man with great flair and ambition.

When the most famous black minstrel star, Billy Kersands, emerged with his own company in 1885, Hicks was its manager. But, as usually happened, within little more than a year, Hicks left to form his own company, this time with A. D. Sawyer, another ambitious black man, as his partner. Again in about a year, Hicks and Sawyer each led rival companies using the same name. At that time, Hicks must have been at one of the lowest points of his career, because he solicited bookings for "dime museums, string shows, or two shows a day." [34] Reverting to the scene of his greatest triumphs, he took his black minstrel company to Australia and New Zealand. Like Johnson, Hicks could succeed only in marginal areas that whites did not covet and control. In a fittingly exotic ending to his colorful and dynamic career, Charles Hicks died in 1902 in Suraboya, Java, while touring with a black minstrel company—doubtless searching for larger audiences and greater glory.[35]

Although black men had to struggle against great odds to own their own companies, black performers inevitably became big stars. The highest paid black minstrel was Kersands, whose fame was based on the comic contortions of his gigantic mouth. Besides such "feats" as dancing with a cup and saucer or several billiard balls in his mouth, he acted out the caricatured role of the ignorant, slow-witted black man. But many other celebrated black minstrel stars did not perform such heavily stereotyped roles. The second highest paid performer with the famous 1882 Callender troupe, Wallace King, was a "Sweet Singing Tenor" noted for his moving renditions of romantic ballads. James and George Bohee and Horace Weston won renown in both England and America as banjo virtuosos. The S. S. Stewart Banjo company even used Weston to endorse its product in a tasteful ad, complete with a dignified photograph of him in formal wear.[36] Black minstrels also won plaudits for "refined" dancing and for song writing. In fact, although within a heavily stereotyped framework, black minstrels clearly demonstrated the diverse talents of black people. In the nineteenth century, minstrelsy was their only chance to make a regular living as entertainers, musicians, actors, or composers.

Although many black minstrels wrote and published songs, James Bland was the most prolific, famous, and influential black minstrel songwriter. Composer of "Carry Me Back to Old Virginny," "In the Evening by the Moonlight," "Dem Golden Slippers," and as many as seven hundred other songs, Bland was also a very popular entertainer. He grew up in Flushing, New York, and Washington, D.C., where his father was a government appointee during Reconstruction. After seeing George Primrose perform in 1874, he decided to become a minstrel. In 1875, he starred in and stage-managed the Original Black Diamonds in Boston. That same year, he published his first songs, "Morning by the Bright Light" and "Carry Me Back to Old Virginny." [37] As a singer, composer, and "refined comedian," Bland quickly rose to stardom, a position he enjoyed for at least fifteen years. After playing with the Bohee Brothers Minstrels in 1876, he was "the Hit" of Sprague's Georgia Minstrels, a troupe that included Billy Kersands and Sam Lucas, two of the greatest black minstrels. In 1880, he joined the Haverly Colored Minstrels and continued his rise to stardom and his outpouring of minstrel songs, which both black and white minstrels used extensively. When the Haverly Colored Minstrels left England in 1882, Bland remained there. He starred with his own troupes and in others, toured widely in

Europe, became the "idol of the Music Halls" in England and a great favorite in Germany, and reportedly earned as much as $10,000 a year, an astronomical minstrel salary. After refusing Charles Hicks's efforts to get him to join Kersands' Minstrels, he returned in 1890 to star with W. C. Cleveland's Colored Minstrel Carnival, one of the successors to Callender. Without doubt, he had proved the black man's talent for songwriting, probably making the way easier for his black successors. But tied to minstrelsy as he was, he played no role in the evolution to Negro musicals. After the 1890's, his career plummeted until his pauper's death in 1911 in Philadelphia.[38]

The career of Sam Lucas revealed the frustrating limits that talented black entertainers faced in the nineteenth century. The son of Ohio free Negroes, he began to travel as a minstrel in 1869 at the age of nineteen. By 1873, Lucas starred as a singer, composer, and character actor specializing in comedy-pathos roles. Throughout his career he continually sought "serious" non-minstrel parts that could diversify the images of the stage Negro, but until the 1890's he had to fall back on minstrelsy to support himself. In 1875, he costarred with the Hyer Sisters in their musical drama *Out of Bondage*, which told the story of the freedman from slavery to his "attainment of education and refinement." But after that show closed he returned to minstrelsy. Later, he rejoined the Hyer Sisters for their production of *The Underground Railroad* but again had to return to minstrelsy.[39]

With the Hyer productions to his credit, Lucas, in 1878, became the first black man to play the title role in a serious production of *Uncle Tom's Cabin*. To save one of their faltering comedy companies, the Frohmans decided to stage the old standby *Uncle Tom* with the added enticement of a black man playing the leading role. "Get me an Eva and send her down with Sam Lucas," Gustave Frohman wired his brother Charles.

"Be sure to tell Sam to bring his diamonds." The Frohmans recognized the value of Lucas's talents as a drawing card and of his diamonds as a financial reserve. After the troupe drew poorly in Richmond, Virginia, the Frohmans sent it to Lucas's home territory in Ohio where they hoped attendance would improve. But the woman playing Little Eva was so fat that when she sat on St. Clair's lap, she not only hid him from view, but also "almost prostrated him." Predictably, the tour ended with Lucas pawning his diamonds to get the company back to Cincinnati.[40]

After this ill-fated venture, Lucas sporadically appeared in minstrelsy until he performed in the shows that transformed black minstrelsy into Negro musicals. In 1890, he played in Sam T. Jack's Creole Show, a production still structured like a minstrel show but the first step to the musical comedies of Bob Cole and J. Rosamund Johnson, Will Marion Cook, Bert Williams and George Walker, and Ernest Hogan. After that, he and his wife toured museums, variety, and vaudeville houses around the country. In 1898–99, when blacks wrote, organized, and produced the first Negro musical to make a complete break with minstrelsy, *A Trip to Coontown*, Lucas was in it. He later played in Cole and Johnson's *Shoo Fly Regiment* and *Red Moon* and on the Lowe vaudeville circuit. Finally, in 1915, as a fitting climax to his career, he was the first black man to star in a film of *Uncle Tom's Cabin*. During the filming he took ill, reportedly from diving into the water to rescue Eva. Although he completed the picture, he died in January 1916. With the long list of firsts in his lengthy, path-breaking career, he certainly deserved the title of "The Grand Old Man of the Negro Stage" that James Weldon Johnson bestowed on him.[41]

The story of black minstrels was much more than the history of troupes, the struggle for ownership, and the careers of stars. It was also the story of thousands of black people who seized the chance to become minstrels but never became stars, and of thousands of others who cheered for them. Unfortunately, woefully little is known about the average black minstrel. It is even uncertain how many there were. Although the 1890 census listed 1,490 blacks as entertainers, more than that must have performed on occasion in the many local troupes and shows. Furthermore, there must have been many who did not support themselves as entertainers but performed when they could get work. Even Sam Lucas, for example, continued to work as a barber while becoming a star. In 1894, when a New York promoter advertised for forty black minstrels, an estimated 2,000 Negroes appeared at his office and 1,012 left their names.[42] But even more important than the lack of information about numbers, there is little biographical data about black minstrels. What there is suggests that they came from all over the country, not primarily the South, and that they were not usually ex-slaves. Some, like Horace Weston, James Bland, and W. C. Handy, were from middle-class homes; others, like Sam Lucas and Tom Fletcher, came from relatively poor farm families. But most are simply of unknown origins—probably typical of the thousands of black people who traveled widely after the Civil War searching for a better life.

Black minstrels had to face all the hazards that nineteenth-century traveling entertainers encountered. They had to play endless series of one-nighters, travel on accident-prone railroads, live in poor housing subject to fires, play in empty rooms that they had to convert into theaters, face arrest on trumped up charges, be exposed to deadly diseases, and endure managers and agents who skipped out with all the troupe's money. On top of all this, black minstrels suffered the painful wounds of racial discrimination in virtually every facet of their lives.

From the outset, black minstrels had great difficulty simply finding food and lodging. Harry Davis, manager of the

Georgia Minstrels in 1865–66, recalled that his greatest problem was feeding and housing his troupe. Although people gladly paid to see them perform, he complained, few were willing to board them. As an example, he cited a discussion he had had with a Maine hotel manager who told him that he believed in the equality of the races. Davis gleefully replied that he had been looking for a landlord with those views for months because he was the agent for the Georgia Minstrels, "genuine negroes," and he usually could not find people to house them. "What," the outraged hotel man screamed, "I keep fourteen black, dirty, greasy niggers? No Sir!" Black minstrels faced such discrimination not because they were minstrels, but because they were Negroes. Between 1871 and 1873, for example the Fisk Jubilee Singers, who were serious, "refined" Negro performers of religious music, were refused housing in Illinois, Connecticut, Ohio, and New Jersey. In Newark, New Jersey, a tavern keeper had booked them in advance, thinking they were a "company of nigger minstrels," by which he meant white minstrels. Even though he did not discover that they were real Negroes until they were settled in their rooms, he still ordered them to leave. Since such problems continually plagued black minstrels, the construction of private railroad cars for them was more a matter of convenience and necessity than a display of opulence. In addition to providing a place to stay, the cars also carried stocks of food and had secret compartments to hide performers who had offended local whites.[43]

Black minstrels experienced the widest possible range of discrimination, from "trivial" to deadly. Tom Fletcher and a number of his fellow black minstrels believed that railroad engineers intentionally jerked the trains early in the mornings to spill the minstrels' coffee, so they bought oilcloth aprons to wear while eating breakfast. Unfortunately, traveling black entertainers had to endure much more than spilled coffee. It was often a matter of survival. When one of the black minstrels in W. C. Handy's troupe contracted smallpox in the 1890's, the entire company was literally corraled outside of the nearest Texas town. They not only were threatened with lynching if they left the compound but were also denied treatment even when the disease spread throughout the company. "County officers came a short while later to inform us that the appearance of only one more case of smallpox among us," Handy recalled, "would be the signal for them to burn the car and carry out the doctor's lynching threat." Denied food, water, and sanitation facilities, they survived only because their train carried water and food reserves in case of just such "emergencies." Finally, under cover of a diversionary show, the troupe smuggled the fourteen sick men out in women's clothing so they could escape from Texas to some place "where the benefits of a hospital might be enjoyed." [44]

Being denied their basic needs and regularly insulted and threatened with things like the "Nigger Read and Run" signs they saw throughout the South were everyday experiences for black minstrels. So was violence. The residents of one Texas town, for example, got their target practice riddling black minstrels' railroad cars with bullets whenever they passed through. During a parade in another Texas town, local "cowboys" lassoed Handy's company while young rowdies bombarded them with rocks. Although incensed, Handy, who realized the frustrating restrictions on blacks' actions, could think of no more satisfying response that to "stoutly" refuse to play a note during the parade. Blacks' fear of being lynched if they fought back was soundly based on reality. After Handy once physically prevented a white man from killing a black minstrel, a lynch mob came after him, and he escaped only by using the railroad car's secret compartment. Defiant blacks were not always that lucky. When a fiercely proud black minstrel, Louis Wright, and his lady friend were snowballed by whites in Missouri, he "retaliated" by cursing at them. With only this "provocation," an angry crowd, threatening to lynch him, invaded the theater. Although he dispersed them by firing his gun at them, later that night a mob surrounded the minstrel railroad car and demanded that Wright give himself up. When he refused, authorities arrested the entire company, several members of which were beaten to force them to identify him. None did, but a member of the crowd recognized Wright, and he was taken into custody. In the middle of the night, the sheriff "released" him to the crowd, which lynched him, cut out his tongue, and shipped his mutilated body to his mother in Chicago.[45] How often such incidents occurred is unknown to us, but they were certainly known to black minstrels. If more of these traveling black entertainers had left personal reminiscences, there doubtless would be much more evidence of such discrimination.

Despite these difficulties, literally thousands of blacks leapt at the chance to become minstrels. Why? First of all, many blacks entered minstrelsy for the same reasons that whites did. There were very few places that minstrelsy did not reach, and especially in small towns minstrels must have seemed dashing figures. After they saw the Georgia Minstrels, many a black boy no doubt practiced strutting as W. C. Handy did in Florence, Alabama. Similarly, whenever a minstrel troupe, white or black, entered Portsmouth, Ohio, Tom Fletcher cut school to carry their banner. Many blacks who were musically inclined must have realized that minstrelsy was the career for them, as James Bland did after seeing his first minstrel show.[46]

But blacks had other reasons. Like W. C. Handy, a number of Negroes must have gotten "a glimpse of another world" and realized that minstrelsy was one of the few ways they could reach it. Minstrelsy, after all, involved Afro-American culture. At the shows, Negroes saw either black people or blackfaced whites doing things that many members of the audience could do. One need not share minstrelsy's stereotype that all blacks were musical to agree with Tom Fletcher that for many blacks "singing and dancing was the way in which they had amused themselves for years." [47] Minstrelsy was one of the few opportunities for mobility—geographic, social, and economic—open to nineteenth-century Negroes. Although the discrimination they suffered made black minstrels much worse off than white minstrels, they were not substantially worse off in that regard than most other blacks, except that they exposed themselves to it more often by traveling into areas where they were not wanted and were more likely to be "reminded" of their places because they were in positions to "be somebody." But at a time when most blacks were moving from slavery to serfdom, a chance to "be somebody" must have seemed worth some extra risks.

Financially, black minstrels seem to have fared worse than whites, but they were in a better position than most Negroes. In 1882, black minstrels reportedly made "pretty good salaries," and the salary list for Callender's Minstrels may have equaled that of first-rate white companies. But this was the *total* payroll when the Callender troupe of one hundred was much larger than white troupes of the day. Furthermore, blacks were in great demand in 1882. Over one-half of all the "Colored Entertainer Wanted" ads found in the *Clipper* between 1865 and 1890 appeared between 1880 and 1884. One advertiser even stated: "NON-COLORED PERFORMERS NEED NOT APPLY." Thus, wages for blacks were probably abnormally high in 1882. The highest paid black man, Billy Kersands, whose salary reportedly jumped from $15 a week in 1879 to $80 a week in 1882, was on a par with the $75 to $100 a week that white minstrel stars earned. But the blacks' salaries dropped off much quicker than the whites'. The white troupes had a number of highly paid

THE ORIGINAL AND ONLY

COLORED MINSTREL TROUPE.

These are a well-dressed group of four automaton figures, which on being wound up go through a variety of entertaining life-like movements, in imitation of playing the Banjo, Bones, Tambourine etc., while the old lady fans herself vigorously and smiles approval to effect is irresi... comical.

...CE $4 50 EACH.

...ROME B. SECOR, BRIDGEPORT, CONN.

performers, but Callender's next highest salary, $60, went to tenor Wallace King, and most of the "other people" made $10 to $35 a week at this high point of black minstrelsy. In 1896, W. C. Handy, starting out as a musician with Mahara's Minstrels, got $6 a week and "cakes," room and board. Even though salaries were modest, they always included room, board, and travel which was more than most blacks had. Tom Fletcher's assessment of the financial benefits of his own and other black minstrels' careers was probably accurate.

> It was a big break when show business started [for blacks].
> . . . Salaries were not large, but they still amounted to
> much more than they were getting [before joining], and
> there was the added advantage of opportunity to travel with
> the company taking care of them.[48]

Whatever their salaries, black minstrels, like their white colleagues, dressed like important people. "I bought smart outfits," W. C. Handy reminisced, "one being a suit, hat, watch fob, umbrella strap and spats all cut from the same bolt of rich brown cloth." James Bland cleverly got his large wardrobe in exchange for free plugs he gave tailors from the stage. A number of black minstrels, like their white counterparts, also invested in diamonds. In 1890, Bland reportedly purchased "the largest diamond ever worn, probably, by a colored performer, its weight being 4¾ carats." Others received eye-catching gifts from their fans. Sam Lucas, for example, got a gold-handled cane in Cincinnati in 1873 and a gold medal and other gifts from fans in Columbus, Ohio, in 1879 and St. Louis in 1886.[49]

12. Besides indicating black minstrels' popularity, this advertisement for windup toys symbolizes the way black minstrels were controlled and manipulated by and for whites.

Advertisement, Bridgeport, Conn., n.d., clipping, Harvard Theatre Collection.

Black minstrels relied on their audiences for much more
than presents. Although black minstrels must have been proud
of the praise they won from white critics and performers, their
greatest source of status and gratification probably came from
their black fans. It was not only black children that looked up
to the well-dressed, swaggering performers who paraded
grandly through town and set everyone buzzing. When Tom
Fletcher entered minstrelsy, his father told him that he would
never be good enough to win a place in a show with Sam
Lucas, who was his father's idol. Furthermore, black minstrels
turned to black communities when they needed places to stay
and people to talk with. Like other traveling entertainers, they
must have delighted in boasting about having seen distant cities
like New York, New Orleans, San Francisco, or even London,
Edinburgh, or Sydney, and of having played for huge
crowds—even for the British Royal Family. Of great importance to these transient men, it was in the black community
that they found star-struck, pretty young women. As Handy
simply put it, "and did we flirt." In short, it was in the black
communities that they could enjoy all the advantages of being
somebody.[50]

From the beginning, black minstrels drew large numbers of
Negroes to their shows. In 1869, Hicks and Height's Georgia
Minstrels reportedly were very popular in Washington, D.C.,
"particularly among the colored people, as the entertainments
were liberally patronized by this class." Two years later in
Pittsburgh, "the colored element of the city turned out en
masse" to see Hicks's Georgia Slave Troupe. In December
1873, Callender's Minstrels enjoyed a good house in New
Orleans, "largely composed of colored people who were
attracted," in the words of the *Clipper* correspondent, "by the
novelty of a corps of 'real nigger' performers." Similarly,
Sprague's Georgia Minstrels owed their fair business in Cincin-

nati in 1879 to "the largely colored audiences." Regardless of the group, the city, or the year, the results were the same. Black minstrels were so popular with Negroes that some theater owners even deviated from their usual practice of restricting blacks to the "Nigger Heaven" section of the gallery. In Galveston, Texas, for the Callender troupe, the "colored population took entire possession of dress circle and galleries." In St. Louis, so many Negroes turned out to see the Haverly Colored Minstrels that a section of the family circle was set apart for them. Billy Kersands proved such a great attraction for blacks, Tom Fletcher recalled, that "prejudice was half forgotten as the owners arranged for colored customers to occupy a full half of the theater from the ground floor or orchestra section right up to the gallery with whites filling the other side." [51]

Although it is impossible to be precise, it seems that black minstrels drew primarily black common people. The Negro press of the nineteenth century, which catered exclusively to the "black bourgeoisie," virtually ignored black minstrels even though it went to great lengths to applaud any semblance of cultural or artistic achievement Negroes made in the formal arts. Furthermore, when Negroes compiled books to record the contributions of the race to American society, black minstrels were usually not included. And when, in 1882, James Monroe Trotter chose to include a chapter on the Georgia Minstrels in his *Music and Some Highly Musical People*, he spent almost half the chapter apologizing for his decision. In the course of his argument, he mentioned that few of the Negroes who condemned black minstrels for giving "aid and comfort to the enemy" had ever seen them perform. Trotter admitted that he himself had been so opposed to black minstrels legitimizing white caricatures that as a boy of fourteen he refused to distribute playbills for a black minstrel company and had not attended a show until he felt obliged to for his book. Although he had nothing but contempt for the "disgusting caricaturing" in the black minstrel show, he was pleasantly surprised by the black minstrels' "high musical culture," which he felt almost compensated for the negative parts of the show. W. C. Handy himself acknowledged that a "large section of upper-crust Negroes" strongly condemned black minstrels.[52] Because there were few black professional entertainers in the late nineteenth century, some members of the black bourgeoisie probably did attend, but there is no indication that it was a regular part of their social and cultural activities. It was probably black common people who flocked to see the black minstrels.

By 1890, because of minstrelsy, blacks had established themselves in American show business. They had made clear to their large black audiences that it was possible for common blacks to become entertainers. And minstrelsy produced all sorts of black artists: Ernest Hogan, an influential ragtime and musical comedy composer and singer; Gussie L. Davis, composer of sentimental songs and the first black man to succeed in Tin Pan Alley; Bert Williams, a star of musicals, vaudeville, and the Ziegfeld Follies; W. C. Handy, one of the first popularizers of blues; Dewey "Pigmeat" Markham, a veteran of fifty years as a comedian; and the Queens of the Blues, Gertrude "Ma" Rainey and Bessie Smith.[53] But black people also had to pay a great price for entering show business. They had to act out white caricatures of Negroes. But since whites had already created and spread these images, it was really less a question of *what* minstrel images of blacks would be than of *who* would portray them. Given the circumstances, participation at least gave blacks a chance to modify these caricatures.

Despite the difficulties, obstacles, limitations, and exploitation that black minstrels had to endure, many of them probably shared W. C. Handy's overall assessment of his experience in minstrelsy.

It had taken me from Cuba to California, from Canada to
Mexico. . . . It had thrown me into contact with a wistful
but aspiring generation of dusky singers and musicians. It
had taught me a way of life I still consider the only one for
me. Finally, it had brought me back after trying days into
the good graces of such home folks as my father and the old
school teacher. The time had been well spent.[54]

NOTES

[1] New York *Clipper*, Nov. 6, 1858.
[2] W. C. Handy, *Father of the Blues* (New York, 1941, Collier
ed.), p. 36.
[3] For a discussion of the content of the black minstrel show, see
Chapter 8.
[4] Eileen Southern, *The Music of Black Americans* (New York,
1971), chapters 2–4 are a fine survey offering considerable detail.
[5] James Monroe Trotter, *Music and Some Highly Musical People*
(Boston, 1882), details the careers of Greenfield, the Luca family,
Blind Tom, and other Negro performers of "serious" music.
[6] "Early Days of Burnt Cork Minstrels," Boston *Globe*, July 18,
1909, clipping, HTC; clipping, n.p., n.d., HTC.
[7] T. Allston Brown, "Early History of Negro Minstrelsy," New
York *Clipper*, July 1, 1912; *Ohio State Journal*, Jan. 17, 1857, quoted in
Carl Wittke, *Tambo and Bones* (Durham, N.C., 1930), pp. 75–76; New
York *Clipper*, Nov. 6, 1858; G. D. Odell, *Annals of the New York Stage*,
15 vols. (New York, 1927–1949), Vol. VI, p. 602, reported the appearance of The Alabama Slaves at the Athenaeum in Brooklyn, May
2, 1857; Seven Slaves Just From Alabama, Springfield, Massachusetts, May 7 [1857?], playbill, HTC.
[8] New York *Clipper*, May 24, 1862, May 31, 1862, Nov. 7, 1863,
Apr. 22, 1865. As long as black minstrels were a novelty, the *Clipper*
commented on almost all of their actions, but after 1870 coverage was
in direct proportion to the amount of advertising placed. Consequently, data on black minstrels is greatest for the largest, most successful troupes and for the most bizarre; Odell, *Annals of the New York*

Stage, Vol. VII, p. 709; *Clipper*, Nov. 1865, July 22, 1865, Dec. 9, 1865.

[9] *Clipper*, Mar. 24, 1866, Feb. 17, 1866; T. Allston Brown, *History of the American Stage* (New York, 1870); *Clipper*, June 2, 1866, July 28, 1866, Aug. 25, 1866.

[10] *Clipper*, Oct. 21, 1865.

[11] *Ibid.*, Jan. 25, 1873; *New York Sunday Mercury*, St. Louis *Republican* and St. Louis *Times*, quoted in Callender's Minstrels, Philadelphia, Jan. 29, 1873, Callender's Minstrels, Chicago, Feb. 26, 1883, programs, HTC.

[12] Brooker and Clayton's Georgia Minstrels, Buffalo, Dec. 18, 1865, playbill, HTC, and many advertisements in the *Clipper; Clipper*, Sept. 1, 1866, Nov. 23, 1867, Oct. 7, 1871; Alabama Minstrels, Newport, Rhode Island, n.d. playbill, HTC; *Buffalo Courier* quoted in Callender's Minstrels, Philadelphia, Jan. 19, 1873, program, HTC; Troy *Whig* quoted in *Clipper*, Dec. 30, 1865.

[13] *Clipper*, Dec. 16, 1865; St. Joseph, Missouri, *Gazette*, Nov. 7, 1875, quoted in Mara's Georgia Minstrel ad in the *Clipper*, Nov. 20, 1875; Callender's Minstrels, Philadelphia, Jan. 29, 1873, program, HTC; *Clipper*, Oct. 8, 1887.

[14] St. Louis *Journal* quoted in Callender's Minstrels, Philadelphia, Jan. 29, 1873, program, HTC, emphasis added; St. Paul press quoted in *Clipper*, Oct. 23, 1875; *Clipper*, July 24, 1880. Similar views were expressed in Louisville, Ky. (*ibid.*, Sept. 14, 1872), Memphis, (*ibid.*, Nov. 28, 1874), Cleveland (Wittke, *Tambo and Bones*, pp. 91–92), and, on many occasions, in New York City.

[15] *Clipper*, Sept. 14, 1872.

[16] *Clipper*, Jan. 29, 1870, Mar. 12, 1870, Apr. 6, 1872; M. B. Leavitt, *Fifty Years of Theatrical Management* (New York, 1912), p. 377.

[17] *Clipper*, Sept. 9, 1873, May 13, 1874.

[18] At least that many black minstrel troupes, headed by different people, appeared between 1872 and 1878; see Appendix I, a chronological list of black minstrel troupes.

[19] *Clipper*, Jan. 16, 1875, Feb. 13, 1875, Mar. 27, 1875, Apr. 7, 1875; Odell, *Annals of the New York Stage*, Vol. IX, p. 634; *Clipper*, Mar. 11, 1876; Daniel Frohman, *Daniel Frohman Presents: An Autobiography* (New York, 1935), pp. 33–34; Frohman never admitted that the troupe he promoted was a black company. Doubtless ashamed of having worked with Negroes, he merely called them minstrels; Brooklyn *Eagle*, Jan. 14, 1877, clipping, HTC.

231

Black Men Take the Stage

²⁰ *Clipper*, Sept. 6, 1879, Aug. 7, 1880; black minstrels did not perform only plantation material (see Chapter 8), but, especially under Haverly, they concentrated their promotions on the plantation aspect of the show.

²¹ *Clipper*, July 19, 1879, June 26, 1880.

²² Baltimore *American* quoted in Haverly ad in the *Clipper*, Sept. 20, 1879; *Clipper*, Sept. 13, 1879; *Haverly's Colored Minstrel Libretto* (London, July 1881).

²³ *Clipper*, Jan. 28, 1882, Mar. 18, 1882.

²⁴ *Ibid.*, Mar. 4, 1882.

²⁵ *Ibid.*, July 8, 1882, Aug. 28, 1882.

²⁶ *Ibid.*, Aug. 18, 1883, Aug. 25, 1883, Sept. 8, 22, 29, 1883.

²⁷ Ike Simond, *Old Slack's Reminiscence and Pocket History of the Colored Profession from 1865–1891* (Chicago, n.d. [1892]), p. 4, dates Johnson's first troupe in 1866; Sam Lucas played with Johnson in 1869: *Sam Lucas' Plantation Songster* (Boston, n.d. [1875?]), pp. 3–4; *Clipper*, Aug. 26, 1882, Oct. 30, 1886, Nov. 13, 1886, Aug. 27, 1870, Jan. 16, 1875, Jan. 13, 1877, July 2, 1881, July 16, 1881, Oct. 23, 1886, Apr. 26, 1890.

²⁸ Simond, *Old Slack's Reminiscence . . . ,* p. 13.

²⁹ *Clipper*, July 23, 1870, July 30, 1870, Oct. 29, 1870, Jan. 28, 1871, April 12, 1873, Aug. 8, 1874, Jan. 2, 1875, Mar. 10, 1875, Dec. 19, 1876.

³⁰ *Ibid.*, Feb. 24, 1877, Mar. 31, 1877, May 19, 1877, July 14, 1877, May 17, 1879, July 5, 1879; Leavitt, *Fifty Years of Theatrical Management*, p. 273.

³¹ *Clipper*, July 31, 1880, July 10, 1880, Sept. 4, 1880, Jan. 15, 1881, Mar. 5, 1881.

³² *Ibid.*, Feb. 18, 1882.

³³ *Ibid.*, Feb. 10, 1883; McIntosh and Sawyer's Colored Minstrels, n.p., n.d. [1883], playbill, NYLC.

³⁴ *Clipper*, Aug. 7, 1886, Aug. 27, 1887.

³⁵ Leavitt, *Fifty Years of Theatrical Management*, p. 40; Edward L. Rice, *Monarchs of Minstrelsy* (New York, 1911), p. 147.

³⁶ *Clipper*, May 24, 1890.

³⁷ Bland is the only black minstrel to have gotten much attention in scholarship, and it is error-laden; see James Daly, *A Song in His Heart* (Philadelphia, 1951); Charles Haywood, ed., *The James A. Bland Album of Outstanding Songs* (New York, 1946); and Kelly Miller, "The Negro Stephen Foster," *Etude* (July 1939), pp. 431–32, 472. Although

these three writers contended that Bland began his career with Haverly's Colored Minstrels (1878), the program for the Original Black
Diamonds, Boston, n.d. [1875], HTC, has "1875" written on it in ink
and contained an ad for his "new" songs "Carry Me Back" and "Morning by the Bright Light," both first published that year. Ike Simond
saw Bland with the Bohee Minstrels in 1876; see Simond, *Old Slack's
Reminiscence . . .*, p. 17.

[38] *Clipper*, Aug. 31, 1878, May 15, 1880; Haywood, "Introduction," n.p.; *Clipper*, Nov. 24, 1883, Sept. 9, 1882, July 3, 1886, Oct.
11, 1890; Daly, *A Song in His Heart*, pp. 65–68.

[39] Lucas, *Sam Lucas' Plantation Songster*, pp. 3–5; *Clipper*, Oct. 11,
1873, Dec. 4, 1875, Jan. 25, 1879, Apr. 10, 1886. Although he played
with almost every black minstrel troupe, he never founded one of his
own. His primary interests were elsewhere.

[40] Harry Birdoff, *The World's Greatest Hit: Uncle Tom's Cabin*
(New York, 1947), pp. 225–26; Tom Fletcher, *100 Years of the Negro in
Show Business* (New York, 1954), p. 71.

[41] Fletcher, *100 Years of the Negro in Show Business*, pp. 74–76;
James Weldon Johnson, *Black Manhattan*, (New York, 1968, Athen-
eum ed.), pp. 90–91, 95, 102.

[42] Lucas, *Sam Lucas' Plantation Songster*, pp. 4–5; New York *Sun*,
July 22, 1894, quoted in Marian Winter, "Juba and American Minstrelsy," *Dance Index*, VI (1947), 43–44.

[43] Charles H. Day, *Fun in Black* (New York, 1874), pp. 19–20;
Clipper, Mar. 22, 1873; J. B. T. Marsh, *The Story of the Jubilee Singers*
(Boston, 1880), p. 35; Fletcher, *100 Years of the Negro in Show Business*,
pp. 10, 57; Handy, *Father of the Blues*, pp. 48–49.

[44] Fletcher, *100 Years . . .*, p. 57; Handy, *Father of the Blues*, pp.
50–52.

[45] Fletcher, *100 Years . . .*, p. xvii; Handy, *Father of the Blues*,
pp. 46–50.

[46] Handy, Father of the Blues, p. 19; Fletcher, *100 Years . . .*,
p. 7; Daly, *A Song in His Heart*, pp. 49–54.

[47] Handy, *Father of the Blues*, p. 17; Fletcher, *100 Years . . .*, p.
xvii.

[48] "How Burnt Cork Pays," Boston, 1882, clipping, Boston Public Library; advertisements tallied from the *Clipper*, 1865–1890; *Clipper*, Feb. 3, 1883; Handy, *Father of the Blues*, p. 35; Fletcher, *100 Years
. . .*, p. xvii.

[49] Handy, *Father of the Blues*, pp. 35–36; *Clipper*, Oct. 11, 1890, Oct. 11, 1873, Jan. 25, 1879, Apr. 4, 1886.

[50] Fletcher, *100 Years . . .* , p. 67; Handy, *Father of the Blues*, p. 38.

[51] Fletcher, *100 Years . . .* , p. 67; *Clipper*, July 24, 1869, Oct. 7, 1871, Dec. 20, 1873, Oct. 28, 1876, Nov. 17, 1877, Oct. 25, 1879, Oct. 9, 1880; Fletcher, p. 62.

[52] Trotter, *Music and Some Highly Musical People*, pp. 273–75; Handy, *Father of the Blues*, pp. 36, 66–67.

[53] Ike Simond saw Ernest Hogan and Gussie L. Davis as minstrels: Simond, *Old Slack's Reminiscence . . .* , pp. 17, 14; Handy's autobiography identifies him as a minstrel; for Markham, see "Pigmeat" Markham, with Bill Levinson, *Here Comes the Judge!* (New York, 1969); for Bessie Smith and Ma Rainey, see Paul Oliver, *Bessie Smith* (New York, 1959); Derrick Stewart-Baxter, *Ma Rainey and the Classic Blues Singers* (New York, 1970).

[54] Handy, *Father of the Blues*, pp. 72–73.

8 Puttin' on the Mask: The Content of Black Minstrelsy

Although black minstrels had always stressed their race and their ties to the plantation, their shows, until the mid-1870's, were almost identical to white minstrels'. The first parts contained more sentimental and romantic songs than Southern Negro material or dialect comedy; the olios were overwhelmingly nonplantation specialities: cornet duets, piccolo solos, clog dances, stump speeches, and topical comedy skits and songs; and the shows concluded with standard farces, like Dan Bryant's "Live Injin" and Leon's "Grand Dutch S." [1]

In the mid-1870's, as white minstrels shifted their emphasis from portrayals of Negroes to lavish productions and general social commentary, black minstrels took an almost opposite direction, leading to a nearly total concentration on Afro-Americans and the plantation. By that time, black minstrels had clearly distinguished themselves from blackfaced whites and had established their primacy as plantation delineators.

Puttin' on the Mask

Stressing these facts, Charles Callender and J. H. Haverly honed an image of black minstrels as "natural" and "spontaneous" representatives of blacks rather than as general entertainers. In the financially chaotic 1870's, this ensured blacks a place in minstrelsy, but it also essentially limited them to portraying Negroes. Thus, while white minstrelsy was reshaped by urban realities and by the new white entertainment forms, black minstrelsy was much more deeply influenced by changes in public interest in blacks and by the way other entertainment forms portrayed them.

In the mid-1870's, when minstrelsy was still concentrated outside the South, there seems to have been a reawakening of the Northern public's curiosity about slave life and the plantation. Since early in the Civil War, Northerners had heard a wide range of conflicting reports about Southern Negroes, not just from the government and from politicians, but also from travelers, from relatives in the army, and from teachers and missionaries. By the mid-1870's, it was clear that whatever else freedmen were they were not a direct threat to Northern whites. No hordes of blacks had emerged from slavery to invade Northern job markets and bedrooms as some demagogues had predicted. Furthermore, the divisive issues of Reconstruction had subsided with at least a tacit agreement that blacks would be kept in their place—in the South as subordinates to whites. Moreover, the genuine black men that Northern whites had seen on stage reinforced the idea that blacks were no threat to whites or to reunification. Thus, general conditions were right for a revival of interest in the plantation.

The spark was provided by the discovery of Southern Negro religious music. During the war, Northerners began to report on the slaves' curious music. In 1867 the first book of *Slave Songs of the United States* appeared, followed two years later by the reprinting of Thomas Wentworth Higginson's collection of slave songs in his *Army Life in a Black Regiment.* Then, in 1871, a group of Negro students from Fisk University, a black school founded by missionaries in 1865, first traveled to the North singing the religious music of the plantation. By mid-1875 they had toured widely, including Europe, and had created a public sensation.[2]

Almost inevitably the "jubilee" groups were associated with minstrelsy, which up to that point had been the public's major interpreter of the plantation and of slave lore. The Fisk Singers, in fact, took the name Jubilee Singers only after being mistaken for minstrels during their first Northern tour.[3] Even after that, the "praise" they won as authentic plantation representatives closely resembled the responses to black minstrels. By 1875 imitators of the Fisk Jubilee Singers flooded the North with the "new" plantation music. Some, like the group from Hampton Institute, another Negro college, presented themselves in a dignified and serious way. But many others made appeals indistinguishable from the black minstrels'. Billing themselves as "genuine slave bands" or "FORMERLY SLAVES," they promised to appear in "full plantation costumes," to play the "rude instruments of the South," and to sing the "quaint and weird" songs that "echoed throughout the Magnolia Groves and Cotton Fields of the bright, Sunny South." Sheppard's Colored Jubilee Singers not only represented themselves as making "no pretensions as to musical abilities, they being unable to read or write," but they also claimed that their leader, Andrew Sheppard, had for thirty years been the "property of General Robert E. Lee." [4] Although jubilee groups claimed to be from Virginia, North Carolina, South Carolina, and Louisiana, some were no more authentic than the Virginia Jubilee Singers who were "guyed off the stage" in Albany, New York, for giving a very poor performance and for being just "a few

Albany coons." [5] Others, like the Louisiana Jubilee Singers, who included "Carve Dat Possum," "Way Down Upon the Swanee River," and "Old Black Joe" in their "Sacred Concert," seem to have been little more than renamed black minstrel troupes. [6]

Regardless of their authenticity, these jubilee groups created a renewed interest in the plantation that had far-reaching effects on minstrelsy. Religion had not been a part of minstrel portrayals of blacks until the 1870's, when for the first time minstrels added religious songs, almost always in dialect. By mid-decade, there were white minstrel "jubilee" singing groups, like the "Ham-Town Students," whose repertoires combined Negro religious songs, popular black minstrel songs, and nostalgia for the plantation. [7] But since black minstrels were by this time the acknowledged experts on plantation subjects and since many black minstrels probably had personal knowledge of spirituals, jubilee songs had a much greater impact on black than on white minstrel shows. Eight white minstrel songsters published in 1880, for example, contained a total of only twelve religious songs, compared to a total of thirty-five in just three black minstrel songsters of the same year. [8]

During 1875–76 jubilee music had its first great impact on the black minstrel show. In February 1875, Callender's Georgia Minstrels gave what to that point was a typical black minstrel show. It contained no religious songs and no jubilee group, devoted less than half of its second part to Southern Negro material, and concluded with a typical nonplantation farce, "The Masquerade Ball." Fourteen months later their show had changed strikingly. The first part contained religious songs like "Angels, Meet Me at the Cross-roads," "Keep Dose Lamps Burning," and "Oh, Rock o' My Soul"; the olio, dominated by plantation material, featured a group singing jubilee songs; and the show concluded with a plantation finale. After that, spirituals remained a permanent black minstrel feature. For at least the next six years, both the Callender and the Haverly troupes always contained a religious singing group, known variously as The Hamtown Students, The Georgian Students, The Blackville Singers, or the Hamtown Quartette, Quintette, or Sextette.[9] Several black minstrel troupes even added "jubilee" to their titles. In late 1874, there was a Callender's Jubilee Minstrels; in 1876, the Alabama Colored Minstrels and Plantation Jubilee Singers appeared; and in 1877, Lew Johnson called his troupe the Original Tennessee Jubilee Singers.[10]

With the introduction of Afro-American religious music, black culture revitalized minstrelsy. But unlike the early years, Negroes now interpreted it. Many black minstrels must have borrowed from black spirituals as Sam Lucas did when he took the melody for "Carve Dat Possum," a secular song, from a tune that "had long been sung in many colored churches."[11] A determination of precisely how heavily indebted black minstrels were to Afro-American melodic tradition awaits a detailed analysis of their music by an ethnomusicologist. It is clear, however, that black minstrels used the antiphonal *form* of Afro-American spirituals: the alteration of lead singer and chorus, the repetition, and the punctuation of each line of the verse with a repeated phrase.

> I'm got a sister in de wilderness,
>   in de wilderness—in de wilderness,
> I'm got a sister in de wilderness,
> Awaiting on de Lord. . . .[12]

Although many of their songs had the ring of authentic folk spirituals, black minstrels very rarely claimed that a specific song was "A Genuine Plantation Song and Melody" as they properly did with "Angels, Meet Me On the Cross-Road":

Puttin' on the Mask

> Angels, meet me on the cross-road, meet me
> Angels, meet me on the cross-road, meet me
> Angels, meet me on the cross-road, meet me
> I ain't gwine to charge any tole.

Some, like "I'm A-Rolling," which both the Fisk Jubilee
Singers and Tom McIntosh sang, appeared authentic and were
credited to no one:

> I'm a-rolling, I'm a-rolling,
> I'm a-rolling through an unfriendly world;
> I'm a-rolling, I'm a-rolling,
> I'm a-rolling through an unfriendly world.
> Oh, brothers [sisters, preachers], won't you
>   help me,
> Oh, brothers, won't you help me to pray;
> Oh, brothers, won't you help me,
> Won't you help me in the service of the Lord? [13]

But whatever their source, nearly all of these songs were either
credited to the performer or to their "author" if they were
copyrighted. Like all entertainers, black minstrels wanted to
enhance their own reputation as creative artists by claiming
their material was original.

But the songs that black minstrels introduced had the content of Afro-American religious music as well as its form. With
the singers of slave spirituals, they sang of an immediate, concrete religion that contrasted greatly to Euro-Americans' other-
worldly, abstract religion. Following African patterns, the black
folk did not divide the world into antithetical spiritual and secular domains. Their religion and their everyday lives were one.
The same "worldly" language could describe them both. Both
black slaves and black minstrels sang of heaven as a paradise of
freedom and plenty. It was where "de white folks must let de

darkeys be," where they would not be "bought and sold,"
where everyone would have three meals a day and occasional
feasts of milk and honey, even if they "ain't got any money."
Again like the black folk, black minstrels felt themselves on intimate terms with God. They asked Him to "open dem doors"
so they could get a glimpse inside, reminded Him that "nobody
knows what trouble we've seen," and implored Him to give
them the means to escape.

> Oh, good Lor' gib me dem wings
> Oh, good Lor' gib me dem wings
> Oh, good Lor' gib me dem wings
> Gib me dem wings to fly away.

And they had no doubt that He would deliver them as He had
Jonah, Daniel, Moses, and the other Old Testament heroes
about whom they sang so often.

> Didn't Moses smote de big red sea
> > Sing glory hallelujah
> For to make some room for you and me
> > Sing glory in my soul.[14]

"I hear dem Angels callin' loud," a black minstrel joyfully
proclaimed in the present tense. With the firm conviction that
salvation was imminent, black minstrels expectantly waited for
Gabriel to summon them on their glorious journey, a trip they
planned for like any other that they knew they would soon be
undertaking. They wondered what to wear ("What kind of garments does de wise men wear?"); they made plans for reunions
on "the other side"; and they cautioned each other to be sure
they were on the right path because "ole Satan stole de com-
pass" and was trying to lure them to "de brimstone lake." But
most of all they rejoiced in their belief that they would inevitably be swept into a "seat in de promise lan' " as if they were

riding the crest of an irreversible wave. They *knew* that they
would ride the "Golden Chariot," the "Gospel Tug," or the
"Gospel Cart"; they *knew* that they would climb the Golden
Stairs and would wear the Golden Crown. They were bound
for glory and no one could stop them.

> An' I'll never turn back no mo'
> An' I'll never turn back no mo'
> I'm a ridin' up in de Chariot
> It's so early in de morning
> An' I'll never turn back no mo'.[15]

Although these spirituals were distinctively Afro-
American, they were consistent with traditional Euro-
American religion. But black minstrels also brought to public
attention much more alien aspects of Afro-American religion
which tended to question the acceptance of Negroes as equal
members of the Christian brotherhood. Reflecting the immedi-
acy of religion in their everyday lives, slaves had used spirituals
as work, social, and marching songs as well as for worship in
the narrow sense. In addition to biblical stories, morality, and
redemption, they had sung of food, clothing, dancing, and jest-
ing [16]—subjects that whites, with their more limited concep-
tion of religion, felt were irreverent or irreligious. Thus, when
black minstrels included such material in their spirituals, they
seemed to be corroborating deeply embedded white minstrel
stereotypes of Negroes. James Bland and others sang of putting
"nice smelling bar's grease" on their hair and donning white kid
gloves, long-tailed coats, and golden or silver slippers for the
glorious journey to heaven in much the same way that pretentious minstrel dandies' preened for balls. Their anticipation of
heavenly feasts of milk, honey, beef steak, sparerib stew, and
"sweetmeat of every kind" reinforced images of blacks as uncontrollable creatures of the appetites. Their interjection of

mocking humor into religious songs allowed audiences to laugh at the idea that blacks were serious about their religion. One version of "Let My People Go," for example, began authentically with Gabriel telling the singer he was bound for glory; the chorus described Moses going down into Egypt land and telling Pharoah to let his people go; but then came:

> Great big nigger on a little fence
> > Let my people go
> A talking to a fat nigger wench
> > Let my people go
> De fence it broke and dey got a fall
> > Let my people go
> Down came fence, nigger, wench, and all.[17]

Black minstrels also described an Afro-American style of worship that differed greatly from Euro-American norms. "Dar we will meet and shout and sing," Tom McIntosh rejoiced, "And won't we make de welcome ring." The minstrel black folk flung themselves wholeheartedly into an intensely emotional praise of God that they thought only the devil would try to stop.

> O some will shout den take a rest
> > Down on de campground
> But when I shout I shout my best
> > Way down on de old campground
> Ole Satan tried to make me hush
> > Down on de campground
> Wid my gospel gun I run him in de brush.
> > Way down on de ole campground.

These services, black minstrels reported, often reached such an emotional crescendo that people lost control of themselves and "cut de pigeon wing." [18]

Black minstrels, who had the chance to shape the initial presentation of jubilee music in minstrelsy, maintained a remarkable degree of authenticity in their religious music, something neither the white minstrel groups like the Hamtown Students nor the "serious" black groups like the Fisk Jubilee Singers did. The former substituted romanticized plantation images for religious themes and the latter "cleaned up" the music to conform to whites' religious ideas and musical criteria in order to create a favorable impression. Black minstrels found that their audiences responded positively to genuine, or at least only moderately adapted, Afro-American religious music. Certainly the black people in the audience would have been knowledgeable critics as well as enthusiastic supporters. But they were only a sizable minority at best. Why did whites accept it?

As the proliferation of jubilee singing groups testified, this newly discovered plantation music intrigued the general public. And the way black minstrels presented it, the religious music did not seriously challenge minstrelsy's plantation mythology. In fact, its positive elements added spiritual and emotional depth to the romanticized Old Darky. At the same time, it also allowed whites to maintain their negative caricatures of blacks by focusing on and exaggerating the alien aspects of Afro-American religion. Descriptions of gaudily dressed, uninhibited blacks singing, shouting, laughing, and dancing in church confirmed minstrelsy's stereotypes of Negroes. And even though songs with these negative elements constituted only a minor part of black minstrels' jubilee music, they were among the most popular of all black minstrel songs. Given whites' ethnocentrism, their deep-seated need to believe blacks were their inferiors, and the real differences between the two cultures, this distortion was an almost inevitable price that blacks had to pay for bringing their culture into the shows.

In the mid-1870's the amount of plantation material in the

black minstrel show increased in direct correlation to the emphasis on jubilee songs. While making the plantation the central appeal of black minstrelsy, Callender and Haverly used religious music as only one aspect of the "songs and ditties" of Southern Negroes. In this process, the word "jubilee" became synonymous with "plantation," and religious meetings became simply more plantation parties. In the summer of 1876, Callender closed with "Jubilee in Georgia, Realistic Pictures of Plantation Life"; a year later, he concluded the shows with the "Characteristic Plantation and Jubilee Melody . . . COON IN DE WOODPILE" and with "a genuine and characteristic Plantation Jubilee Walkaround, THE FREEDMAN'S FROLIC." In 1880, Haverly titled his entire first part "The Grand Opening Jubilee Chorus." In it, he mixed religious songs like "Clear de Track, Moses," "Dese Bones Will Rise Again," and "Silver Slippers" with songs like "Massa's in de Cold Cold Ground" and the usual dialect comedy. After 1875 such plantation scenes, which included spirituals, regularly opened and closed black minstrel shows.[19]

When black minstrels began performing plantation material, they inherited the heavily stereotyped images that had already become virtually synonymous with minstrelsy. In the nineteenth century, white minstrels continued to reinforce these images in the specialty acts of men like J. W. McAndrews and Milt Barlow and in the plantation farces that most troupes still regularly performed. Although there was some variation in these skits, they usually focused on the Old Darky: Uncle Rufus, Old Pompey, Uncle Eph, or Old Black Joe. Against the background of the plantation in shambles, he stood alone—his beloved master, mistress, wife, and family all departed. Often his "dreams" of happy times were reenacted on-stage, effectively contrasting images of youth and age, happiness and sadness, companionship and loneliness. Played to maximize emotions, these skits frequently concluded with sentimental reunion scenes. After the Old Darky had reconciled himself to a lonely wait for death, a young white "stranger" appeared, revealed that he or she was the young child the old man had once held on his knee, and told him that either his master or mistress was still alive and would take care of him for the rest of his life. As the two walked off, the Old Darky usually sang a final song, like "Old Black Joe." [20] In white minstrels' views, then, the decrepit old black man even with much of his world tragically destroyed still had "a place" with his beloved white folks.

Although black minstrels began with and regularly portrayed these typical themes, they also significantly modified them. In the plantation material they themselves wrote, the black minstrels, like their white counterparts, featured the Old Darky nostalgically recalling the happy days of his youth, the frolicking children, the tasty possum, the bright cotton fields, the perfume of magnolia blossoms, the lively banjo music, and the comforting warmth of his family. Most of all, he deeply missed the "loving presence" of his "mudder, father, sister, or brudder." But in striking contrast to the songs written by whites, black minstrels' songs rarely mentioned their masters and mistresses! Instead, they focused all their affection on their black relatives and friends and on the warm memories of their youth, feelings many older Negroes must have shared.[21]

Besides omitting whites from their nostalgic songs, blacks further modified white plantation images by expressing strong antislavery feelings. Even though white minstrels no longer voiced opposition to slavery, the existence of this tradition combined with the abolition of slavery made this form of protest acceptable to whites, whereas protests that challenged existing white discrimination would not have been. Moreover, these black protests were only undercurrents in a broader stream of nostalgic plantation material. Some of them were "snuck" into nonprotest songs. In an otherwise innocuous song about romance on the plantation, for example, Pete Devonear complained that there were "two oberseers to one little nigger." Similarly, several of the religious songs looked forward to heaven as the place "where there is no overseer," where blacks would be free men, and from which some whites would be excluded. Since such indirect and covert jibes were common in black folk culture but not in white, many blacks in the audience would have been sensitized to hear and enjoy even such surreptitious barbs, while most whites might not even have noticed them.

Black minstrels also used overt, direct protest material. Recalling the moving antislavery images white minstrels had used over twenty years earlier, black minstrels focused on the threatened black family. In unmistakable language, George Bohee, for example, sang of a tormented mother who cried that if there was "any room in heaven for a poor black slave," she hoped her baby would die rather than live for her brutal master.

> Hark! baby, Hark! your mama is dying,
> For saving her child from cruel master's blows
> Oh! cruel, cruel slavery! hundreds are dying.
> Please let my baby die and go.

Tom McIntosh vowed that he would even return to slavery and "bear de whip and chain" if he could have his beloved wife back again. Another black minstrel sang of roaming "de darkey nation" in search of Chloe, the wife that had been torn away from him during slavery. Although never himself a slave, Sam Lucas recounted a story that many ex-slaves might have told. When he thought of his "dear old home," he recalled sitting on his mammy's knee and being told about "dose Northern men, Dat soon would set us free." As an adult, he experienced the anguish of slavery but also the joy of freedom.

> I remember now my poor wife's face,
> Her cries ring in my ear;
> When they tore me from her wild embrace,
> And sold me way out yere.
> My children sobbed about my knees,
> They've all grown up since then,
> But bress de Lord de good time's come;
> I'se freed by dose Northern men.[22]

If white minstrels quickly forgot the importance of emancipation to slaves, black minstrels did not. "We ain't going home any more, Down t' the Peach-blow Farm," vowed James Grace, one of the leading black minstrel tenors. Invoking the "religious" theme of release from suffering, he concluded: "Ain't I glad to get out the wilderness, Get out the wilderness, Get out the wilderness, Oh my lamb!" Black minstrels, like their white colleagues, drew on Harrigan and Hart for material, but unlike whites, they used the team's antislavery, proemancipation songs: "Sing de jubilee; ev'ry body free/ Welcom, welcom, Mancipation." Blacks also resurrected songs that white minstrels had long since discarded. Using Henry Clay Work's "Kingdom Coming," they mocked the planter for running away during the war and disguising himself as a "contraband," while his slaves took over the plantation, locked up the overseer, and waited in splendor for the "Linkum Sojers." Again unlike white minstrels, Sam Lucas and other black minstrels wrote songs praising Lincoln for freeing the slaves. But the focus of these songs was always the joy of emancipation. "I nebber shall forget, no nebber," Lucas concluded his praise of Lincoln, "De day I was sot free." [23]

Some black minstrels movingly combined the nostalgic

Old Darky with the exuberance for freedom. One of Sam Lucas's songs, for example, began with "Old Uncle Jasper" reminiscing about his happy days in Virginia before the war. Having decided that he preferred the "good old sunny south" to "de north dat am so cold," Jasper vowed to return so he could hear the banjos ring again and see the old folks at home. But he expressed no desire to be a subordinate and no affection for whites. He concluded the song by thanking God:

> Dat I've lived to see de things,
> Of de great Cen-ten-nial year,
> And de 'mancipation day, I hab lived
>   to see dat too,
> De happiest day de colored man e'er knew.[24]

Since black minstrels also performed the white-centered, nonprotest material written by whites, they conveyed at best a mixed message. Perhaps their modifications are of greater historical significance than they were of contemporary impact. But many of the black people in the audience probably heard and understood this undercurrent of protest and independence. Had they realized that black minstrels, like folk tricksters, had taken white stereotypes of blacks and refashioned them into jibes at whites, they would have appreciated them even more. It is also possible that whites wanting to confirm their caricatures of blacks overlooked this strain.[25] In any case, it is clear that black minstrels themselves did not feel the devotion and subservience to white folks that whites chose to believe they did.

Although dominated by the plantation and religious songs, black minstrelsy also evolved other distinctive features, particularly the uniformed black marching unit, which began as just another act that black and white minstrels shared. In 1875–76 Callender's Minstrels closed the first part of their show with a "ludicrous military burlesque." Such lampoons of black soldiers had been occasional minstrel features since the Civil War, but this skit proved so popular that it became the standard finale for the first part of the black minstrel show. Throughout 1876, Callender, cashing in on the Southern Negro craze, titled it "Georgia Brigadiers." But in mid–1877, while in New York, he capitalized on a popular Harrigan and Hart feature and re-named the "Brigadiers" the "Ginger Blues." Part of Harrigan's regular black cast, the Skidmore Guards and the Ginger Blues, were black social and marching clubs that provided the major drill team competition for Dan Mulligan's Irish Mulligan Guards. Although playing them for laughs, Harrigan did not just ridicule the blacks. They were not portrayed as military men, but neither were the Mulligans. Composed of barbers and servants, they were excellent marching units that took great pride in themselves, their uniforms, and the parties they threw.[26] Since Billy Kersands, who excelled at low comedy, starred in the Callender feature, it is likely that Callender por-trayed the Ginger Blues as laughable dandies.

When Haverly took over the Callender troupe, he retained the uniformed sketch as the first-part finale. Whether empha-sized earlier or not, comedy became the major feature of the skit, with either Tom McIntosh or Billy Kersands winning reg-ular praise for "gymnastic drumming" that kept audiences con-vulsed with laughter. Haverly also exploited the popular craze for military-type bands by adding a brass band and renaming the sketch "Recruits for Gilmore." Patrick S. Gilmore, after serving as a bandmaster in the Union army, had won renown touring the nation with his military band. Gilmore's band sparked a movement that by 1890 had seen as many as 10,000 towns and cities establish municipal bands based on the brassy military model. Reflecting this boom, the Haverly brass band by mid-1880 had become the principal attraction of the uniformed sketch, which remained a fixture closing the first part.[27]

During the troupe's British tour in 1881–82, Haverly retained the Gilmore sketch and temporarily departed from the normal plantation ending by closing the show with "The Coonville Guards Review" featuring Sergeant William Simms of the Massachusetts 6th Volunteers, in an exhibition of precision drilling with the musket. In contrast to Simms's military proficiency, the songs about the Guards laughed at them as soldiers, resurrecting the old charge that blacks preferred running to fighting:

> For those who fight and run away,
> Least so the proverbs tell
> Will live to fight another day
> And run away as well—a-ha-a, ha!

Although the song mockingly joked that they were such "wonderful shots" that they could occasionally hit a haystack at twenty yards, it praised their uniforms, their skills at marching, dancing, singing, banjo playing, courting, and party-giving.[28] Whatever they might seem, the songs told the audience, these were not military men; they were party-loving blacks.

These uniformed routines remained standard black minstrel features well into the 1890's. After 1882 the Callender troupe made an expanded Guards unit a regular feature of their olio. When Tom McIntosh tried to establish his own troupe in 1883, he starred as bass drummer with a brass band. Similarly, one of the most widely praised acts in Kersands' Minstrels was his marching band, which led the Mardi Gras parade in 1886. Kersands even offered $1,000 to any group that could beat them in drilling and parading. In 1890, the two major white-owned black minstrel troupes still featured high-stepping band units. Cleveland's Collossal Colored Carnival Minstrels offered the "March of the Mozambique Gladiators," and Richard and

Puttin' on the Mask

Pringle's Georgia Minstrels featured "The Vestibule Car Porters and Drum Majors," starring Billy Kersands. In 1894 a Callender troupe closed with "Life on the Tented Field," a display of military life and marching, directed by Sergeant Simms.[29] From an act whose primary function was to lampoon black soldiers, black minstrels had evolved a popular feature combining the public's taste for brass bands, marching units, and the idea that Negroes were harmless strutters.

Individual black minstrels also evolved their own specialty acts, many of which paralleled the standard white minstrel roles. There were black "sweet" singers, graceful prima donnas, refined dancers, pompous interlocutors, and wisecracking endmen. Similarly James Bland wrote songs that closely coincided with the white minstrel songwriters' "Negro Songs." His nostalgic Old Darkies expressed great love for their masters and mistresses; his plantation songs were free from antislavery protests and from praise of freedom; his religious songs contained many stereotyped images of flashy dressers and of overindulgent parties; and his Northern Negroes strutted, sang, danced, and had flapping ears, huge feet, and gaping mouths.[30] Although others, like Sam Lucas, presented images of blacks almost as diverse as Harrigan's Irish, Bland predictably was the most popular black songwriter in white-controlled minstrelsy.

Black minstrels also developed distinctive specialty acts of their own. For at least seven years, beginning in 1877, Bob Mack performed his unique act with both the Callender and Haverly troupes. Variously billed as the Hen Convention, Barnyard Antics, Henatics, and Hen Frolics, the act consisted of Mack, dressed as a rooster, clucking out a song about a hen convention where Mr. Rooster Shanghai cut "the biggest swell of all," boasted of his success with the hens, and threatened to show the other roosters he was "one of the boys" if they wanted trouble. The only change in his act over the years was the addi-

13. This dignified portrait of the leading black minstrel composer and the romanticized images associated with these three songs represent favorable but still stereotyped presentations of black minstrels.

"James Bland's 3 Great Songs," Boston, 1879, Harvard Theatre Collection.

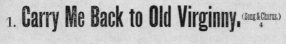

BRIGHT LIGHT MEDLEY QUICKSTEP, Full Military Band, introducing "Golden Slippers," "I Must Go," and "In the Morning by the Bright Light," arr. by August Damm, of the Boston Cadet Band.   Price 50 cents, postpaid.

AS SUNG BY LOTTA AND ED MARBLE IN " MUZETTE" AND " ZIP."

1. **Carry Me Back to Old Virginny.** (Song & Chorus.) 4

2. **In the Morning** by the **Bright Light.** (End Song.) 4

3 **Oh dem Golden Slippers.** (Song & Chorus.) 4

Words and Music by JAMES BLAND, of Sprague's Georgia Minstrels.

BOSTON:

JOHN F. PERRY & Co., Music Publishers.

13 West Street.

Copyright 1879, by John F. Perry & Co.

J. E. Simonds, Printer, 50 Bromfield St.

GARFIELD VERSION of "Bright Light in the Morning," Song and Chorus.   40 cents postpaid.

14.   Grotesque physical caricatures of Negroes persisted and were even used for the normally romanticized reunion scene. Note the huge feet, lips, and noses and also the contrasting images used by two different music publishers for the same man's songs.

James Bland, "Oh Dem Golden Slippers," Boston, 1879, Harvard Theatre Collection.

tion in 1880 of "Little Dick," the "only Trained Chicken in the world." Combining images of Negroes as dandies with mildly sexual allusions and presenting them in the inherently funny form of a grown man dressed as a rooster singing to a dancing hen, Mack made a career for himself while reinforcing stereotyped images of blacks.[31] Other unique black specialties were equally replete with caricatures. Billed in 1880–81 as "the Natural Curiosity," Alex Hunter, the "Old Alabama Slave," imitated bagpipes, bass viols, Barnum's steam Calliope, a saw and planing mill, tugboats, freight trains, and riverboats. For his finale, he placed a lighted candle on top of his head and blew it out "by throwing out his big lips." [32]

Billy Kersands rose to fame in the early 1870's playing heavily caricatured roles that he continued to perform throughout his forty-year career. Although he was an excellent dancer, perhaps the originator of Essence of Old Virginia (forerunner of the soft shoe) and of the Buck and Wing, his principal claim to fame was his slow-witted character with, what one critic called, a "copiousness of mouth and breadth of tongue that no white man could ever expect to rival." Emphasis on the black man's supposedly large lips and mouth was not new. From the beginning of minstrelsy, white minstrels had made themselves up to appear to have huge mouths, an important part of the physical stereotype that set blacks off from whites. Kersands, however, made his own unusually large mouth one of the central features of his act. W. C. Handy vividly recalled him putting an entire cup and saucer in his mouth to prove its size. He also danced with a mouthful of billiard balls and reportedly quipped to Queen Victoria that if his mouth had been any larger, they would have had to move his ears.[33] One of his most popular songs, "Old Aunt Jemima," contained a verse about a bullfrog courting a tadpole's daughter, the last line of which was "He smacked his lips and then he kissed her." Kersands

BILLY KERSANDS.

CALLENDER'S (GEORGIA) MINSTRELS.

15. Besides demonstrating the heavily caricatured context black minstrels
had to work in, this poster also suggests how Negroes reinforced these images
by acting them out.

Callender's (Georgia) Minstrels, n.p., n.d. [early-1870's],
Theatre Collection, The New York Public Library at
Lincoln Center. Astor, Lenox and Tilden Foundations.

must have played this "smack" for all the grotesque facial contortions he could muster, because his audiences howled at such
manipulations. "The slightest curl of his lip or the opening of
that yawning chasm termed his mouth," a typical commentator
observed, "was of itself sufficient to convulse the audience." [34]

Another of Kersands' most popular songs, "Mary's Gone
with a Coon," reinforced another negative image of blacks. In
it, an old man lamented his daughter's choice of a husband in
unmistakable terms:

> He's as black, as black as he can be
> Now I wouldn't care if he was only yaller,
> But he's black all o'er, he's a porter in a store,
> My heart it is tore, when I think de matter o'er
> De chile dat I bore, should tink ob me no more
> Den to run away wid a big black coon. [35]

Although such antiblack sentiments were a part of Afro-
American folk tradition, minstrelsy did not present the pro-
black sentiments that were at least as common. Thus, Kersands's
song legitimized the whites' distaste for blacks by testifying that
blacks, too, shared these feelings. Furthermore, since minstrels
did not portray "yellow" men, condemnations like Kersands's
in effect precluded any positive images of young Negro men
being presented in black minstrelsy.

Yet Kersands was a great hit with black people in the audience. Both W. C. Handy and Tom Fletcher noted his extreme
popularity with blacks in the South and Midwest. "In the
South," Fletcher recalled, "a minstrel show without Billy Kersands was like a circus without elephants." Fletcher also reported that Kersands's popularity with blacks forced theater
managers in the South to deviate from their normal segregation
pattern. His type of slow-witted, big-mouthed character was
equally popular with New York blacks. In 1891, a white re-

viewer complained about Tom McIntosh, a Kersands-type comedian, who based his act on "facial contortions and mouthings, which are neither funny nor pleasing." But, the puzzled writer observed, the "goodly number of colored people [in the audience] . . . seemed to vastly enjoy the ludicrous portion of the program." Similarly, Fletcher considered "Mary's Gone with a Coon" "very funny" and felt no need to apologize for Kersands's antics.[36] Why?

Black people must have laughed at these characters for some of the same reasons whites did. The physical humor used in the "mouth routines" and the literalism that these "ignorant" characters employed were comic devices of great general appeal. Bert Williams, who carried on the basic Kersands tradition, minus the mouth, explained that he based most of his successful material on the idea that he was "getting the worst of it." In other words, audiences, black and white, could laugh down at characters who were worse off and/or more ignorant than anyone in the audience. Furthermore, laughing at these stereotypes might have softened their negative impact on black people. But some Negroes, like James M. Trotter, complained that when black minstrels presented these caricatured images they legitimized white stereotypes. A quarter-century later, a Negro college instructor wrote to Bert Williams charging that he was doing a disservice by not presenting positive images to inspire black youth. Williams's reply suggested some of the reasons for the contrast between these objections and the laughter of the blacks in the audiences. Williams argued that black entertainers had a difficult task because whites only wanted to see them portray "the antebellum 'darkey' " and many Negroes only wanted to see "such characters as remind [them] of 'white folks.' " Although he acknowledged that there were truly exceptional Negroes, he pointed out that he was trying to create black characters drawn "from the mass and not the few." [37]

The blacks that attended minstrel shows were basically "from the mass." Unlike Trotter and the others, they were probably not concerned with what impression whites would get from the show or with how well blacks measured up to white standards. It was the difference between the black bourgeoisie with their eyes focused on whites and on middle-class standards and the·masses of black people whose perspectives were essentially confined to their group and to Afro-American culture. Certainly, all blacks could recognize that Kersands, McIntosh, and Williams performed caricatures—distorted images greatly exaggerating a few prominent features. Unlike whites, they *knew* the diversity of black people; they knew all blacks were not like these stage images and that no blacks were exactly like them. But they also probably knew black people who shared some of these traits. They laughed at the familiar in exaggerated form. At least in part, theirs was in-group laughter of recognition, even of belonging. Bert Williams's reputation for making blacks laugh rested in large part on his dialect. Yet, offstage he did not speak with a dialect. A native of the West Indies raised in San Francisco, he learned how to portray common black people by observing and listening to them in bars and on street corners. When blacks "from the mass" heard him, then, they heard their own dialect, their own slang, their own jokes: in short, their own culture. They did not worry about what whites thought of it. Feeling a common bond with the performer, they laughed and cheered.[38]

Although this phenomenon of laughing at the familiar is difficult to explain, what it suggests is the affirmation of group belonging. The live recordings of Moms Mabley, a contemporary black comedienne who has played to black audiences for fifty years, reveal the process at work. She usually opens her show by establishing a very close relationship with her audience. To begin with she is "Moms" and they are her "children," and she tells them how glad she is to be back home with them (the ghetto is her home, blacks her family). In Washington, D.C., in 1964, she opened by telling her "children" that she had just had her "first *real* meal in months." Her niece had cooked her "some hog ma-a-ws [laughter], some crackling corn-bread [laughter and screams], and a batch of greens on the side [laughter and screams]." After the audience finally quieted down, she capped it all by shouting: "*Thank* the Lord, I'm talking to people that know what I'm talking about! [screams]." She had become one with the audience simply by testifying that they shared the same culture and that others (mainly whites) did not understand it. Although doubtless much less explicit and perhaps even less conscious, much the same process must have taken place when early black comedians used black dialects and humor, when Kersands and others performed dance steps blacks knew were their own, when blacks sang spirituals and rejoiced in emancipation, and when Sam Lucas and others sang of the joys of eating mouthwatering possum, cabbage, and sweet potatoes.[39]

Besides all of this, blacks in the minstrel audiences also heard bits of Afro-American folklore, especially from Billy Kersands. "Old Aunt Jemima," the song that by 1876–77 Kersands had reportedly already performed 2–3,000 times and one he continued throughout his long career, abounded with black folk culture. Kersands apparently improvised verses for the song as he performed. Three different texts of the song appeared in black minstrel songbooks, two in 1875 and one in 1880.[40] The first verses of each were about going to church. Although the two 1875 versions described the active worship in Negro churches—singing, dancing, and "getting tight," the 1880 version placed the singer in a white church which he quickly left because they "prayed so long." These verses, which contrasted black folk to white worship, suggest the differentiated appeal

Afro-American culture could have to racially and culturally mixed audiences. Whites and some Negroes could look down on the black folk for making their religious service into a party and being unwilling to pray "properly," while "common blacks" could laugh at sanctimonious whites.

The three texts of the song also used verses and motifs found in later Afro-American folklore collections. One of the 1875 versions used the familiar:

> My old missus promise me,
> > Old Aunt Jemima, oh, oh, oh [after each line]
> When she died she-d set me free,
> She lived so long her head got bald
> She swore she would not die at all.[41]

Although the refrain after each line was peculiar to Kersands's version, the verse was common in both early minstrelsy and black tradition. Its overt protest message and its lack of even a face-saving comic "victory" for the black character both suggest that it originated in white minstrelsy. Black tradition characteristically utilized symbolic indirection and contained "victories" for black characters, even if nothing more than momentary psychological reversals. But by the time Kersands used this verse, white minstrels had long since discarded it. Although it had lost its function for them, it had real meaning for blacks, who could endorse its protest against whites' broken promises while they laughed at the idea of a bald white woman (perhaps also a jibe at the idea of whites having "good hair").

Like the anonymous black folk, Kersands blended this white-derived protest verse with elements typical of Afro-American tradition, including animal verses in which the weak outsmarted or defeated the strong. One of Kersands's animal verses began like most of the folk and minstrel versions of it:

> Dar was a bull-frog dress'd in soldier clothes,
> He went out to drill dem crows.

In the black folk versions, the bullfrog went out to *shoot* crows, who in typical trickster fashion smelled the powder and flew away leaving a "mighty mad," frustrated bullfrog. Instead, Kersands sang:

> But de bull-frog he made such a mighty splutter,
> Dat I up with my foot and kicked him in de water.[42]

Putting himself in place of the crow, a symbol of the black man, Kersands may have been identifying with his character as twentieth-century urban blacks do when they substitute "I" for the characters in their stories and songs.[43] Kersands also used aggressive action instead of the frustrating trick. But Kersands's aggression, which was directed against a symbolic animal, not a white man, retained the indirection of black folk tradition. In the 1880 version of the same song, he substituted "monkey" for "bullfrog," thereby making both animals black symbols. Rather than complete the verse by attacking the monkey, Kersands shifted to the first and last lines of another familiar verse:

> The jaybird hung on the swinging limb
> I up with a stone and hit him on the shin.[44]

In this case, he omitted the middle two lines describing the sparring back and forth to get directly to the action. In both versions, he used Afro-American folk symbols, described overt, violent victories, and personalized the triumphs. Whether he consciously manipulated Afro-American folklore by making its aggressive theme more explicit or just unconsciously did it, much of his black audience would have recognized and enjoyed these features of their culture.

Although only a small part of it showed through, elements

of Afro-American subculture clearly surfaced in black minstrelsy. Doubtless much more was included in the shows than ever appeared in print, but the full expression of Afro-American culture came only in later years when professional black entertainers performed for all-black audiences. By that time, whites, to a considerable extent, had channeled blacks into expressive forms and actions that seemed to confirm traditional white stereotypes of blacks. To survive, blacks had developed masks and façades that allowed whites to indulge their racial fantasies, while blacks created their own hidden culture within. Thus, the same words and actions could have very different meanings for whites, for the black bourgeoisie, and for members of the black subculture.[45] In this, as in many other ways, black minstrelsy was a microcosm of black history.

Black minstrelsy culminated in the summer of 1895 when the plantation literally came to Brooklyn. In Ambrose Park, recently refurbished for the Buffalo Bill Cody Show, Nat Salisbury, Cody's manager, constructed a "Negro Village" of real log cabins. He stocked it with hen yards, haywagons, mules, and chickens, surrounded it with bushes dotted with cotton balls, and peopled it with 500 blacks, all, Salisbury boasted, "genuinely southern negroes" brought "direct from the fields" of Virginia and the Carolinas. Emphasizing its absolute authenticity, Salisbury billed it "an ethnological exhibit of unique interest." Any of the "participants" (he never called them entertainers) who exhibited any artifice or affectation would be immediately discharged, he promised, thereby assuring the audiences that they would see "no imitations, nothing but what is real." Before the "show," audience members were invited to wander among the cabins, where the cast lived, so that they could observe the plantation for themselves. It "might have been hundreds of miles from civilization," one typical critic observed. And again the familiar adjectives, "authentic," "genuine," "natural," flowed from pens of writers who marveled at seeing the black man living on the plantation, "just as one might see him in a journey to the land of cotton." [46] Almost half a century after the Virginia Minstrels first took to the stage, Northern audiences could witness firsthand the "oddities, peculiarities, eccentricities, and comicalities of that Sable Genus of Humanity."

The show itself epitomized the stereotyped plantation. Mammoth choruses set the grounds ringing with "Kentucky Home," "Roll, Jordan, Roll," "Carry Me Back to Old Virginia," and "Old Black Joe." When a watermelon cart entered the performance arena, the entire cast broke ranks and descended on the melons, "uninhibitedly" breaking them open and gorging themselves on the sweet contents. After this "natural and uncontrolled" outburst, the first part concluded with a cakewalk. The cakewalk was not a performance, the program assured the audience. It had originated on Southern plantations when Negroes dressed in their masters' and mistresses' discarded finery and competed for a prize, usually a cake. This was, then, simply another feature of plantation life. Since the audience decided the winner by shouting out the number of its favorite couple, the black people threw themselves into a frenzied series of contortions—almost like puppets on strings. After an intermission, diverse specialty acts, including the marching of a Negro army regiment on leave, built up to the climax of the show, a contest of Buck and Wing dancers, who literally danced until they collapsed from exhaustion. [47] The "Black America" show left nowhere else for the plantation-centered black minstrel show to go. It embodied the ultimate in white fantasies about Southern Negroes and brought the living proof to Northerners. Because of this and because it was part of the transition to Negro musicals, it symbolized the final culmination of the minstrel show.

NOTES

[1] Brooker and Clayton's Georgia Minstrels, Buffalo, Dec. 18, 1865; Georgia Minstrels, n.p., n.d. [1866–67], New York, Sept. 10, 1867; Georgia Minstrels Slave Troupe, Hartford, Sept. 15, 1868; Georgia Minstrels, n.p., n.d. [1868]; programs and playbills, HTC.

[2] Collections of slave songs during the Civil War are conveniently reprinted in: Bruce Jackson, ed., *The Negro and His Folklore in Nineteenth Century Periodicals* (Austin, Tex., 1967), Bernard Katz, ed., *The Social Implications of Early Negro Music* (New York, 1969), *Slave Songs of the United States*, (New York, 1965, Oak ed.), and Thomas Wentworth Higginson, *Army Life in a Black Regiment* (Boston, 1962, Beacon ed.); J. B. T. Marsh, *The Story of the Jubilee Singers with Their Songs* (Boston, 1880), G. D. Pike, *The Jubilee Singers* (Boston, 1873).

[3] Marsh, *Story of the Jubilee Singers . . .* , pp. 25–26, 29.

[4] *Ibid.*, p. 78; Carl Wittke, *Tambo and Bones* (Durham, N.C., 1930), pp. 91–92; New York *Clipper*, Jan. 22, 1876; Louisiana Jubilee Singers, Woburn and Boston, Massachusetts, Oct. 17, 1877, Oct. 28, 1877, program and playbill, HTC; *Clipper*, Sept. 25, 1877; Virginia Colored Jubilee Singers, Boston, n.d., playbill, HTC; Sheppard's Colored Jubilee Singers, Boston, Jan. 30, [1879?], playbill, HTC.

[5] *Clipper*, Dec. 22, 1877.

[6] Louisiana Jubilee Singers, n.p., Nov. 4, 1877, playbill, HTC.

[7] *Ham-Town Students Songster* (New York, 1875).

[8] Content analysis of 65 minstrel songsters published before 1870 revealed religious themes in only seven of nearly 3,500 songs. Religious content in white minstrel songsters increased in the late 1870's. Three songsters in 1877 contained six; eight in 1880 had twelve; and three in 1885 had seven. Similarly, two 1875 black minstrel songsters contained a total of only two religious songs, but four that appeared in 1880–81 contained a total of 44.

[9] Callender's Georgia Minstrels, Brooklyn, Feb. 1, 1875, program HTC; *Clipper*, Feb. 27, 1875; Callender's Georgia Minstrels, Rochester, Aug. 25, 1876, Boston, April 2, 1877, New York, April 22, 1877; Haverly's Colored Minstrels, New York, Aug. 18, 1879, and many other playbills and programs, HTC.

[10] *Clipper*, Nov. 12, 1874, Nov. 18, 1876, Jan. 13, 1877. Jubilee groups also were featured in many of the heavily minstrelized versions

of *Uncle Tom's Cabin* that toured the nation in the late nineteenth century; see Harry Birdoff, *The World's Greatest Hit* (New York, 1947), pp. 226–27; Francis P. Gaines, *The Southern Plantation* (New York, 1924), pp. 103–5; George Odell, *Annals of the New York Stage*, 15 vols. (New York, 1927–49), Vol. X, pp. 367, 516–17; Vol. XII, p. 265; Vol. XIII, pp. 404–5.

[11] Letter to the editor, *Clipper*, Sept. 4, 1875.

[12] "Awaiting on de Lord," *Haverly's Genuine Colored Minstrels Songster* (Chicago, 1880), p. 25; *Slave Songs*, pp. 45–46. Although Anglo-American folk music used some of these stylistic devices, black minstrels almost certainly drew their form from Afro-American tradition.

[13] "Angels Meet Me on the Cross-Road," "I'm A-Rolling," Haverly, *Songster*, pp. 10, 24; Marsh, *Story of the Jubilee Singers . . .* , p. 131.

[14] For an analysis of slaves' sacred world-view, see Lawrence Levine, "Slave Songs and Slave Consciousness: An Exploration in Neglected Sources," in Tamara Hareven, ed., *Anonymous Americans* (Englewood Cliffs, N.J., 1971), pp. 99–130. Sam Lucas, "Children I'm Gwine to Shine," Boston, 1881, sheet music, HTC: "Talk about Your Moses," "Put On My Long White Robe," "Open Up Dem Doors," "Dem Silver Slippers," *Tom McIntosh's Plantation Songster* (Boston, 1880), pp. 19, 15, 40, 13; "Medley of Jubilee Hymns," "Angel Gabriel," Haverly, *Songster*, pp. 26–27, 12; "The Whale Got Jonah Down," *Plantation Songs and Jubilee Hymns* (Boston, 1881), n.p.; *Willie E. Lyle's Great Georgia Minstrel Song Book* (New York, 1875), p. 30.

[15] "Keep in de Middle ob de Road," Haverly, *Songster*, p. 61; "Angels Meet Me at the Crossroads," "Dem Silver Slippers," "All De Darkies Gittin' Up," "Hail Dat Gospel Tug," "The Golden Chariot," *McIntosh*, pp. 15, 24, 13, 23, 39; Frank Dumont, "De Gospel Raft," (dedicated to Billy Kersands), New York, 1878, sheet music, HTC; "I'se Gwine in de Valley," *Sam Lucas' Plantation Songster* (Boston, n.d. [1875], p. 15.

[16] Levine, "Slave Songs . . . ," pp. 111–22.

[17] "Dem Golden Slippers," Haverly, *Songster*, p. 7; "Dem Old Shoes," *The Callender Minstrel Program and Libretto* (n.p, n.d.) [London, 1884?], pp. 10–11; "In the Morning by the Bright Light," Charles Haywood, ed., *The James Bland Album of Outstanding Songs*

(New York, 1946), pp. 24–25; Sam Lucas, "Dem Silver Slippers," Boston, 1879, sheet music, HTC and in *McIntosh*, p. 13; "Hail Dat Gospel Tug," *McIntosh*, p. 18; "Let My People Go," Haverly, *Songster*, p. 45; for a sample of irreverent black folk humor, see Newman I. White, *American Negro Folk Songs* (Cambridge, Mass., 1928, 1965 reprint), pp. 130–47.

[18] "When We Meet in the Sweet Bye and Bye," "Down on De Campground," *McIntosh*, pp. 35, 39; "Angel Gabriel," Haverly, *Songster*, p. 12; Sam Lucas, "Dem Silver Slippers," Boston, 1879, sheet music, HTC, and in *McIntosh*, p. 13.

[19] Callender's Georgia Minstrels, Rochester, Aug. 25, 1876, Boston, April 2, 1877, New York, April 22, 1877, New York, July 2, 1877; Haverly Genuine Colored Minstrels, Cleveland, Jan. 1880, New York, July 19, 1880, programs and playbills, HTC.

[20] The most popular of these was: Charles White, *Uncle Eph's Dream* (Chicago, 1874); Bryant's Minstrels, New York, 1874–75, programs, HTC; Emerson's Mammoth Minstrels, San Francisco, Nov. 11, 1884, program, NYLC; *Clipper*, Dec. 2, 1876; for some other examples of such skits, see: "Uncle Pete," *Dick's Ethiopian Scenes* (New York, 1879); "Old Black Joe," *Ham-Town*, pp. 4–5; F. Cutler, *Old Pompey* (Clyde, Ohio, 1883); Dan Collyer, *Christmas Eve in the South* (Chicago, 1882).

[21] For a sample of such songs, see: "The Old Home Ain't What It Used To Be," *Lyle*, p. 47; "On the Levee by the River Side," *McIntosh*, p. 25; "Since I Saw de Cotton Grow," *Lucas*, pp. 25–26; "Sleeping Where the Cotton Plant Doth Grow," *James A. Bland's De Golden Wedding Songster* (New York, n.d. [mid-1880's]), p. 59.

[22] Pete Devonear, "Dere's a Meetin' Here Tonight," Boston, 1875, sheet music, HTC; "Uncle Ruff," Haverly, *Songster*, p. 18; "Hark! Baby Hark," *Haverly's Genuine Troupe of Blacks* (London, 1881), p. 13; "Times of Long Ago," *McIntosh*, p. 42; *"Dem Days Am Passed For Everymore,"* Haverly, *Songster*, p. 52; "My Dear Old Southern Home," *Lucas*, p. 30.

[23] "Balm of Gilead," "My Cotton Pickin' Days Am Ober," "Emancipation Day [by Edward Harrigan]," Haverly, *Songster*, pp. 5, 17, 54; "Kingdom Coming," *Bland's Golden Wedding*, p. 43; "Emancipation Day," *Lucas*, p. 7; Sam Lucas, "De Day I Was Sot Free," Boston, 1878, sheet music, HTC.

[24] C. A. White, "Old Uncle Jasper," Boston, 1876, sheet music, HTC, and in *Lucas*, p. 6.

[25] For the workings of "selective perception," see Gordon All-port, *The Nature of Prejudice* (New York, 1958, Anchor ed.), pp. 300–301.

[26] For white minstrel treatment of black soldiers see Chapter 4; Callender's Georgia Minstrels, Rochester, Aug. 25, 1876, Boston, April 2, 1877, New York, Apr. 22, 1877, programs and playbills, HTC; "The Ginger Blues," *Cool Burgess' I'll Be Gay Songster* (New York, 1880), pp. 44–45, and in William Delehanty, *I Hope I Don't Intrude* (New York, 1877), p. 47.

[27] *Clipper*, July 19, 1879; Haverly's Genuine Colored Minstrels, New York, July 12, 1879, program, HTC; on Gilmore, see Irving Sablosky, *American Music* (Chicago, 1969, paperback ed.), pp. 99–103; *Clipper*, Sept. 13, 1879, June 26, 1880.

[28] Haverly's Genuine Colored Minstrels, Glasgow, Scotland, Jan. 24, 1882, program, NYLC; *Haverly's Blacks*, p. 31; "Gentleman Coon's Picnic," *Bland's Golden Wedding*, p. 37.

[29] Callender's Consolidated Colored Minstrel Festival, Chicago, Aug. 28, 1882, program, NYLC; Boston, Jan. 15, 1883, program, HTC, among others; McIntosh and Sawyer's Colored Callender Minstrels, n.p., n.d. [New Jersey, 1883?] playbill, NYLC; *Clipper*, Dec. 26, 1885, July 3, 1886; Cleveland's Colossal Colored Carnival Minstrels, Fresno, California, Nov. 5, 1890; Richard and Pringle's Georgia Minstrels, Nov. 20–22, [1890?], programs, NYLC; Callender's Original Georgia Minstrels, n.p. [New York?], June 1894, playbill, HTC.

[30] For a sample of his repertoire, see Bland and Haywood.

[31] Callender's Georgia Minstrels, Boston, Apr. 2, 1877, and other programs and playbills for Callender's and Haverly's black minstrel troupes in HTC and NYLC; "Hen Convention," *Haverly's Blacks*, p. 28, *Callender's Libretto*, pp. 19–20; Haverly's Genuine Colored Minstrels, n.p., 1880–81, programs, HTC.

[32] Haverly's Genuine Colored Minstrels, New York, July 19, 1880, playbill, HTC.

[33] *Clipper*, Feb. 22, 1879; Tom Fletcher, *100 Years of the Negro in Show Business* (New York, 1954), pp. 61–62.

[34] "Old Aunt Jemima," Haverly, *Songster*, p. 13; *Clipper*, Oct. 8, 1887.

[35] "Mary's Gone With a Coon," *Haverly's Blacks*, p. 13; the publisher advertised it as "The Greatest End Song" sung by Milt Barlow and Billy Kersands, *Clipper*, Oct. 30, 1880.

[36] Fletcher, *100 Years of the Negro in Show Business*, p. 62; *Clipper*, Mar. 7, 1891.

[37] Bert Williams, "The Comic Side of Trouble," *American Magazine*, 85 (Jan. 1918), p. 33; James W. Trotter, *Music and Some Highly Musical People* (Boston, 1882), pp. 273–74; exchange of letters between Williams and Albert Ross of Western University, Quindaro, Kansas, printed in *Variety*, Dec. 14, 1907.

[38] Williams, "Comic Side," pp. 33, 60; Booker T. Washington, "Bert Williams," *American Magazine*, 70 (Sept. 1910), p. 600; Mabel Rowland, ed., *Bert Williams: Son of Laughter* (New York, 1923), pp. 12, 15. Nathan Huggins argues that these characters were outlets for the tensions felt by black versions of Horatio Alger, like Booker T. Washington. He does not, however, distinguish between different black groups and does not demonstrate that middle-class blacks constituted a large part of the black minstrel audience. But he does make the important point that recognition was part of the reason for black laughter. See *Harlem Renaissance* (New York, 1971), pp. 248–63.

[39] Moms Mabley has recorded many live comedy albums for Chess and Mercury Records; quotations are from: Moms Mabley, "Out on a Limb," Mercury SR60889, recorded live in March 1964 in Washington, D.C.; "Hannah, Boil Dat Cabbage Down," *Lucas*, p. 41; "Carve Dat Possum," *Lucas*, p. 11, *Bland's Golden Wedding*, p. 32; for a black folk version of the latter, see Thomas Talley, *Negro Folk Rhymes* (New York, 1922), pp. 23–24.

[40] *Lyle*, p. 20; *Lucas*, p. 31; Haverly, *Songster*, p. 13.

[41] *Lyle*, p. 20; among the many black folk versions are: Talley, *Negro Folk Rhymes*, p. 26; *Frank C. Brown Collection of North Carolina Folklore*, 7 vols. (Durham, N.C., 1952), Vol. III, p. 503; Dorothy Scarborough, *On the Trail of Negro Folksongs* (Cambridge, Mass., 1925, 1963 reprint), pp. 164–65; White, *Negro Folk Songs*, p. 152; the verse was also common in early minstrelsy, for example: Elias Howe, *Ethiopian Glee Book #4* (Boston, 1850), n.p.

[42] *Lucas*, p. 31; for black folk versions, see: Talley, *Negro Folk Rhymes*, p. 20; Scarborough, *On the Trail of Negro Folksongs*, p. 111; *Frank C. Brown*, Vol. III, p. 496; for an early minstrel version, see: "Clare De Kitchen," Foster S. Damon, *Series of Old American Songs* (Providence, 1936), n.p.

[43] For a black folk verse in which whites hate crows for being black, see Talley, *Negro Folk Rhymes*, p. 183; *Frank C. Brown*, Vol. III,

pp. 203–4. For a discussion of the "Intrusive I" in Afro-American folklore, see Roger Abrahams, *Deep Down in the Jungle* (Chicago, 1970, rev. ed.), pp. 58–59.

[44] Haverly, *Songster*, p. 13; black folk versions are in: Talley, *Negro Folk Rhymes*, p. 15; *Frank C. Brown*, Vol. III, pp. 201–2; Scarborough, *On the Trail of Negro Folksongs*, p. 191; for the signifying monkey in black tradition, see Abrahams, *Jungle*, pp. 142–43.

[45] The best discussion of the interrelationships between white stereotypes of blacks and blacks' creative and aggressive responses is Roger Abrahams, *Positively Black* (Englewood Cliffs, N.J., 1970).

[46] "Interview with Nate Salisbury," *Boston Transcript*, July 1895; this and other commentary on the "Black America" show are from a clipping collection in NYLC.

[47] "Black America," Boston, 1895, program, HTC.

Conclusion

Minstrelsy's unprecedented success demonstrated the great, almost unlimited, demand for popular entertainment that spoke for and to the great masses of middling Americans. It also exposed some of the central strains in American popular culture. Intensely nationalistic and aggressively egalitarian, minstrelsy took common people as its central characters and employed a robust humor to ridicule foreigners' "strange" ways and to debunk the pretentious. Besides laughter, minstrelsy also contained a wide variety of attractions that virtually anyone could understand and appreciate along with a strong current of sentimentalism. Cutting across all boundaries—age, sex, literacy, region, and national origin—it provided a lighthearted diversion that continually adjusted itself to public moods, desires, and tastes.

But minstrelsy was much more than merely amusing. As it entertained, it served critically important social and psychological functions. To please their widespread, vociferous audiences, minstrels constantly worked on new material, dropping the unpopular and retaining, honing, and expanding anything that evoked laughter and/or applause. Although they always tailored their material to suit their audiences, they did much more than just reflect a particular group's ideas. They created concrete images out of abstract notions and beliefs, and performed them throughout the country. Furthermore, minstrel material that was familiar and "old-hat" in one area or to one audience might be strange and new when minstrels introduced it to others. A great many nineteenth-century Americans must have gotten their first, and perhaps only, exposure to such subjects as plantations, cities, Negroes, Irishmen, or Germans while watching a minstrel show. In the same informal and even unconscious ways that basic social and cultural values are transmitted to children, minstrels communicated their implicit messages to their audiences as part of their performances. The jokes that were told and retold, the songs that were on everyone's lips, and the vivid, literally living, characters that minstrels created all embedded minstrels' images and symbols into the structure and assumptions of American popular thought. While building their repertoires, minstrels in effect evolved a kind of "national folklore"—a constellation of images, definitions, symbols, and meanings that most white Americans could and did share.

From the beginning, minstrels helped audiences cope with their concerns, frustrations, and anxieties. Lambasting aristocrats and making extensive use of frontier language and lore, minstrels asserted the worth and dignity of the white American common man. They created ludicrous Northern Negro characters that assured audience members that however confused, bewildered or helpless they felt, someone was much worse off than they were. These ridiculously stupid black characters, who had to learn everything the hard way, also enabled minstrels to answer their audiences' need for information about modern life—inventions, natural laws, the proper use of language, urban problems, and interpersonal relations—without threatening or insulting them. Similarly, minstrelsy's ethnic caricatures made America's first "foreign" immigrants seem understandable. Their caustic jokes about such topics as women's rights or the problems of urban living made threatening matters seem less ominous by letting people laugh at them. Their maudlin, sentimental songs reaffirmed traditional values while also providing emotional release. And their unwavering patriotism gave all "good Americans" a sense of belonging to the greatest country on earth.

Perhaps most important of all its social and psychological functions, minstrelsy provided a nonthreatening way for vast numbers of white Americans to work out their ambivalence about race at a time when that issue was paramount. Consistent with their nationalism, egalitarianism, and commitment to the status of whites, minstrels ultimately evolved a rationalization of racial caste as a benevolent fulfillment of, not a contradiction to, the American Creed. If Negroes were to share in America's bounty of happiness, minstrels asserted, they needed whites to take care of them. To confirm this, minstrels created and repeatedly portrayed the contrasting caricatures of inept, ludicrous Northern blacks and contented, fulfilled Southern Negroes. Besides providing "living" proof that whites need not feel guilty about racial caste, the minstrel plantation also furnished romanticized images of a simpler, happier time when society was properly ordered and the loving bonds of home and family were completely secure. Minstrelsy, in short, was one of the few comforting and reassuring experiences that nineteenth-century white Americans shared.

Beginning with early blackface entertainers who adapted

Conclusion

aspects of Afro-American music, dance, and humor to suit white audiences, minstrelsy also brought blacks and at least part of their culture into American popular culture for the first time. The enthralling vitality of this material, even as adapted by white performers, accounted in large part for minstrelsy's great initial impact. Although minstrel use of black culture declined in the late 1850's as white minstrels concentrated on caricatures of blacks, when Negroes themselves became minstrels after the Civil War, they brought a transfusion of their culture with them. Again, Afro-American culture intrigued white Americans. But black minstrels had to work within narrow limits because they performed for audiences that expected them to act out well-established minstrel stereotypes of Negroes. Within these restrictions, however, black minstrels began to modify plantation caricatures and first attracted large numbers of black people to American popular entertainment.

By the turn of the twentieth century, the popularity of the minstrel show was waning and black minstrelsy was generally restricted to a Southern and primarily rural base, including blacks. Tin Pan Alley, musical comedies, and vaudeville became the major vehicles through which blacks could reach a national audience. Bert Williams, for example, began his career with one of Lew Johnson's black minstrel troupes, but achieved national eminence in musical comedies, vaudeville, and the Ziegfeld Follies. But Williams and the handful of other black stars and celebrities were exceptions. Generally as minstrelsy declined so did opportunities for Negroes to participate in the mainstream of American popular entertainment. Before long, black entertainers were basically limited to performing for largely Negro audiences. Although this nourished Afro-American culture and laid the foundation for the professional black entertainment circuits that flourished virtually underground in the twentieth century, it also meant that blacks again became just the unpaid sources of the material—music, dance, and humor—that periodically revitalized American popular culture and made white entertainers famous and rich.

Despite its great impact and extensive influence on both popular thought and popular culture, minstrelsy lost its dominance of the entertainment business in the 1890's. From its inception, its portrayals of the plantation and of Negroes, especially Southern Negroes, had been its greatest asset and its distinguishing characteristic. Its popularity directly coincided with public curiosity, concern, and interest in these subjects. When these waned, minstrelsy was doomed. White minstrels, caught between their "authentic" black competitors and the versatility of variety and musical shows, prolonged the life of their form by shifting to more lavish productions, greater variety, urban topics, and even an abandonment of blackface. But these changes simply made it easier for vaudeville to absorb the blackface act and take minstrelsy's place as the most popular and therefore the most significant entertainment form in the country. But like the Cheshire Cat in the topsy-turvy world through the looking glass where appearances offered few clues to reality, the minstrel show, long after it had disappeared, left its central image—the grinning black mask—lingering on, deeply embedded in American consciousness.

Appendix

CHRONOLOGICAL LIST OF BLACK MINSTREL TROUPES, 1855–1890 [1]

Name	Date And Place of First Appearance	
Mocking Bird Minstrels *	1855–56	Philadelphia
Alabama Slaves *	1856	Northeast
Apollo Minstrels *	1857	Ohio
Anon. *	1858	New Hampshire
Sam Pride's Minstrel Party *	1862	San Francisco

[1] Only the first appearance of each troupe is listed. Since many toured for years, the list does not indicate how many black minstrels were touring in any given year. Obvious duplications have been deleted, but due to the similarity of names and the lack of data errors are inevitable. The list includes only Negro, not Caucasian, troupes.

* Indicates that there is no evidence the troupe lasted over a month. Many of these appeared and disappeared in the same week. Others doubtless survived but left no record.

275

Anon. *	1863	St. Louis
Smallwood's Great Contraband Minstrels and Brass Band	1865	Detroit
Norton's Oriental Minstrels (from San Domingo) *	1865	New York
Anon. *	1865	Cincinnati
Brooker and Clayton's Georgia Minstrels **	1865	Northeast
Griffin and Rogers' Georgia Minstrels *	1866	Connecticut
Lew Johnson's Minstrels **	1866	Chicago
Georgia Minstrels and Brass Band *	1866	
Georgia Minstrels' Slave Troupe [Charles Hicks]	1866	Rhode Island
Charles Hicks' Original Georgia Minstrels	1867	Northeast
Hicks and Height's Georgia Minstrels	1869	
Neal Moore's Minstrels *	1869	Lower South
Anon.*	1870	Boston
Diamond and Wellington's Georgia Minstrels *	1870	Michigan
Billy Anderson's Minstrels *	1870	Nebraska
Georgia Quadroon Minstrels *	1870	New Jersey
Davenport's Original and Only Georgia Minstrels	1871	Northeast
Marshall and Smith's Georgia Minstrels *	1871	Pennsylvania
Original Georgia Minstrels **	1871	St. Louis
Lew Johnson's Plantation Minstrels **	1871	Iowa
Georgia Minstrels and Slave Troupe	1871	Cincinnati
Callender's Original Georgia Minstrels **	1872	Ohio
Henry Hart's Alabama Minstrels	1872	Indiana

** Indicates an important and/or long-running troupe.

Appendix I

Charles Hick's African Minstrels *	1873	
Charles White's Great Troupe of Georgia Minstrels *	1873	
Emmet and Ripley's Georgia Minstrels *	1873	
Raynor's Georgia Minstrels *	1873	
Alabama Minstrels *	1873	
Louisiana Slave Troupe *	1873	
Hardman's African Minstrels *	1873	
Henry Hart's Colored Minstrels *	1874	Indiana
Harry Davis' Alabamas *	1874	Cincinnati
Callender's Jubliee Minstrels	1874	New York
Charles Hick's Georgia Minstrels	1874	Midwest
Old Kentucky Minstrels *	1874	California
W. A. Mara's Georgia Minstrels	1875	Midwest
Louisiana Slave Troupe and Brass Band	1875	Indiana
Original Georgia Minstrels * [John E. Warner]	1875	
Original Black Diamonds *	1875	Boston
Colored Plantation Minstrel Combination *	1875	Chicago
Slavin's Georgia Jubilee Singers	1876	New York
Maguire and Haverly's Georgia Minstrels	1876	Nevada
Harry Leslie Colored Congress and Brass Band *	1876	Illinois
Alabama Colored Minstrels and Plantation Jubilee Singers	1876	
Old Dominion Slave Troupe	1876	Wisconsin
Sprague and Blodgett's Georgia Minstrels **	1876	Missouri
The Bohee Minstrels *	1876	Philadelphia
Corbyn's Georgia Minstrels *	1876	
Lew Johnson's Original Tennessee Jubilee Singers	1877	Illinois
George Montague's Virginia Minstrels *	1877	New Jersey

Slavin's Original and Only Georgia Cabin Singers	1877	
Brown's Slave Cabin Minstrels *	1877	New Jersey
Original Virginia and Old Dominion Slave Troupe	1878	New York
New Orleans and Georgia Colored Minstrels *	1878	Memphis
Stoddart's Original Alabama Sable Minstrels (Pure Negro) *	1878	Washington, D.C.
Haverly's Colored Minstrels **	1878	Northeast
Sprague's Georgia Minstrels **	1878	
Tom Granger's Georgia Minstrels *	1878	Midwest
Henry Hart's Colored Minstrels	1878	Indiana
Sine's Virginia Slave Troupe Minstrels *	1879	Philadelphia
Original Dixie Minstrels (Colored)	1879	Richmond, Va.
Bishop's Female Georgia Minstrels * (Lew Johnson, manager)	1879	Chicago
Alabama Colored Minstrels *	1879	Massachusetts .
Kentucky Jubilee Singers and Combination Troupe *	1880	California
Cross' Original Mastodon Minstrels *	1880	
Cross' Virginia Mastodon Minstrels *	1880	Connecticut
Alabama Minstrels and Blackville Family *	1880	Michigan
Hall and Thompson's Slave Troupe *	1880	Albany
Hart's Colored Georgia Minstrels *	1881	Cincinnati
Crescent City Minstrels and Louisiana Jubilee Singers *	1881	New Orleans
Lew Johnson and William Smallwood's Colored Combination	1881	Midwest
East Tennessee Colored Minstrels *	1881	
Original New Orleans Minstrels *	1881	
Callender's Consolidated Minstrels **	1882	Chicago
Simond and Allen's Minstrels *	1882	New York
McIntosh and Sawyer's Coloured Callender Minstrels	1883	New Jersey
Richard and Pringle's Georgia Minstrels **	1883	Midwest

Appendix I

Alexander's Colored Minstrels *	1883	
Dixon's Alabama Minstrels *	1883	Toronto
Liverman's Genuine Colored Minstrels *	1883	Minnesota
Press and Jones' Genuine Colored Minstrels *	1883	Pennsylvania
Bishop's Colored Minstrels *	1883	Maine
Gales and Hagger's Minstrels *	1884	Cincinnati
Sawyer's Georgia Minstrels	1885	New Jersey
Kersands' Colored Minstrels **	1885	New York
Charles Taylor's Alabama Minstrels *	1885	Kansas
Virginia Coloured Minstrels *	1886	New York
World Minstrels [Integrated?] [2]	1886	New York
McCabe, Young and Hun Brothers Refined Colored Minstrels ** [Integrated?]	1886	Philadelphia
Hicks and Sawyer's Consolidated Colored Minstrels	1886	Midwest
McIntosh's Georgia Minstrels *	1886	New York
McCabe, Young, and Gray's Pavilion Minstrels ** [Integrated?]	1886	Pennsylvania
Professor Henderson's Minstrels	1886	Chicago
Minor, Eaton, and Williams' Alabama Minstrels *	1886	
Halliday and Company's Colored Georgia Minstrels *	1887	Missouri
Shultz's Georgia Minstrels *	1887	Kansas
Lew Johnson's Black Baby Boy Minstrels	1887	San Francisco
Yarber's Colored Minstrels	1887	New York
Pennington's Georgia Minstrels	1887	
Howard's Novelty Colored Minstrels *	1888[3]	New York
Roscoe and Swift's Minstrels *	1888	
Colored Parlor Georgia Minstrels *	1889	New York
Bohee Brothers Minstrels	1890	London, England

[2] The "integrated" troupes evidently gave separate shows by black and white minstrels traveling under one name. This did not become widespread.

[3] Data incomplete for 1888 and 1889.

Parkis' Colored Carnival *	1890	
W. S. Cleveland's Colored Minstrels **	1890	Chicago
Cash and Newburne's Colored Minstrels *	1890	
Eden and Hogan's Minstrels	1890	Chicago

A Note on Method

Frustrated by the narrow limitations of their traditional methods, many scholars are searching for ways to uncover the history of "common people." Using computers to process vast stores of statistics, they are beginning to reconstruct the lives of average Americans. But they have yet to find ways to recapture common people's thoughts, concerns, desires, fears, and hopes. The problem, of course, is sources. Average people rarely kept diaries, wrote letters, or authored books. But they were far from inarticulate. Swapping stories, singing songs, laughing at jokes, and retelling their history, they shared their folk culture with their friends and neighbors. They also joined with strangers in crowded theaters to shape the performances of professional entertainers whose major goal was to please as many people as possible. If scholars can learn to use the surviving records of these folk and popular expressive forms, they can gain at least partial access to the vehicles that spoke for and to average Americans. Folklore, simply defined as communication within an in-group, is of greatest value for studies of American sub-cultures. Popular culture, designed to appeal to the widest possible audience, can provide broad, general insights. But these materials, which are virtually the only sources for the popular thoughts and feelings of the past, are "new" kinds of documents that challenge scholarship to expand its analytical and conceptual tools.

The scholar cannot simply assume that popular culture accurately reflects popular thought. If it is a mirror at all, it is like a funhouse mirror that presents distorted or partial images of the subject. To decipher these images requires a thorough understanding of the mirror. Thus, the scholar seeking to uncover the unique social insights that popular culture can provide must carefully analyze every facet of the popular art form, not just its content. Since the social significance of any source depends on its links to a broad segment of the public, the scholar must first establish the relationship between the popular form and its patrons. He must define the nature and scope of its audience to determine its social base. He must also closely examine the process by which the form is created and shaped. The more immediate the interaction between the consumers and the producers or performers, the more likely it is that the content of the form directly embodies the thoughts, feelings, needs, or desires of its patrons. The farther the formative role is removed from the audience, the more important it becomes to study the form's creators and its conventions and structures as filters for, not as expressions of, popular tastes. Especially in a performing art, the institutional format and the way material is presented are part of the message. Furthermore, the conventions of the form dictate to a considerable extent the selection of material to be performed. And for a form like the minstrel show, which evolved its structure and norms from its interaction with its au-

A Note on Method

diences, institutional developments are socially significant in themselves as well as being the necessary context for analysis of the form's content.

A sound interpretation of a popular culture form requires analysis of large amounts of primary sources so that atypical variations and individual idiosyncrasies are not mistaken for broadly representative patterns. Fortunately, a vast array of minstrel primary material has been preserved. In fact, the poster, program, playbill, and clipping collections of the Harvard Theater Collection and the Theater Collection of the New York Public Library at Lincoln Center, together with the playlets, jokebooks, sheet music, and songbooks housed there and in the Boston Public Library, the Buffalo and Erie County Library, the Brown University Library, the Harvard University libraries, and several branches of the New York Public Library constitute such a wealth of material that the research for this study could be concentrated there.

Because of the abundance of minstrel songbooks, playlets, and sheet music and because the repetition in them created a point of diminishing returns, a representative sample weighted to reflect minstrel popularity patterns—for decades, troupes, and geographical areas—was chosen. The New York *Clipper*, the major theatrical journal of the nineteenth century, furnished the information on which the selection was made as well as a wealth of other data. The posters, programs, and playbills provided a basic record of the shows and insights into minstrelsy's appeals to the public. And the jokebooks, songbooks, playlets, and sheet music divulged the actual content of minstrels' repertoires. The sample included over 160 one-act farces, hundreds of pieces of sheet music, uncounted thousands of playbills and programs, and the 5 to 6,000 songs in the 140 selected songbooks.

To effectively process this disparate data and to discover

the actual patterns in minstrel material rather than just extracting data to answer preconceived questions, a thematic and topical checklist was prepared in advance and then revised after a short trial run. One checklist was used for each book and at least one tally was recorded for each song or joke. A non-dialect sentimental love song, for example, got one mark after "Non-Negro Romance"; "Old Folks At Home" was tallied under both "Old Darky" and "Longing for the Plantation". Although inexact, this technique, when applied to the large sample, revealed the general configurations in minstrel content and recorded them in a flexible format that allowed the same data to be easily compared chronologically, topically, geographically, or by troupes.

No charts and few statistics have been used in this study. They would be too misleading. Besides the checklist method being too imprecise to justify the implied "certainties" of tables and graphs, numbers simply can not convey the emotional impact of the material nor can they capture the dynamics of the minstrel show—a potpourri of songs, dances, jokes, gestures, and ad-libs. For similar reasons, business data are held to a minimum. The institutional analysis and the rough quantitative content analysis were intended only to provide a solid foundation for the qualitative judgments that underlie this social interpretation.

Bibliography

MINSTREL PRIMARY SOURCES

(1) SPECIAL COLLECTIONS: PROGRAMS, CLIPPINGS,
SCRAPBOOKS, AND UNCATALOGUED BOOKS

Boston Public Library.
Buffalo and Erie County Public Library.
Harris Collection, John Hay Library, Brown University.
Harvard Theatre Collection, Harvard University. (HTC)
Houghton and Widener Libraries, Harvard University.
Dance Collection, New York Public Library at Lincoln Center.
Main Branch, New York Public Library.
Music Collection, New York Public Library at Lincoln Center.
Schomberg Collection, New York Public Library.
Theatre Collection, New York Public Library at Lincoln Center.
    Astor, Lenox and Tilden Foundations. (NYLC)

(2) *JOKEBOOKS AND SONGBOOKS*

Baird, I. W. *Original New Orleans Songster*. New Orleans, 1880.

Barlow Brothers and Frost's Minstrel Songster. New York, 1887.

Billy Birch's Ethiopian Melodist. New York, 1862.

The Boys of New York Minstrel Guide and Jokebook. New York, 1880.

Black Diamond Songster. New York, 1840.

Bland, James A. *James A. Bland's De Golden Wedding Songster*. New York, n.d. [1880's].

Brower, Frank. *Black Diamond Songster*. New York, 1863.

Bryant, Dan. *Bryant's Essence of Old Virginny*. New York, 1857.

——. *Bryant's Songs from Dixie Land*. New York, 1861.

——. *Dan Bryant's New Songster*. New York, 1864.

——. *Dan Bryant's "Shoo Fly" Songster*. New York, 1869.

Buckley's Ethiopian Melodies, #4. New York, 1857.

Buckley's Melodist. Boston, 1864.

Buckley's Song Book for the Parlor. New York, 1855.

Burgess, Cool. *Cool Burgess' Oh! Don't Get Weary Children Songster*. New York, 1877.

——. *Cool Burgess' I'll Be Gay Songster*. New York, 1880.

Callender Minstrels (Colossal, Spectacular, Coloured). London, 1884.

Carey, Thomas. *Brudder Gardner's Stump Speeches and Comic Lectures*. New York, 1884.

Carncross and Dixey's Minstrel Melodies. Philadelphia, 1865.

Christy, E. B. *Christy's New Songster and Black Joker*. New York, 1863.

Christy, E. P. *Christy's Plantation Melodies #1*. New York, 1851.

——. *Christy's Plantation Melodies #2*. New York, 1851.

——. *Christy's Plantation Melodies #3*. New York, 1851.

——. *Christy's Plantation Melodies #4*. New York, 1851.

——. *Christy's Plantation Melodies #5*. New York, 1851.

Christy, George. *Christy and White's Ethiopian Melodies*. Philadelphia, 1854.

——. *Christy's Bones and Banjo Melodist*. New York, 1865.

——. *Christy's Panorama Songster*. New York, 1860.

——. *George Christy's Essence of Old Kentucky*. New York, 1864.

——. *George Christy and Wood's Melodies*. New York, 1854.

Bibliography

Converse, Frank. *Frank Converse's "Old Cremona" Songster*. New York, 1863.

Deacon Snowball's Negro Melodies. New York, 1843.

Delehanty, William. *Delehanty and Hengler's Song and Dance Book*. New York, 1874.

———. *I Hope I Don't Intrude*. New York, 1877.

Devere, Sam. *Sam Devere's Burnt Cork Songster*. New York, 1877.

———. *Sam Devere's Combination Songster*. New York, 1876.

De Witt, Clinton. *Bones: His Gags and Stump Speeches*. New York, 1879.

Dick, W. B. *Ethiopian Scenes*. New York, 1879.

Dixey, Edward F. *Dixey's Essence of Burnt Cork*. Philadelphia, 1859.

Dixon, George Washington. *Dixon's (The Celebrated Buffo Singer) Oddities*. Ithaca, N. Y., 1846.

The Dockstader's T'Shovel Songster. New York, 1880.

Dumont, Frank. *Lew Benedict's Far West Song Book*. Philadelphia, 1871.

———. *Charles Duprez's Famous Songster*. New York, 1880.

Emerson, Billy. *Billy Emerson's Nancy Fat Songster*. Washington, D.C., 1880.

Ethiopian Serenaders. London, 1846.

Field, Al G. *Field and Co.'s Minstrels Songster*. New York, 1890.

Foley, M. H., and C. H. Sheffer. *Big Pound Cake Songster*. New York, 1878.

Fox, Charles. *Charley Fox's Bijou Songster*. Philadelphia, 1858.

———. *Charley Fox's Minstrel Companion*. Philadelphia, 1863.

———. *Fox's Ethiopian Comicalities*. New York, 1859.

———. *Sable Songster*. Philadelphia, 1859.

Gorton, Joseph. *Gorton's Original New Orleans Minstrel Songster*. New York, n.d. [*1883*].

Great American Song and Dance Songster. New York, 1870.

Ham-Town Students Songster. New York, 1875.

Hart, Bob. *Bob Hart's Plantation Songster*. New York, 1862.

Haverly, J. H. *Haverly's Genuine Colored Minstrels Songster*. Chicago, 1880.

———. *Haverly's Genuine Colored Minstrels Songster*. New York, 1879.

———. *Haverly's Genuine Troupe of Blacks*. London, 1881.

———. *Haverly's Mastodon Minstrel Songster*. Chicago, n.d. [1880?].

————. *Haverly's Minstrel Libretto*. Buffalo, 1888.

————. *Musical Album*. New York, n.d.

————. *Haverly's United-Mastodon Minstrels Song Book*. Chicago, 1880.

————. *Negro Minstrels: A Complete Guide*. Chicago, 1902.

————. *Unequaled Haverly's Mastodon Minstrels*. Chicago, 1882.

Hooley, R. H. *Hooley's Opera House Songster*. New York, 1863.

Horn, Eph. *Eph Horn's Own Songster*. New York, 1864.

Howard, Rollin. *Queen and West's Corporal Jim and I Songster*. New York, n.d.

Howe, Elias. *Ethiopian Glee Book #1*. Boston, 1850.

————. *Ethiopian Glee Book #3: Christy Minstrels*. Boston, 1849.

————. *Ethiopian Glee Book #4: The New Orleans Serenaders*. Boston, 1850.

————. *100 Ethiopian Songs*. Boston, 1877.

James, Ed. *Amateur Negro Minstrel Guide*. New York, 1880.

Jim Along Josey Roarer. New York, n.d. [1830's].

Joe Lang's Old Aunt Jemima Songster. New York, 1873.

Johnson and Bruno Mania Monia Nigs Songster. New York, 1875.

Kentucky and Virginia Minstrel. New York, 1850.

Lloyd and Bideaux Minstrels. *Gems of Minstrelsy*. New York, 1867.

Lucas, Sam. *Sam Lucas' Careful Man Songster*. Chicago, n.d. [1881].

————. *Sam Lucas' Plantation Songster*. Boston, n.d. [1875?].

Lucy Long's Nigga Humming Bird. New York, n.d. [1840's].

Lucy Neale's Nigga Warbler. New York, n.d. [1840's].

Lyle, Willie. *Willie E. Lyle's Great Georgia Minstrels Song Book*. New York, 1875.

McCauley, Stewart. *Songs of Kunkel's Nightingale Opera Troupe*. Baltimore, 1854.

McIntosh, Tom. *McIntosh's Plantation Songster*. Boston, 1880.

McIntyre and Heath's Scenes on Mississippi Songster. New York, 1885.

Madame Rentz's Female Minstrel Songster. New York, 1874.

Marble, Ed. *The Minstrel Show or Burnt Cork Comicalities*. New York, 1893.

Minstrel Gags and End Men's Hand-Book. New York, 1875.

Morris, William. *Billy Morris's Songs*. Boston, 1864.

Negro Forget Me Not Songster. Philadelphia, n.d. [*mid-1840's*].

Bibliography

Negro Melodies No. 1. Philadelphia, 1864.

Negro Melodies No. 2. Philadelphia, 1864.

Negro Melodies No. 3. Philadelphia, 1864.

The Negro Melodist. Cincinnati, n.d. [1850's].

De Negro's Original Pianorama. New York, 1850.

Newcomb, Bobby. *A Guide to the Minstrel Stage.* New York, 1882.

———. *Bobby Newcomb's Love Letters and Pocket of Poems Songster.* New York, 1880.

———. *Bobby Newcomb's San Francisco Minstrel's Songster.* New York, 1868.

———. *Tambo: His Jokes and Funny Sayings.* New York, 1882.

New Minstrel and Black Face Joke Book. New York, 1907.

New Negro Band Songster. Philadelphia, n.d. [1850's].

New Negro Forget-Me-Not Songster. Cincinnati, 1848.

Nigger Melodies. New York, 1848.

Old Folks at Home Songster. Philadelphia, n.d. [1860?].

Old Plantation Songster. Philadelphia, n.d. [1840's].

Old Uncle Ned Songster. Philadelphia, n.d. [1850's].

Pell, Harry. *Harry Pell's Ebony Songster.* New York, 1864.

The People's New Songster. New York, 1864.

Plantation Songs and Jubilee Hymns. Chicago, 1881.

Pop Goes the Weasel Songster. Philadelphia, n.d. [1853?].

Purdy, S. S. *Paul Pry Songster and Black Joker.* New York, 1865.

Queen and West's Popular Songster. New York, n.d. [1878?].

Rial, Jay. *Jay Rial's Ideal Uncle Tom's Cabin Song Book.* San Francisco, 1883.

Rosa Lee's Sable Songster. New York, n.d. [1850's].

De Sable Harmonist. Philadelphia, n.d. [1850's].

Sanford, Sam. *Popular Ethiopian Melodies.* Philadelphia, 1856.

Schoolcraft, Luke. *Shine On Songster.* New York, 1873.

Shaw, W. F. *Gems of Minstrel Songs #2.* New York, 1882.

"Shoo-Fly, Don't Bodder Me" Songster. New York, 1871.

De Susannah and Thick Lip Songster. New York, 1850.

Thatcher, Primrose, and West Consolidated Mammoth Minstrel's Songster. New York, n.d. [1885?].

Thatcher, Primrose, and West's Latest Songster. New York, n.d. [1885].

Thayer, Ambrose. *Morris Brothers, Pell, and Trowbridge Songs.* Boston, 1860.

Turner, Ned. *Ned Turner's Bones and Tambourine Songster.* New York, 1869.

Uncle True Songster. Philadelphia, n.d. [1850's].

De United States Screamer and Rousing Nigga Rouser. Philadelphia, n.d. [1840's].

Unsworth's Burnt Cork Lyrics. New York, 1859.

Webman's Minstrel Sketches, Conundrums, and Jokes. New York, n.d. [1882?].

White, Charles. *Charley White's Ethiopian Joke Book.* New York, 1855.

———. *New Ethiopian Song Book.* New York, 1850.

———. *New Illustrated Melodeon.* New York, 1848.

———. *White's New Book of Plantation Melodies.* Philadelphia, 1849.

———. *White's Serenaders Song Book.* New York, 1851.

White, Hank. *Burnt Cork Songster.* Montpelier, Vt., 1868.

Wilson, Fred. *Fred Wilson's Book of Original Songs as Sung by Morris Brothers, Pell, and Trowbridge Minstrels.* Boston, 1860.

Wilson, George. *George Wilson's World Champion Minstrel Songster.* New York, 1891.

Wood's Minstrel Songs. New York, 1855.

Wood's New Plantation Melodies. New York, 1855.

World of New Negro Songs. Philadelphia, 1856.

(3) FARCES, PLAYLETS, AND BURLESQUES

Arnold, John. *Glycerine Oil.* New York, 1874.

———. *Obeying Orders: Ethiopian Military Sketch.* Chicago, 1874.

Back from Californy. Chicago, 1895.

Baker, Robert. *Black Magic.* Boston, 1889.

Barking up the Wrong Tree. New York, 1886.

Black Mail. New York, n.d.

Bones at a Raffle. New York, 1875.

Bowers, E. *Man About Town.* Boston, 1894.

Bryant, Dan. *The Live Injin, or Jim Crow.* Chicago, 1874.

Buckley's Minstrels. *Scenes on the Mississippi.* n.p., n.d.

Bibliography

Christy, E. *Box and Cox*. New York, n.d. [1860's].
Coes, George. *Black Blunders*. Boston, 1893.
———. *The Faith Cure*. Boston, 1895.
———. *Here She Goes; There She Goes*. Boston, 1893.
———. *Intelligence Office*. Boston, 1893.
———. *Mrs. Didymus' Party*. Boston, 1893.
———. *Our Colored Conductors*. Boston, 1893.
———. *Perplexing Predicament*. Boston, 1895.
———. *The Police Court*. Boston, 1895.
———. *Scenes in a Sanctum*. Boston, 1895.
———. *Sublime and Ridiculous*. Boston, 1893.
———. *Tricks Upon Travellers*. Boston, 1894.
Collyer, Dan. *Christmas Eve in the South*. Chicago, 1882.
———. *The Milliner's Shop*. New York, 1872.
Courtright, William. *Private Boarding*. New York, 1872.
———. *The Motor Bellows*. New York, 1877.
Crossey, J. S. *Eh? What Is It?* New York, 1871.
———. *Hemmed In*. New York, 1870.
———. *Tricks*. New York, 1871.
———. *Wrong Woman in the Right Place*. New York, 1874.
Cutler, F. L. *Cuff's Luck*. Clyde, O., 1883.
———. *Old Pompey*. Clyde, O., 1883.
———. *That Boy Sam*. Clyde, O., 1878.
Darkey Plays. 2 vols. New York, 1874.
Darkey Tragedian. New York, 1874.
Don't Get Weary. Chicago, 1885.
Dumont, Frank. *Absent Minded*. New York, 1881.
———. *An Awful Plot*. Chicago, 1880.
———. *Black Brigands*. New York, 1884.
———. *Cupid's Frolics*. New York, 1881.
———. *Dodging the Police*. Chicago, 1889.
———. *Election Day*. New York, 1880.
———. *Gambrinus, King of Lager Beer*. New York, 1876.
———. *Helen's Funny Babies*. New York, 1878.
———. *Making a Hit*. New York, 1876.
———. *Midnight Intruder*. Chicago, 1876.

——. *Noble Savage*. New York, 1880.

——. *Norah's Goodbye*. Chicago, 1884.

——. *The Painter's Apprentice*. New York, 1876.

——. *Pleasant Companions*. New York, 1880.

——. *The Polar Bear*. New York, 1876.

——. *Rival Barber Shops*. Chicago, 1880.

——. *Scenes in Front of a Clothing Store*. New York, 1889.

——. *Sulpher Bath*. New York, 1884.

——. *The Two Awfuls*. Chicago, 1876.

——. *Vinegar Bitters*. New York, 1875.

——. *What Shall I Take?* New York, 1876.

An Elephant on Ice. New York, 1875.

Emmett, Dan. *Hard Times*. New York, 1874.

Evans, Henry. *Meriky, or Old Time Religion*. New York, 1883.

Field, A. *The Popcorn Man*. Clyde, Ohio, 1880.

——. *Those Awful Boys*. Clyde, Ohio, 1880.

Gallus Jake. New York, 1874.

Griffin, George W. H. *The Actor and the Singer*. New York, 1867.

——. *Black Crook Burlesque*. New York, n. d. [1881?].

——. *Camille*. New York, n.d. [1860's].

——. *Fenian Spy: John Bull in America*. New York, 1873.

——. *The Great Arrival*. New York, 1867.

——. *Hamlet The Dainty*. New York, n.d. [1880's].

——. *Haunted House*. New York, n.d. [1890's].

——. *Jake's the Lad*. New York, n.d. [1870's].

——. *Les Misérables*. New York, n.d. [1860's].

——. *Othello*. New York, n.d. [1870's].

——. *Nobody's Son*. New York, n.d. [1870's].

——. *Sports on a Lark*. New York, n.d. [1880's].

——. *The Troublesome Servant*. New York, n.d. [1870's].

——. *The Unhappy Pair*. Chicago, n.d.

——. *William Tell*. New York, 1881.

Hockenbery, Frank. *Professor Black's Phunnygraph, or Talking Machine*. Chicago, 1886.

Hunter, Wesley, *Strawberry Shortcake*. Clyde, Ohio, 1887.

293

Bibliography

Ingram, C. *The Best Cure*. Clyde, Ohio, 1888.
Leavitt, Andrew. *Academy of Stars*. New York, n.d. [1870's].
————. *The Arrival of Dickens*. New York, n.d. [1860's].
————. *Blinks and Jinks*. New York, n.d. [1870's].
————. *Big Mistake*. Chicago, 1875.
————. *The Black Ole Bull*. New York, n.d.
————. *The Body Snatchers*. New York, 1879.
————. *Boarding School*. New York, n.d. [1870's].
————. *Bruised and Cured*. New York, 1874.
————. *The Coming Man*. New York, 1877.
————. *Cousin Joe's Visit*. New York, n.d. [1870's].
————. *The Dead Alive*. New York, n.d. [1870's].
————. *Deaf as a Post*. New York, 1863.
————. *The Deserter*. New York, n.d. [1870's].
————. *High Jack the Heeler*. New York, 1875.
————. *In and Out*. New York, 1875.
————. *The Last Will*. New York, 1875.
————. *No Pay No Cure*. Chicago, 1882.
————. *Rigging a Purchase*. New York, 1875.
————. *Squire for a Day*. New York, 1875.
————. *Two Pompeys*. New York, n.d.
————. *Upper Ten*. Chicago, n.d. [1890].
————. *Who Died First?* New York, 1874.
Luster, James O. *Dutchey vs Nigger*. Clyde, Ohio, 1887.
McBride, H. *Poisened Darkies*. New York, 1877.
McCarthy, Harry. *Deeds of Darkness*. New York, 1876.
Maffitt, James. *Mutton Trial*. New York, 1874.
Mowery, Phil H. *The Musical Servant*. New York, 1875.
Mysterious Stranger. New York, 1874.
A Night with Brudder Bones. New York, 1874.
Othello and Darsdemoney. Chicago, n.d.
Richards, Bert. *Colored Senators*. Clyde, Ohio, 1887.
Rose Dale. New York, n.d. [1870's].
Ryman, Addison. *Julius, the Snoozer*. New York, 1876.
Sambo's Return. New York, n.d. [1870's].

Shockell, G. *Chops*. Clyde, Ohio, 1886.

Shaw, J. S. R. *How Sister Paxey Got Her Child Baptized*. Clyde, Ohio, 1880.

Sheddan, W. B. *Joke on Squinim*. Chicago, 1883.

Stanton, F. *The Select School*. Clyde, Ohio, 1883.

Stewart, J. *Eh What Is It?* New York, 1871.

———. *Hemmed In*. New York, 1871.

———. *Last of the Mohicans*. New York, 1870.

———. *Two Black Roses*. New York, 1871.

———. *Wrong Woman in the Right Place*. Chicago, n.d.

Stout, George. *Rival Tenants*. Chicago, 1874.

Townsend, Charles. *Darky Wood Dealer*. New York, 1890.

Up Head. New York, 1874.

Vautrot, George S. *Black vs. White, or Nigger and Yankee*. Clyde, Ohio, 1890.

Wallace, F. K. *Pete and the Peddler*. Chicago, 1876.

White, Charles. *African Box*. New York, 1875.

———. *Black Chemist*. New York, 1874.

———. *Black Shoemaker*. New York, n.d. [1870's].

———. *The Black Statue*. New York, 1856.

———. *The Bogus Indian*. New York, 1875.

———. *Daguerreotypes*. New York, 1874.

———. *Darkey's Stratagem*. Chicago, 1875.

———. *The Draft*. New York, 1875.

———. *Excise Trials*. New York, 1875.

———. *Fisherman's Luck*. New York, 1875.

———. *Hippatheatron Burlesque Circus*. New York, 1875.

———. *Hop of Fashion*. New York, n.d. [1870's].

———. *Jealous Husband*. New York, 1874.

———. *Laughing Gas*. New York, 1874.

———. *Malicious Trespass*. New York, 1874.

———. *Oh Hush!, or The Virginny Cupids*. New York, 1873.

———. *Old Dad's Cabin*. Clyde, Ohio, n.d. [1890?].

———. *100th Night of Hamlet*. New York, 1874.

———. *Policy Players*. New York, 1874.

———. *Recruiting Office*. New York, 1874.

————. *Sam's Courtship*. New York, 1874.

————. *Sausage Makers*. New York, 1874.

————. *Siamese Twins*. New York, 1874.

————. *Storming the Fort*. New York, 1874.

————. *The Streets of New York*. New York, 1874.

————. *Uncle Eph's Dream*. Chicago, 1874.

Wild, John. *One, Two, Three*. New York, 1875.

Williams, Henry. *The Black Forrest*. New York, 1882.

————. *Bobolino the Black Bandit.* New York, 1880.

————. *The Darkey Sleepwalker*. New York, 1880.

————. *Go and Get Tight*. New York, 1880.

————. *Moko Marionettes*. New York, 1880.

Wilton, M. *Mickey Free*. New York, n.d. [188?].

(4) AUTOBIOGRAPHIES AND REMINISCENCES

Alderman, Joseph. "Story of an Old Timer," *Dance Magazine*, 36 (1962), 50–52.

"Authentic Memoir of E. P. Christy," *New York Age*, April 1848.

Davis, A. W. "Past Days of Minstrelsy, Variety, Circus, and Side Show," *Americana*, 7 (June 1912), 529–47.

Dillon, William A. *Life Doubles in Brass*. New York, 1944.

Dockstader, Lew. "Dockstader's Ideas," n.p., July 1893. Clipping, HTC.

————. "Mr. Lew Dockstader Explains the Popularity of Minstrelsy," New York *Herald*, Dec. 23, 1906. Clipping, NYLC.

Dumont, Frank. "The Golden Days of Minstrelsy," n.p., 1914. Clipping, NYLC.

————. "Letter to the Editor," Philadelphia *Morning Telegraph*, Dec. 19, 1911. Clipping, NYLC.

————. "The Origin of Minstrelsy: Its Rise and Fall Since 1842," *Philadelphia Enquirer*, Apr. 5, 1896. Clipping, NYLC.

————. "The Younger Generation in Minstrelsy," New York *Clipper*, n.d. [191 ?]. Clipping, NYLC.

Field, Al G. *Watch Yourself Go By*. Columbus, 1912.

Fletcher, Tom. *One Hundred Years of the Negro in Show Business*. New York, 1954.

Frohman, Daniel. *Daniel Frohman Presents: An Autobiography*. New York, 1935.

———. *Charles Frohman: Manager and Man.* New York, 1916.

Handy, W. C. *Father of the Blues*. Paperback ed. New York, 1970.

Jennings, J. J. *Theatrical and Circus Life*. St. Louis, 1882.

Keeler, Ralph. "Three Years as a Negro Minstrel," *Atlantic Monthly*, XXIV (July 1869), 71–85.

———. *Vagabond Adventures*. Boston, 1872.

Leavitt, Andy. "One of the Old Minstrels," Boston *Herald*, Nov. 24, 1889. Clipping, Boston Public Library.

Leavitt, M. B. *Fifty Years of Theatrical Management*. New York, 1912.

Markham, Dewey "Pigmeat," with Bill Levinson. *Here Comes the Judge*. New York, 1969.

"Merry Minstrels," n.p., Oct. 21, 1879. Clipping, NYLC.

Pike, Marshall S. "Early Minstrelsy in Boston," n.p., Mar. 21, 1891. Clipping, NYLC.

Sanford, Sam. "American Minstrelsy," Boston *Globe*, Oct. 28, 1882. Clipping, Boston Public Library.

Sawyer, Eugene T. "Old Time Minstrels of San Francisco, Recollections of a Pioneer," *Overland Monthly*, LXXXI (1923), 5–7.

Spinney, Frank. "A New Hampshire Minstrel Tours the Coast," *California Historical Society Quarterly*, 20 (1941), 243–58.

Sutherland, James M. *From Stage to Pulpit by Bob Hart* [*pseud*]. New York, 1883.

Sweatnam, Willis P. "Interview with Willis Sweatnam," n.p. [New York *Clipper?*], January 22, 1898. Clipping, NYLC.

Taylor, Justus Hurd. *Joe Taylor*. New York, 1913.

Toney, Lamuel. *What A Life*. New York, 1934.

Williams, Bert. "The Comic Side of Trouble," *American Magazine*, 85 (January 1918), 33–35, 58–61.

Wilson, Francis. *Francis Wilson's Life of Himself*. New York, 1924.

Wood, William B. *Personal Recollections of the Stage*. Philadelphia, 1855.

SELECTED MINSTREL SECONDARY SOURCES [1]

Brown, T. Allston. "Early History of Negro Minstrelsy," New York *Clipper*, 1913–1914.

———. "The Origin of Negro Minstrelsy," in Charles H. Day. *Fun in Black*. New York, 1874, pp. 5–10.

Browne, Ray B. "Shakespeare in American Vaudeville and Negro Minstrelsy," *American Quarterly*, 12 (1960), 374–91.

Daly, John J. *A Song in His Heart*. Philadelphia, 1951.

Damon, Foster S. "The Negro in Early American Songsters," *Papers of the Bibliographical Society of America*, 28 (1934), 132–63.

———. *Series of Old American Songs*. Providence, 1936.

Davidson, Frank C. "The Rise, Development, Decline, and Influence of the American Minstrel Show." Unpublished Doctoral Dissertation. New York University, 1952.

Eaton, W. P. "Dramatic Evolution and the Popular Theatre; Playhouse Roots of Our Drama," *American Scholar*, 4 (1935), 148–59.

Edwall, Harry R. "The Golden Era of Minstrelsy in Memphis: A Reconstruction," *Western Tennessee Historical Society Papers*, 9 (1955), 29–48.

Fletcher, Tom. *One Hundred Years of the Negro in Show Business*. New York, 1954.

Green, Alan W. C. " 'Jim Crow,' 'Zip Coon': The Northern Origins of Negro Minstrelsy," *Massachusetts Review* (1970), 385–97.

Haywood, Charles. "Negro Minstrelsy and Shakespearean Burlesque," in Bruce Jackson, ed. *Folklore and Society*. Hatsboro, Pa., 1966, pp. 77–92.

"How Burnt Cork Pays," Boston, 1882. Clipping, Boston Public Library.

Howard, John Trasker. *Stephen Foster America's Troubadour*. Paperback ed. New York, 1962.

Huggins, Nathan. *Harlem Renaissance*. New York, 1971, pp. 244–302.

[1] Of the great many articles written about minstrelsy only the most useful for this study are listed.

Hutton, Lawrence. *Curiosities of the American Stage*. New York, 1891, pp. 87–145.

Johnson, James Weldon. *Along This Way*. Paperback ed. New York, 1968.

———. "Black Geniuses," n.p., Feb. 15, 1931. Clipping, HTC.

———. *Black Manhattan*. Paperback ed. New York, 1968.

Kahn, E. J. *The Merry Partners: The Age and Stage of Harrigan and Hart*. New York, 1955.

Kendall, John Smith. "New Orleans Negro Minstrels," *Louisiana Historical Quarterly*, 30 (1947), 128–48.

Kinnard, J. "Who Are Our National Poets?" *Kinckerbocker Magazine*, XXVI (1845), 331–41.

Kmen, Henry A. "Old Corn Meal: A Forgotten Urban Negro Folksinger," *Journal of American Folklore*, 75 (1962), 29–34.

Logan, Olive. "The Ancestry of Brudder Bones," *Harper's*, LVIII (1879), 687–98.

Miller, Kelly. "Negro Stephen Foster," *Etude*, July 1939, pp. 431–32, 472.

Moody, Richard. *America Takes the Stage: Romanticism in American Drama*. Bloomington, Ind., 1955.

———. "Negro Minstrels," *Quarterly Journal of Speech*, 30 (1944), 321–28.

Nathan, Hans. *Dan Emmett and the Rise of Early Negro Minstrelsy*. Norman, Okla., 1962.

Nathanson, Y. S. "Negro Minstrelsy—Ancient and Modern," *Maga Social Papers*. New York, 1867, pp. 277–96.

Nevin, R. P. "Stephen C. Foster and Negro Minstrelsy," *Atlantic Monthly*, XX (1867), 608–16.

Paskman, Dailey, and Sigmund Spaeth. *Gentlemen Be Seated! A Parade of the Old Time Minstrels*. New York, 1928.

Patterson, Cecil L. "A Different Drummer: The Image of the Negro in Nineteenth Century Popular Song Books." Unpublished Doctoral Dissertation. University of Pennsylvania, 1961.

Revett, Marion S. *A Minstrel Town*. New York, 1955.

Reynolds, Harry. *Minstrel Memories: The Story of Burnt Cork Minstrelsy in Great Britian from 1836–1927*. London, 1928.

Rice, Edward LeRoy. "Minstrelsy That Was and Is," New York Morning *Telegraph*, Feb.–Mar. 1909. Clipping, HTC.

————. *Monarchs of Minstrelsy*. New York, 1911.

Rourke, Constance. *American Humor*. Paperback ed. New York, 1953.

Rowland, Mabel, ed. *Bert Williams, Son of Laughter*. Reprint ed. New York, 1969.

Simond, Ike. *Old Slack's Reminiscences and Pocket History of the Colored Profession from 1865 to 1891*. Chicago, n.d. [1892].

Stearns, Marshall and Jean. *Jazz Dance*. New York, 1968.

Trotter, James Monroe. *Music and Some Highly Musical People*. Boston, 1882. Chapter XX.

Washington, Booker T. "Bert Williams," *American Magazine*, 70 (1910), 600–604.

White, Charley. "Negro Minstrelsy: Its Origin and Progress," New York *Clipper*, April 28, 1860.

White, Newman. "White Man in the Woodpile," *American Speech*, IV (1929), 207–15.

Winter, Marian. "Juba and American Minstrelsy," *Dance Index*, VI (1947), 28–47.

Wittke, Carl. *Tambo and Bones*. Durham, N. Car., 1930.

SELECTED SECONDARY LITERATURE ON NINETEENTH-CENTURY AMERICAN POPULAR CULTURE

Bier, Jesse. *The Rise and Fall of American Humor*. New York, 1968.

Birdoff, Harry. *The World's Greatest Hit: Uncle Tom's Cabin*. New York, 1947.

Blair, Walter. *Native American Humor*. Paperback ed. San Francisco, 1960.

Bode, Carl. *Anatomy of American Popular Culture, 1840–1861*. Berkeley, 1959.

Chase, Gilbert. *America's Music*. New York, 1955.

Crandall, John. "Patriotism and Humanitarian Reform in Children's

Literature, 1825–1860," *American Quarterly*, XXI (Spring 1969), 3–23.

Dorson, Richard M. *American Folklore*. Chicago, 1959.

———. "Mose the Far-Famed and World-Renowned," *American Literature*, XV (1943), 288–300.

———. "The Question of Folklore in a New Nation," in Bruce Jackson, ed. *Folklore and Society*. Hatboro, Pa., 1966, pp. 21–33.

———. "Sam Patch Jumping Hero," *New York Folklore Quarterly*, I (1945), 133–51.

———. "The Yankee on the Stage," *New England Quarterly*, XII (1940), 467–93.

Dulles, Foster R. *A History of Recreation*. 2nd ed. Paperback ed. New York, 1965.

Elson, Ruth. *Guardians of Tradition: American Schoolbooks of the Nineteenth Century*. Lincoln, Neb., 1964.

England, J. Merton. "The Democratic Faith in American Schoolbooks, 1783–1860." *American Quarterly*, XV (1963).

Gilbert, Douglas. *American Vaudeville: Its Life and Times*. New York, 1940.

Goldberg, Isaac. *Tin Pan Alley: A Chronicle of the American Popular Music Racket*. New York, 1930.

Grimsted, David. *American Melodrama, 1800–1850*. Chicago, 1968.

Handlin, Oscar, "Comments on Mass and Popular Culture," in Norman Jacobs, ed. *Culture for the Millions?* Princeton, N.J., 1961, pp. 63–71.

Heaps, Williard and Porter. *The Singing Sixties*. Norman, Okla., 1960.

Hodge, Francis. *Yankee Theatre: The Image of America on the Stage, 1825–60*. Austin, 1964.

Kmen, Henry A. *Music in New Orleans*. Baton Rouge, La., 1966.

McLean, Albert F. *American Vaudeville As a Ritual*. Louisville, Ky., 1965.

Moody, Richard. *America Takes the Stage: Romanticism in American Drama*. Bloomington, Ind., 1955.

———. *The Astor Place Riot*. Bloomington, Ind., 1958.

Nye, Russell. "The Juvenile Approach to American Culture, 1870–1930," in Ray B. Browne, ed. *New Voices in American Studies*. Lafayette, Ind., 1966, pp. 69–99.

———. *The Unembarrassed Muse: The Popular Arts in America.* New York, 1970.

Odell, George C. D. *Annals of the New York Stage.* 15 vols. New York, 1927–49.

Quinn, Arthur H. *A History of the American Drama before the Civil War.* 2nd ed. New York, 1943.

———. *A History of the American Drama since the Civil War.* 2nd ed. New York, 1943.

Rourke, Constance. *American Humor.* New York, 1931.

Sablosky, Irving L. *American Music.* Paperback ed. Chicago, 1969.

Schlesinger, Arthur M. *Learning How to Behave: A Historical Study of American Etiquette Books.* New York, 1946.

Smith, Cecil. *Musical Comedy in America.* New York, 1950.

Sobel, Bernard. *A Pictorial History of Burlesque.* New York, 1956.

Spaeth, Sigmund. *A History of Popular Music in America.* New York, 1948.

Stearns, Marshall and Jean. *Jazz Dance.* New York, 1968.

Zeidman, Irving. *The American Burlesque Show.* New York, 1967.

SELECTED SECONDARY LITERATURE ON RACIAL STEREOTYPING IN AMERICA

Abrahams, Roger. *Positively Black.* Englewood Cliffs, N. J. 1970.

Allport, Gordon. *The Nature of Prejudice.* Cambridge, Mass., 1954.

Baldwin, James. *Notes of a Native Son.* Boston, 1955.

———. *Nobody Knows My Name.* New York, 1961.

Brown, Sterling. "Negro Characters As Seen By White Authors," *Journal of Negro Education,* II (Jan., 1933), 180–201.

———. *The Negro in American Fiction.* Washington, D.C., 1937.

———. *Negro Poetry and Drama.* Washington, D.C., 1937.

Clark, Kenneth. *Prejudice and Your Child.* 2nd ed., Boston, 1963.

Dollard, John. *Castle and Class in a Southern Town.* New Haven, Conn., 1937.

Frederickson, George M. *The Black Image in the White Mind.* New York, 1971.

Friedman, Lawrence. *The White Savage: Racial Fantasies in the Post-bellum South*. Englewood Cliffs, N.J., 1970.

Gossett, Thomas. *Race: The History of an Idea in America*. New York, 1965.

Herndon, Calvin. *Sex and Racism in America*. New York, 1965.

Jordan, Winthrop. *White Over Black*. Chapel Hill, N.C., 1968.

Kovel, Joel. *White Racism: A Psychohistory*. New York, 1970.

Logan, Rayford L. *The Betrayal of the Negro*. New York, 1965.

Myrdal, Gunnar. *An American Dilemma*. 2 vols. New York, 1944.

Powdermaker, Hortense. "The Channeling of Negro Aggression by the Cultural Process," *American Journal of Sociology*, 48 (1943), 750–58.

Silberman, Charles. *Crisis in Black and White*. New York, 1964.

Index

Note: references to illustrations are italicized. See individual dance names under Dances, and stereotyped characters under Stereotypes.

305

Index

Negroes, portrayals of: (*continued*)
strels questioned by white critics, 202.
See also Dandies, Negro; Northern Negroes; Plantation; Old Darky; Southern Negroes; Stereotypes

Negrophobes, 78, 119

New Orleans, 45, 46, 250

New York City, 4, 15, 16, 19-20, 28, 32, 116, 137; end of resident minstrelsy in, 152; first minstrel show opened in, 30; parodies of *Uncle Tom's Cabin* in, 92, 94

New York *Clipper*, 57, 114, 171, 195, 200

Newcomb, Bobby, 186

Newcomb Minstrels, 77

Newspapers, popularization of, 6

Nichols, George, 27, 44-45

Northern Negroes: as buffoons in drama, 28-29, 88; as buffoons in minstrelsy, 56-57, 66, 71, 120, 124, 125-26, 215, 254, 256-57, 271-72; as dandies in minstrelsy, 27, *35*, 68-69, 85, *122*, 124, 183, 241; no place for, in free society, 68, 71, 78, 85, 125; portrayals of, compared to Irish and Germans, 179, 180

Nostalgia, 165, 187, 245-46; for past minstrelsy, 155

Octoroons, 29, 76, 77, 81, *141*; source of female impersonation in minstrelsy, 139-40

"Old Aunt Jemima," 254, 256, 259-61

"Old Black Joe," 237, 244, 245, 263

"Old Corn Meal," 45, 196

Old Darky: as emotional symbol, 37, 78-79; as escapist fantasy figure, 187; fixture in plantation myth, 244-45; used against slavery, 81-82, 248. *See also* Plantation; Southern Negroes

"Old Folks at Home," 36

"Old Uncle Ned," 36, 78

Olio, 55, 135, 147

Oratory, minstrel. *See* Dialect; Stump speech

Out of Bondage, 217

Parade, minstrel, 135, 146

Pelham, Frank, 30

Philadelphia, 4, 32, 94-95

Phillips, Wendell, 112, 114, 126

Plantation: central theme of minstrelsy, 274; decreasing importance of, in white minstrelsy, 154; destruction of black families on, 72, 80-82, 246; finales in white minstrelsy, 52, 56-57, 244-45; as model happy home, 37, 72-73, 75-80, 97; myth as white fantasy, 86, 97, 127, 168, 187; myths modified by black minstrels, 245-48; party as central minstrel feature of, 72-73, 244. *See also* Old Darky; Slavery; Southern Negroes

Plays, popular, 14-16, 28-29, 90-92, 164, 169, 177-78, 217-18

Popular culture, 3-5, 7-8, 13, 16-18, 20-21

"Possum Up a Gum Tree," 26, 42

Prima donna. *See* Female impersonator

Primrose, George, 152, 216

Primrose and West, 152-54

Promoters. *See* Barnum, P. T.; Callender, Charles; Frohman, Charles; Haverly, J. H.; Hicks, Charles; Johnson, Lew; Primrose and West

Promotional techniques, 136, 146, 200, 201, 209

Puns, 54. *See also* Humor

Racial equality, 66-68, 118, 125

Racial stereotypes. *See* Caricatures, Chinese, Germans, Indians, Irish, Japanese, Stereotypes

Radical Republicans, 112, 126

Rainey, Gertrude ("Ma"), 228

"Raw Recruits," 120, *121*

Reconstruction, Radical, 125-26, 235

Red Moon, 218

Reed, Dave, 44, 45

Reunification of North and South, 127

Rhythm, syncopated, 46, 50

Rice, Thomas D. "Jim Crow," 27-28, 36, 42, 43, 45; as Uncle Tom, 92

Riverboatsmen, 9; in minstrelsy, 40-41

Romanticism, 7, 8. *See also* Families; Motherhood, cult of; Nostalgia; Sentimentalism

Runaway slaves, 84-85, 88

Salisbury, Nate, 262
Sam Hague's British Minstrels, 152, 154
Sam T. Jack's Creole Show, 218
San Francisco, 31, 92; black minstrels popular in, 210
San Francisco Minstrels, 149-52, 166-67, 186
Sanford, Sam, 94-96, 154
Sanford's Minstrels, 32, 106
Santley, Mabel, 138
Sawyer, A. D., 214, 215
Scenery. *See* Staging
Secession, 105, 112, 127. *See also* Confederates; Davis, Jefferson
Sentimentalism, 15, 36, 88; black mother as model of, 84; as escapism, 161, 186-87; focused on white suffering in the Civil War, 109-111, 118; in love songs, 37, 53-54; Old Darky as proslavery expression of, 78-79; used against slavery, 80-81; white men omitted from Civil War songs of, 111-12
Shoo Fly Regiment, 218
Simms, William Gilmore, 29
Simond, Ike, 212
Size, as minstrel attraction, 135-36, 147-48
Slave rebellions, 83-84
Slavery: benevolence of, for Negroes, 72-73, 75-76, 78-79, 97; immediate threat to Northerners in 1850's, 66, 87; key to minstrel popularity, 65, 274; minstrel ambivalence about, 66, 72, 84, 86-87; opposition to, in minstrelsy, 66, 73-75, 80-84, 88, 119, 245-48. *See also* Plantation; Southern Negroes
Slaves. *See* Southern Negroes
Smith, Bessie, 228
Social commentary, 128, 160, 163, 183, 186
Social problems, as minstrel topics, 56, 68-72, 115-16, 161, 179-87, 272
Southern Negroes, *35, 207, 208, 252, 253;* antebellum white minstrel concentration on, 30, 52, 56-57, 65; black minstrel concentration on, 198, 201-2, 205-6, 234-35; mistreatment of, 72, 80-84, 119, 245-48; observed by early

minstrels, 46-47; as playful children, 66, 73, 76, 86, 187. *See also* Old Darky; Plantation; Slavery; Stereotypes
Specialty roles, minstrel, 53-56, 139-45
Spirit of the Times, 6, 38
Spirituals, 235-44. *See also* Afro-American folk religion
Sprague's Georgia Minstrels, 216, 226, 227, *253*
Stage shows, 9-10, 18, 134-35. *See also* Plays, popular
Stagecraft. *See* Staging
Staging: of minstrel shows, 36, 51-52, 55-57, 106, 147-48, 152, *153,* 154, 205, 206, 262-63; of popular plays, 14, 15, 18, 90
Stereotypes, plantation myth: Jasper Jack, 75; Mammy, 79; Old Auntie, 79; Old Uncle, 78-79. *See also* Caricatures; Plantation; Old Darky; Southern Negroes
Stowe, Harriet Beecher, 28, 96-97, 138
Stump speech, 52, 55-56, 162. *See also* Humor
Sullivan, John L., 137, 179
Summer, Senator Charles, 116, 126
Superstition, 47-48

Tall tales, 41
Tambo, Brudder, 54. *See also* Endmen; Humor
Temperance, 56, 176. *See also* Social problems
Thatcher, George, 33
Thatcher, Primrose and West Minstrels, 152, *153,* 172
Theater, compared to minstrelsy as form, 177-78. *See also* Plays, popular; Stage shows; Staging
Theaters, 11, 32, 137
Thompson, Lydia, 138
Tights. *See* Female minstrel troupes
Traveling minstrel troupes, 31-32, 135, 139, 145-52, 184, 204-5, 211
Tricksters, slave, 50, 73-75, 88, 261. *See also* Afro-American folk culture; Plantation; Slavery; Southern Negroes
Trip to Coontown, A, 218

Trotter, James M., 227; critical of black minstrels, 257-58

Uncle Tom's Cabin, 28-30, 89-90; issue in the sectional conflict, 87; minstrel parodies of, 93-96; stage versions of, 90-93, 210, 217-18
Underground Railroad, The, 217
Unionism. *See* Nationalism
Urbanization, 4-5, 9, 179, 180-82

Variety shows, 134, 139. *See also* Olio; Vaudeville
Vaudeville, 273, 274
Verbal arts, 5, 19. *See also* Afro-American folk culture; Anglo-American folk culture; Frontier lore
Virginia Minstrels, 30-31, 38, 40, 45, 154, 263; concentration on Southern Negroes, 35; performance style of, 36; early minstrel show structured by, 51-52
Virginia Serenaders, *39*

Walker, George, 218
Washington, George, 96, 106, 117
"Way Down Upon the Swanee River," 237
Weston, Horace, 203, 206, 219
"When This Cruel War Is Over," 110
White House, minstrels performing in, 31
Whitlock, Billy, 30, 45-46
Williams, Bert, 203, 218, 228, 257-58, 273
Women, 183-84; Negro, as butt of jokes, 77
Women's rights, 56, 162-64
Wood's Minstrels, 32, 56, 198; parody of *Uncle Tom's Cabin* by, 94-95

"Yaller gals." *See* Yellow girls
Yankee, 9, 40; on stage, 13-14, 29
"Yankee Doodle," 11
Yellow girls, 76, 77, 81; source of female impersonator role, 139-40, *141*

Ziegfeld Follies, 273
"Zip Coon," 27, 34, *123*